AF754600

St Antony's Series

General Editor: **Richard Clogg** (1999–), Fellow of St Antony's College, Oxford

Recent titles include:

E.K. Dosmukhamedov
FOREIGN DIRECT INVESTMENT IN KAZAKHSTAN
Politico-Legal Aspects of Post-Communist Transition

Felix Patrikeeff
RUSSIAN POLITICS IN EXILE
The Northeast Asian Balance of Power, 1924–1931

He Ping
CHINA'S SEARCH FOR MODERNITY
Cultural Discourse in the Late 20th Century

Mariana Llanos
PRIVATIZATION AND DEMOCRACY IN ARGENTINA
An Analysis of President–Congress Relations

Michael Addison
VIOLENT POLITICS
Strategies of Internal Conflict

Geoffrey Wiseman
CONCEPTS OF NON-PROVOCATIVE DEFENCE
Ideas and Practices in International Security

Pilar Ortuño Anaya
EUROPEAN SOCIALISTS AND SPAIN
The Transition to Democracy, 1959–77

Renato Baumann *(editor)*
BRAZIL IN THE 1990s
An Economy in Transition

Israel Getzler
NIKOLAI SUKHANOV
Chronicler of the Russian Revolution

Arturo J. Cruz, Jr
NICARAGUA'S CONSERVATIVE REPUBLIC, 1858–93

Pamela Lubell
THE CHINESE COMMUNIST PARTY AND THE CULTURAL REVOLUTION
The Case of the Sixty-One Renegades

Mikael af Malmborg
NEUTRALITY AND STATE-BUILDING IN SWEDEN

Klaus Gallo
GREAT BRITAIN AND ARGENTINA
From Invasion to Recognition, 1806–26

David Faure and Tao Tao Liu
TOWN AND COUNTRY IN CHINA
Identity and Perception

Peter Mangold
SUCCESS AND FAILURE IN BRITISH FOREIGN POLICY
Evaluating the Record, 1900–2000

Mohamad Tavakoli-Targhi
REFASHIONING IRAN
Orientalism, Occidentalism and Historiography

Louise Haagh
CITIZENSHIP, LABOUR MARKETS AND DEMOCRATIZATION
Chile and the Modern Sequence

Renato Colistete
LABOUR RELATIONS AND INDUSTRIAL PERFORMANCE IN BRAZIL
Greater São Paulo, 1945–60

Peter Lienhardt (*edited by Ahmed Al-Shahi*)
SHAIKHDOMS OF EASTERN ARABIA

John Crabtree and Laurence Whitehead (*editors*)
TOWARDS DEMOCRATIC VIABILITY
The Bolivian Experience

Steve Tsang (*editor*)
JUDICIAL INDEPENDENCE AND THE RULE OF LAW IN HONG KONG

Karen Jochelson
THE COLOUR OF DISEASE
Syphilis and Racism in South Africa, 1880–1950

Julio Crespo MacLennan
SPAIN AND THE PROCESS OF EUROPEAN INTEGRATION, 1957–85

Enrique Cárdenas, José Antonio Ocampo and Rosemary Thorp (*editors*)
AN ECONOMIC HISTORY OF TWENTIETH-CENTURY LATIN AMERICA
Volume 1: The Export Age
Volume 2: Latin America in the 1930s
Volume 3: Industrialization and the State in Latin America

St Antony's Series
Series Standing Order ISBN 0–333–71109–2
(*outside North America only*)

You can receive future titles in this series as they are published by placing a standing order. Please contact your bookseller or, in case of difficulty, write to us at the address below with your name and address, the title of the series and the ISBN quoted above.

Customer Services Department, Macmillan Distribution Ltd, Houndmills, Basingstoke, Hampshire RG21 6XS, England

Foreign Direct Investment in Kazakhstan

Politico-Legal Aspects of Post-Communist Transition

E.K. Dosmukhamedov
Honorary Professor,
Kazakh American University

palgrave macmillan

in association with
St Antony's College, Oxford

© E.K. Dosmukhamedov 2002

All rights reserved. No reproduction, copy or transmission of this publication may be made without written permission.

No paragraph of this publication may be reproduced, copied or transmitted save with written permission or in accordance with the provisions of the Copyright, Designs and Patents Act 1988, or under the terms of any licence permitting limited copying issued by the Copyright Licensing Agency, 90 Tottenham Court Road, London W1T 4LP.

Any person who does any unauthorized act in relation to this publication may be liable to criminal prosecution and civil claims for damages.

The author has asserted his right to be identified as the author of this work in accordance with the Copyright, Designs and Patents Act 1988.

First published 2002 by
PALGRAVE MACMILLAN
Houndmills, Basingstoke, Hampshire RG21 6XS and
175 Fifth Avenue, New York, N. Y. 10010
Companies and representatives throughout the world

PALGRAVE MACMILLAN is the global academic imprint of the Palgrave Macmillan division of St. Martin's Press, LLC and of Palgrave Macmillan Ltd. Macmillan® is a registered trademark in the United States, United Kingdom and other countries. Palgrave is a registered trademark in the European Union and other countries.

ISBN 0–333–98798–5

This book is printed on paper suitable for recycling and made from fully managed and sustained forest sources.

A catalogue record for this book is available from the British Library.

Library of Congress Cataloging-in-Publication Data

Dosmukhamedov, E.K., 1968–
Foreign direct investment in Kazakhstan: politico-legal aspects of post-Communist transition/E.K. Dosmukhamedov.
p. cm. – (St. Antony's series)
Includes bibliographical references and index.
ISBN 0–333–98798–5 (cloth)
1. Investments, Foreign – Law and legislation – Kazakhstan. 2. Investments, Foreign – Political aspects – Kazakhstan. 3. Post-communism – Kazakhstan. I. Title. II. St. Antony's series (Palgrave (Firm))

KLR321.3 .D67 2002
346.5845'092–dc21

2002025100

10 9 8 7 6 5 4 3 2 1
11 10 09 08 07 06 05 04 03 02

Printed and bound in Great Britain by
Antony Rowe Ltd, Chippenham and Eastbourne

Contents

Acknowledgements

I am grateful to the many good people who made this publication possible. I only regret that I am unable to name them all individually. Their help is truly appreciated.

My mentors in St Petersburg University in Russia, my *alma mater*, Professor Lidiya A. Nikolayeva, Professor Vladimir F. Popondopulo, Nadezhda A. Chechina, Dmitrii M. Chechot, Alexander K. Yurchenko and all the members of the Law Faculty have made a significant contribution to the foundations of this project. It is they who sparked and nurtured my interest in the newly emerging area of Gorbachev's dynamic legislation. The St Petersburg stage of my life was the crucial milestone on my road towards *terra academia*. Any modest achievement of mine should be attributed to my teachers at the northern capital of Russia, with her polar nights, foggy mornings and ever-inspiring architectural ensembles, wounded during the last war, but nevertheless always proudly carrying a title of the intellectual capital of Russia bestowed upon her by Peter the Great.

My two supervisors at Oxford University – Professor Daniel D. Prentice and Professor Archie Brown – have become my true friends, in good times and bad times. These two renowned academics, with never ageing hearts, rightfully personify that centuries-old spirit of Oxford.

George Soros has played an important role in my life on two occasions. Firstly, the Soros Foundation was my hosting organization when I won the US Congress' Benjamin Franklin Scholarship to study Law in the United States. Secondly, when I came to England to read for a doctoral degree in Law, I was provided with a Soros Foundation Scholarship. After having met with Mr Soros in New York back in 1994, my main impression of him was that even a multi-trillion fortune will never pacify his rebellious spirit. Unlike other financiers, the business of making money for Soros is an exercise driven by deeply spiritual motives.

The British Institute of Petroleum awarded me a Paul Frankel Prize. Besides being a great honour, its financial component enabled me to finalize the project within the planned time schedule. My special thanks go to Dr Robert Mabro, OBE, Director of the Oxford Energy Institute, whose continuing support of scholars from the former USSR, Middle East, Africa and Latin America deserves admiration and respect.

I wish to sincerely thank the Saudi Royal family for their generous support. I am indebted to Sir and Lady John Morgan, and the Flitter, Wilson and Lin families for their friendship.

Finally, I am grateful to my family, especially, my mother, Bibi Orazimbetovna Shingisbayeva, brother Nurlan and sisters Aizhan, Asylkhan and Raikhan.

Introduction

The collapse of the centrally planned systems of the Eastern bloc was undoubtedly one of the most important global events of the twentieth century. The transformation of highly centralized economic systems into market economies over such a massive geographical area was historically unprecedented. For western corporations this created a major opportunity to enter markets whose accessibility had been very limited, and for scholars it provided a powerful impetus for in-depth studies of post-Communist development.

This book studies the post-Communist transition of the former Soviet Union. It stakes out different ground from previous works in that it approaches transition by analysing the legal regulation of foreign direct investment (FDI) through a politico-legal lense. Rapidly emerging legislation in the post-Soviet states provides fertile ground for the application of political science concepts to transition. Until recently the political context in the former Soviet Union (FSU) was implied by but never interwoven into legal analysis. Equally, political studies of the post-Soviet transition have used law only as an auxiliary analytical instrument to illustrate a point or support an argument. By contrast the central contention of this book is that the expanding mass of laws, in many cases controversial and confusing, and related political practices must be placed within a coherent and interrelated framework. The ultimate goal is to uncover the driving forces, the overall direction and the dynamics of the post-Soviet transition.

The book draws on previous theories and concepts of transition in order (i) to offer insights to readers who wish to understand the inner workings of the governments of transitional countries and are seeking to learn more about the interaction between the evolving political, economic and legal realms, and (ii) to analyse topics of interest to those who wish to evaluate the merits of governmental regulatory strategies and understand legal reforms. An important implication of this is that the book will be equally useful to legal scholars, political scientists, economists, business practitioners and public decision-makers.

To date no fundamental studies have been conducted on foreign direct investment in the former Soviet Union. This could indicate a belief by scholars that studies of this kind are unnecessary, given the extensive body of literature on political and economic transition and on foreign direct investment in other parts of the world. Such a view is not entirely without merit as certain transnational and historical factors are of relevance to all transitional countries. At the same time, however, there are fundamental differences between the experiences of the countries of the FSU and those of other nations, as will be shown.

There is also considerable academic debate on whether transition, as an analytical construct, is of any value to the search for a coherent understanding of the historical forces that are shaping the legal reality in the former Soviet Union. Few studies of transition offer a systematic narrative that distinguishes between events that are transitory and developments that signal a transformation of the nature, form and prospects of legal systems in the former Soviet Union. In acknowledging the deficiencies of existing approaches, this book seeks to develop a distinctive account of transition that is both historically grounded and informed by a rigorous analytical framework.

Recent studies of FDI in the former Soviet Union depart from three general assumptions[1] when dealing with the legal superstructure.[2] First, they perceive the process of transition as a constant in that they assume that the process is a straightforward move from totalitarianism to western democracy. Second, when dealing with post-Soviet law they appear to accept the argument in western economic studies that the goal of post-Soviet social and legal policy is economic efficiency. In other words they view the emerging legal system as rational in the sense that its goal is economic efficiency. Third, they tend to view the state as a monolithic entity that accords with their assumptions of rationality. Hence they expect the state's behaviour to remain consistent. Accordingly, in analyses of entire legal systems or particular branches of law the influence of the state on the substance of newly emerging laws is ignored.[3]

This book suggests that these perceptions are erroneous. It argues that the changes in the underpinning principles of FDI legislation are a manifestation of a gradual shift away from the western-type, rational-based model conceived towards the end of the Gorbachev era. The overall aim is to develop an understanding of the dynamics of legal regulation of FDI in the circumstances of a transitional society. It is suggested that the pattern of transition, which can differ according to the pursued objective (economic efficiency or short-term political considerations), governs the evolution of FDI legislation. This approach to transition is used to develop a framework that integrates a number of factors underlying legal regulation that are often omitted or treated separately in the literature. An important aspect of this approach is that it allows identification of the direction in which the legal system is evolving. The settled nature of politicoeconomic determinants in established democracies explains the differences between legal scholars' methodological approaches to problems associated with FDI in industrialized and transitional countries.[4]

As this study draws on the methodologies of three major disciplines (law, economics and political science) a few basic points need to be made on the relevance of these disciplines to this undertaking.

A legal dimension of our approach is based on methodologies employed by the law and economics school, particularly the neo-institutionalist stream. Methods provided by the sociology of law, comparative law and legal anthropology are also applied. In fact, the decision to base this study in these fields rather than in international law arises from the lack of analytical utility in the international law paradigm for understanding the legal aspects of foreign investment in the conditions of post-Soviet transition. By contrast, the above fields are concerned with the nature of law and its relationship to its particular social or national context. As noted above, this study employs the new institutionalist approach. However, this does not mean that we will overlook the methods suggested by the law and society school, which is considered in current literature as something opposite to neo-institutionalism. On the contrary, as observed elsewhere, these schools both originate from the same Weberian notion of legal rationality.[5] Thus, the issue of current debates between the two movements seems to lie not in substance, but in the different levels of abstraction which are employed by these approaches. For the purpose of this study, the tools of the institutionalist approach will form the core of the methodology adopted. In particular, they can be helpful in understanding the nature of the law-making process, especially, in understanding the institutions and mechanism of their interaction. The law and society approach will be useful in the analysis of those issues associated with the political aspects relevant to the regulation of FDI.

Our study draws on economic theories and concepts of FDI in order first, to identify the nature of this purely economic phenomenon; and, second, to outline the economic implications for and underpinnings of the legislation on FDI and to define the contours of a legal regime that will be conducive to FDI – that is, one which provides an equilibrium between the domestic and foreign interests such that it allows the extraction of the maximum benefit from FDI by a host state and a foreign investor.

This work employs political science methodologies because it sees legal regulation as part of the broader process of social regulation, which is indisputably a political process. Legal regulation involves a contest for power, the study of which, as such, lies at the heart of the interests of political scientists. The study of the legal regulation of foreign investment in conditions of a highly fluid contest for a new balance of power offers an important opportunity for a reconciliation between the long-divorced disciplines of law and political science. Yet, it should be noted that the reason for applying political science methods here differs from the purpose commonly pursued by students of politics of transition.[6] Our reason for applying a political perspective is not only to achieve an understanding of power per se or simply to understand what kind of sociopolitical organization is likely to be achieved, given the present characteristics of transition. It is more important to find out why and how a certain kind of organization leads to the establishment of a particular model for the legal regulation of FDI.

As noted earlier, this book seeks to develop a distinctive account of transition which is both historically grounded and informed by a rigorous analytical framework. It does not aim to present the precise legal state of the legislation relating to FDI. Rather, in order to count the variety of crucial factors involved in the legal regulation of FDI, the foreign investment laws of Kazakhstan enacted during the post-independence period – the Law on Foreign Direct Investment of 1994, the Law on State Support of Direct Investment of 1997, and the 1997 Amendments to the 1994 Law on Foreign Investment – are employed as analytical milestones. Furthermore, relevant clauses of other statutes will be also considered in order to illustrate the correlation between a particular model of legal regulation and the evolving arrangements between the state and a foreign investor provided by domestic law. Such an analysis may demonstrate a shift from one model of legal regulation of FDI to another, more or less optimal, one.

Thus, to understand events in the former USSR a multidisciplinary approach is necessary. The 'value-free' analysis of actual legislation is unlikely to be a fruitful academic exercise. The forces affecting the law-making process in transitional society naturally reflect the unsettled nature of the institutions that either emerge, undergo transformation or die. Accordingly, the analysis of the emerging law must be firmly based on a clear understanding of the complexity of the context that underlies the legal phenomena. At the same time, as is clear from the above, this study's focus is on the dynamics rather than on the statics of laws. The final goal is not to make a portrait, but to explain the nature and dynamics of the legal regulatory system for FDI in conditions of post-Soviet transition.

In order to analyse the subject in-depth from the perspective of the ongoing process of sociopolitical, economic and legal transformations, this book employs a case-study approach, focusing primarily on the Republic of Kazakhstan. This is the second largest country of the former Soviet Union, located in both Europe and Asia, and has been a part of the Russian Empire for more than 250 years. It is well endowed with natural resources such as oil, natural gas, gold, silver, and ferrous and non-ferrous ores, to name but a few. Given this natural wealth, the republic was one of the major agro-industrial backbones of the Soviet economy before it gained independence in 1991. Since ancient times the country has been located between the three major religions of the world, lying on the Great Silk Road. Kazakhstan displays a positive attitude towards foreign investment. This results from the fact that religion has never played an important role in this secular country; Kazakh women have never veiled their faces and Shariah has never been a source of the country's law. The fact that it is different from other Central Asian nations in lifestyle and in its distinctive geoclimatic conditions has also contributed to the formation of an openness to international dialogue and tolerance towards a variety of ethnic groups and religions.[7] Partly because of this contemporary Kazakhstan has not been infected by inter-ethnic conflict and has provided a degree of stability which has contributed to its becoming perhaps the most successful post-Soviet state in the attraction of FDI. At the same time, the legacy of the past – a colonial-type economic organization, aggravated by a failed post-independence privatization which has not resulted in a restructured economy and has thus not created the internal sources for the generation of investment – made foreign direct investment the only source of much-needed finances to keep the country's economy afloat. Equally important, these facts presupposed the pivotal role which foreign investment can play in this country's further development. Thus, the significance of FDI for the country, the vested interests of the major multinational companies, as well as the state's geopolitical importance in the region, are some of the key reasons to consider Kazakhstan as a focus of this book.

The subject of the law on foreign direct investment has generally been a topic of inquiry for scholars of international law. Because the prime concern of their studies has been the insulation of multinational enterprises out of the reach of national laws, the latter remained unexplored and has been treated as an externality generating risk and thus, in academic terms, as a constant variable in legal research.[8] Bilder and Murphy, in their review of the recent fundamental study on FDI undertaken by Sornarajah, have noticed:

> The major problem is that [Sornarajah] spends an excessive amount of time on expropriations and very little time on the great variety of other topics arguably of equal or greater concern to persons interested in foreign investment. One possible reason for the imbalance in Sornarajah's focus is that he has chosen as his topic the 'international law' on foreign investment. International law is not the only, nor necessarily the most important, component of the law on foreign investment. As every international business person can attest, national statutes and regulations are likely to loom large.[9]

Recent practice, in particular unsuccessful attempts to promulgate the OECD-sponsored Multilateral Agreement on Investment (MAI), confirms the above observation. The rather cool response of non-OECD states to MAI proves that the domestic level of the legal regulatory framework for FDI will continue to play an increasingly important, if not a driving role in shaping the international legal framework governing the international flows of investment. Hence, the need to understand the rationale and the hidden processes which stand behind the visible surface of legislative policies of newly emerging states of the former USSR mean that this book particularly timely.[10]

The choice of legal regulation of *foreign direct investment* represents a new and fruitful field for the analysis of post-Communist transition. First, FDI is a new phenomenon in the economies of the former Soviet republics. As a result, the legislation designed to deal with FDI is also a new phenomenon in the Soviet as well as post-independence legal practice and scholarship. Second, because foreign direct investment is a measurable phenomenon – that is, it has a quantitative nature – the impact of laws on overall FDI inflows are easy to verify, based on both domestic and international, that is to say more independent, statistical data.[11] The third is based on the previous point. For the purely profit-maximization reasons which lie behind the decision of a multinational enterprise to undertake an FDI, the need to promote economic efficiency can also be detected in the emerging national legislation on FDI. Correspondingly, generalizations can be made about the overall direction of the legal system's evolution. Finally, because of its increasing importance for the national economy, FDI is also becoming a highly politicized issue. By analysing the legal regulation of FDI one may reveal the processes occurring in a transitional society, and thus the prospects for the development of democracy and the rule of law that allow scholars studying 'settled' legal systems to focus on the so-called 'value-free' analysis of legal phenomena.

The first two chapters of this book outline its methodological framework. They explain the necessity and validity of adopting a multidisciplinary approach to the phenomenon of transition; the criteria for drawing upon particular of disciplines and levels of analysis; and the significance of applying a political context to the study of legal phenomena during transition.

Chapter 3, 'The Law on FDI in Kazakhstan: Origins, Principles and Structure', moves on to provide an analysis of the evolution of the legislation on foreign direct investment from 1920 to the present day. It suggests that the post-independence law on foreign investment is a continuation of the processes conceived within the Soviet period of *perestroika*. By pointing out the qualitative difference between the nature of FDI-related laws both before and after the dissolution of the USSR, the study displays the significance of the underpinning state policy and centrality of political factors to the formation of FDI legislation. Based on this, the chapter suggests a methodological approach to the 1995 Constitution, the fundamental law of Kazakhstan, in the context of the economic efficiency analysis which holds together the present study.

Chapter 4, 'The Types and Choice of the Model for the Legal Regulation of FDI', provides a definition of the models of legal regulation with a particular focus on the outcomes of possible bargaining between a host state and a foreign investor. It then outlines the country-specific factors shaping the contours of the regulatory framework for FDI. The chapter proceeds to formulate the criteria for the choice of an optimal model for Kazakhstan. Finally, on the basis of the previous cases of transition, an explanation of the actual workings of the chosen institutions is offered.

In Chapter 5, 'The Kazakh Model for the Legal Regulation of FDI', the relevant conclusions from the previous chapter are utilized in an analysis of the post-independence laws designed to regulate FDI – the 1994 Law on Foreign Investment and the 1997 Law on State Support of Direct Investment. It is suggested that after the collapse of the Soviet Union, the evolution of the legislation on FDI reflected largely the momentum which originated in the period of *perestroika* before the disintegration of the USSR. Later, the pattern of evolution was reversed, as the book will argue, by an executive which had been driven by motives of concentration of power and rent-seeking considerations. The chapter argues that the enactment of the 1997 law was a confirmation of this change in the country's mode of regulation of FDI.

Chapter 6, 'The Legal Regulation of FDI in the Context of Legal Reforms', seeks to prove the assumptions of the previous chapter by shedding light on the correlation between the realms of law and politics in the context of the regulation of FDI. In particular, it suggests an approach to the ongoing legal reform in Kazakhstan which, in turn, explains the fundamental changes in the legislation governing FDI which occurred within the transitional period.

Chapter 7, 'The State as the Regulator of FDI', further elaborates these propositions. In particular, it builds its argument on the basis of analysis of the 1995 Constitution which reflects a new balance of power and thus a new institutional set-up. The chapter emphasizes the changes in the nexus 'state–society', and between the branches of power within the state itself. By so doing, it analyses the workings of the institutions involved in the formulation of economic strategy, part of which is the legislation on FDI. There is an explanation of how, by whom and why the legal changes have been taken to reflect the metamorphoses in the policy towards FDI. The Conclusion summarizes the book's findings, identifies those points that may be generalized in an assessment of the process of evolution of FDI laws in conditions of post-Soviet transition, and provides a paradigm for understanding the nature of the post-Soviet law on FDI.

1
Methodological Approach

1.1 Introduction

Foreign direct investment is a complex phenomenon and the history of international investment law, particularly over the last three decades, 'reflects economic and political debate and conflict':[1] This explains the attention paid to the subject by scholars from a wide range of disciplines, including law, the social sciences, business and management. These studies have contributed to the understanding not only of the various facets of FDI, but also the evolution of FDI as a phenomenon.

Earlier legal studies on FDI in the developing world tended to focus on the international public law aspects of relations between host states and foreign investors.[2] As a result a popular subject of academic discussion has been the liability of host states when they violate their contractual obligations to foreign investors. This book takes a different approach in that it focuses on normal, rather than conflictual, aspects of FDI-related interactions between host states and foreign investors. It is interested in the content of this relationship *vis-à-vis* property rights and in the host state as 'law taker' in this relationship, as well as in the state as decision maker in the process of creating and executing property rights associated with FDI. In contrast with previous studies, therefore, the emphasis is not on the liability of the state but on its role in a proprietary relationship.

1.2 The nature of legal analysis

Wallace, in her study of legal controls on multinational enterprises (MNEs), notes:

> In developed states, where a reasonably stable political structure has existed long enough to give government policy and legal solutions

> sufficient continuity to be of interest in our study, the development of legal means of dealing with the multinationals are more easily traceable and more juridicially significant than in the developing world where, due to historical forces, such a continuity is often lacking ... The investment problem of the less developed nations and those of the advanced industrialized states differ substantially in kind – those of developing nations tending to fall more into the politico-socio-economic sphere, and those of the developed states arising generally in the legal arena.[3]

It is evident from the above that different analytical approaches are required for industrialized and transitional countries. So far analyses of the legal regulation of FDI in transitional countries have been limited to case studies or have focused on international legal mechanisms to insulate FDI from the reach of host states. The lack of a paradigm applicable to FDI in transitional states has led to the conclusion that 'international law is not the only, nor necessarily the most important component of the law on foreign investment and national statutes and regulations are likely to loom large';[4] and that 'the existing national regimes are critical for an understanding of what international regulation can accomplish'.[5] In other words the legal regulation of FDI in the non-industrialized world has remained an analytical 'black box'. The absence of an appropriate framework to deal with the 'investment problem' emanating from the 'politico-socio-economic sphere', to borrow Wallace's words, becomes particularly obvious when one considers studies of post-Soviet law. As Lev, in his recent review of a book by Hendley, accurately notes:

> Trying to identify all the variables that make law count is as likely to obscure as to clarify matters. References to cultural factors, which are always easier to assert than to prove, actually weaken Hendley's political analysis of the common scepticism surrounding legal process and imply that reform is unlikely at best. Habitual as it is in the literature, we probably ought to re-think the uses of cultural analysis in explaining legal evolution, for it tends to circularity and confusion, diverting attention from the structural sources of relevant values.[6]

The challenge is to treat the 'black box' as an object of analysis in order to identify a framework to assess the legal regulation of FDI in a transitional state. In this regard a prime objective is to formulate a systematic approach to the numerous phenomena that are shaping the laws on and regulation of foreign investment in the former Soviet Union. What should be the starting point for such an undertaking? Wallace argues that the continuity of government policy and legal solutions to protect property rights in the developed world is due to a 'reasonably stable political structure', which explains why 'the development of legal means of dealing with the multinationals is more easily traceable and more juridicially significant than in the developing world'.[7] We shall use this point as a platform for further discussion. Questions to be addressed are: does stability of the political structures in the developed world explain the diverging approaches to the study of the legal aspects of FDI in the developed and industrializing world, and why and how does it matter in the legal regulation of FDI?

1.3 Political stability

Political stability is an important factor in investment in industrialized countries as well as in less developed ones, and even in the home countries of investors, such as Sweden and the United States.[8] Indeed changes and uncertainties in the political environment have always had an impact on the conduct of business. Nonetheless not all such changes/uncertainties can properly be considered as risks. Furthermore a political risk for one firm may not be a political risk for another. Political instability, as represented for example by an unexpected change in government leadership, may or may not involve political risk for international business. In other words political instability, depending on how it is defined, is a separate phenomenon from political risk.[9] Therefore it is worthwhile to clarifying the definition of political risk.

There have been many attempts to provide a comprehensive definition of political risk in respect of FDI.[10] For the purpose of this study we shall define political risk as host government actions (expressed in legal form) that limit the time frame planned or envisaged by a foreign investor. In other words we shall focus only on the effects of government actions that interrupt the normal flow of business activities or curtail the time allocated for certain activities.

The above definition and others of a complementary nature focus on the interplay between 'risk' and 'uncertainty'. In particular, Williams and Heins define risk as objective doubt about the outcome of a given situation, and uncertainty as subjective doubt.[11] Similarly Pfeffer defines risk as a combination of hazards measured by probability, while uncertainty is measured by degree of belief. Risk is to do with the state of the world and uncertainty is a state of mind.[12] Willet, a pioneer of risk analysis, argues that risk is the objective correlate of subjective uncertainty.[13] Thus political stability matters in legal analyses of FDI inasmuch as it affects the subjective perceptions of foreign investors as holders of property rights.

However the authors mentioned above, perhaps because of the methodological limitations of their respective disciplines, fail to identify the point at which risk and uncertainty become crucial in changing foreign investors perception of the property rights associated with direct investment in a foreign host state. Or to put it more pointedly, what makes subjective perception of objective risks – which theoretically are possible in any country – so different in the developed and developing worlds and consequently so crucial for the overall effectiveness of a host state's legal regulation of FDI? If the probability of a political risk or its intensity are not sufficient to change the perception of investors, then what is? What is it that separates the effect of uncertainty on the execution of the property rights associated with FDI in the developing world from that in the developed world?

1.4 Externalities

It follows from the above that the theories on FDI and their interpretations conform to the postulations of transaction cost economics.[14] They allow us to look at a decision to undertake FDI (f) as a combination of two basic factors: transaction costs (a) and foreign-market environment (b). FDI occurs when this combination is likely to produce an economic benefit for a foreign company. This can be formulated as:

$$f = (a + b)$$

This equation, however, reflects the ideal situation and in reality, as in any transaction, FDI is not free from externalities (x). This can be formulated as:

$$f = (a + b) : x$$

According to this equation, the greater the value of x the less likely it is that FDI will take place. In fact if $x = (a + b)$ the basic economic reason for investment evaporates. Hence for FDI to be made in a given country the following must pertain:

$$([a + b] : x) > 1$$

Consequently the ideal host country legal regulation is one that not only offsets the negative effects of x, but also maintains it at less than the sum of a and b. A simple logical deduction implies that an underlying difference in analysis of FDI in the developed and developing worlds, pointed out by legal scholars, lies in the nature of x, or rather in the possibility of x becoming equal to or more than $a + b$. But at what point can x be said to exceed $a + b$ and how should a legal student approach this task, if it can be dealt with by legal methodology at all?

Before answering this question, account should be taken of two crucial features of FDI. First, FDI is above all an economic phenomenon in that an MNE will only finance a foreign investment if the net value of future earnings is likely to exceed the cost of the initial investment. Second, FDI involves the movement of capital, technology and the like across national borders, and in contrast to portfolio investment it also involves the active management of and control over property. This requires us to consider the property rights assigned by the host state. These two characteristics mean that a suitable analytical framework should combine law and economics. Posner, one of the most eminent proponents of the law and economics approach, aptly observes that 'economic analysis of law need not be conducted at a high level of formality or mathematization. The heart of economics is insight rather than technique'.[15] Bearing this in mind, let us now formulate a set of assumptions to serve as the basis of further discussion.

1.5 The law and economics approach

Conceiving FDI as a form of property implies 'a set of social relationships which ties the future to the present through expectations of stabilized behaviour regarding other persons and things'.[16] Indeed, the success of any new investment project depends on the future state of the world, which usually deviates from that which is expected due to primary uncertainty (event uncertainty) and secondary uncertainty (market uncertainty). The former does not depend on the will of parties involved in the transaction. The latter exists 'when certain facts about the present or future are known to some people but not to other people'.[17] Law allows for the construction of an adequate decision-making model and provides rules that facilitate the construction of individual pictures of the world. By reducing secondary uncertainty it produces common knowledge and makes it possible for expectations to converge. This convergence of expectations is part of the equilibrating force of law. As North puts it: 'the major role of institutions in a society is to reduce uncertainty by establishing a stable ... structure to human interaction'.[18] In this sense the task of law, as viewed in the context of the present work, is not to maximize the wealth of individuals, but to facilitate cooperation and interaction. Hence if an FDI legal regime is viewed as a set of property rights designed to reduce information assymetry between a foreign investor and a host state, it becomes clear that the environments of both decision-makers are important to achieving a mutually defined outcome. Therefore our first assumption is that *efficient law* serves to improve the ability of the agents correctly to anticipate each other's behaviour. In this respect it is important for the law to be 'rather certain than to be right'.[19] The second assumption allows us to view transition as an exogenous variable that constitutes an information environment on the side of the host state.

Next, an FDI-related relationship involves exchange: the host state assigns property rights to a foreign investor, and in return the latter delivers a wealth-producing asset and its associated activities. Obviously, a clear profit-maximization (or utility-maximization) objective, which explains the reasons for the MNE and the host state to embark on an FDI transaction, presupposes a mutually desired outcome. The assignment of a certain regime of property rights by a host state is exchanged for certain behaviour by the foreign owner of an asset. Hence the relationship is a bargained one and is thus assumed to be rational. Presumably the host nation's laws should display a rationality that corresponds with the foreign investor's notion of rationality. Why then do clashes of interest arise, leading to instability (and uncertainty) and affecting foreign investors' decisions?

The law and economics approach also implies that one should look at the relationship between a foreign investor and the host state as being in equilibrium. Accordingly the exogenous underlying factors, jointly referred to in this study as transition, can be treated within an equilibrium framework. This in turn raises another question – what kind of equilibrium is implied in this study? Obviously 'any state of affairs can be efficient if the run is taken as long or short enough. Efficiency is relative to a model. It is not surprising, then, that by manipulation of the time frame one can transform an inefficient situation into an efficient one'.[20] Do the foreign investor and host state have the same perception of the time framework needed for efficiency?

What makes or should make the perceptions of host state and foreign investor match?

To answer this question one needs to consider the following point. Assuming that FDI will be long term and thus continuing, it is expected that a time frame should be one which perpetuates perceptions materialized by a set of a host country's property rights and its overall legal regulation.[21] The continuing nature of FDI also implies that equilibrium depends on environmental factors – the shorter the duration of a transaction, the fewer the negative effects of externalities. Hence when analysing a continuing relationship the effects of multiple factors over time do matter as opposed to short-term transactions where the dynamics of a system and its environment do not have such an impact. Consequently the notion of such a state of the world which produces the more stable net equilibrium associated with and conducive to the long-life period of FDI is becoming of a particular significance in our analysis. Thus the continuing nature of FDI requires particular consideration of equilibrium achieved between one individual investor and a host state at a certain point of time but necessarily within the context of the bigger net equilibrium. We assume that a certain state of the institutional set-up of a transitional society can be treated as such a net equilibrium. This point will be elaborated on in a subsequent section.

The above presupposes another assumption. Let us assume that a foreign investor and a host state, both of whom are looking for an efficient long-term relationship, face an efficient rule A and an inefficient rule B. Will exchanging rule B for rule A result in equilibrium of their whole relationship system? Obviously not, because this prediction requires the dynamic forces of the system to drive it into the new equilibrium. Furthermore the efficiency of rule A is a necessary but not sufficient condition for introducing it because a transition cost may be attached to this rule. According to the Coase theorem (one of the central ideas in the economic analysis of law), if there are positive transaction costs an efficient outcome may not occur under every legal rule. Rather the preferred legal rule is that which minimizes both transaction costs and inefficient choices made to avoid these costs. Two important points can be made here. It is implied that an efficient rule should be viewed as an element of a larger system of rules. However, what is more important is to focus on the *dynamics* rather than the statics of this bigger system which shapes a certain type of equilibrium in a particular investment relationship. Second, we are required to look more closely at the nature of a larger system in order to find out why and how it imposes certain costs on a sub-system (in our case the legal regulation of FDI) in the process of transition towards more efficient rule(s).[22]

The previous section sets up a ground for the next assumption, which is that may treat FDI as a decision-making process on the basis of the notion that costs are always opportunity costs. They are defined as 'the highest-valued opportunity necessarily forsaken', which is 'a logical implication of choice among available options'.[23] This definition implies that the notion of costs may only be used sensibly in the context of decision situations. The cost of choosing any alternative is the cost incurred *by* the decision-maker; though, 'in actual practice the measurement is very imprecise in that it involves estimates of uncertain future events'.[24] Nevertheless, what is important for this study is 'that the only interpretation one can give to the concept of opportunity cost as the value of the next best alternative is a subjective one'.[25] This allows us to integrate into one analytical picture the subjects involved in the execution of property rights associated with FDI along with their environmental context. In other words, we may consider both decision-makers – foreign investors and a host state – as actors who have an image of their relevant environment.[26] This picture of the world shapes the decision models, the implications of which, as we argue in this study, may be calculated.[27] Differences in the approach to FDI in developed and developing countries makes us interested in how this picture about means and ends does in fact develop. Socially relevant decisions are only made during the construction of this picture of the world, referring to the relevant constraints and preferences. Law is one of those constraints. In other words, the impact of a bigger system can be detected through the analysis of the decision-making process associated with the *actual* execution of property rights. But the issue is why, and to what extent, an agent decides about law as a constraint, rather than accepting it as a predetermined parameter for any decision-maker? The distinction between imperfect information and imperfect decisions using the available information is of central relevance here. There is a difference between the real world and the decision-maker's perception. In fact, people must decide both about the relevant set of legal rules in a specific context and the meaning of these rules. This explains why a system of rules, supposed to lead to mutually compatible individual expectations, may in fact produce a serious incompatibility of actions.

Finally, the law and economics approach allows us to incorporate the notion of *goals* in our analysis of decision-makers. Lindblom says: 'Decision-making is ordinarily formalized as a means–ends relationship:

means are conceived to be evaluated and chosen in the light of ends finally selected independently of and prior to the choice of means.'[28] Breyer, in turn, explains that his approach to the question of the choice of a regulatory instrument, 'is built upon a single axiom for creating and implementing any programme: determine one's objectives, and choose the best method for doing so'.[29] He then suggests that the best method is 'the least restrictive one'.[30] Thus, the difference in the final outcome being pursued will inevitably result in a mismatch (or 'under-match') of behaviour and pictures (prescribed by property rights) planned in their expectations of the future. Equally, the state's actual behaviour may be inconsistent during the period of investment; that is, it may pursue different goals even while being a 'law taker'. Thus, account should be taken that more than one pattern of property right can exist and that profit (or wealth) maximization is not assured. This explains the incorporation into our study of the notion of an FDI relationship as a goal-oriented one and why our objective is to study contracting processes, not mainly in ex ante and ex post respects but rather in their entirety.

To sum up, the law and economics approach provides useful insights which allow us to focus on crucial features of the relationship between a host state and foreign investors. Undoubtedly, the nature of the research phenomenon in question perfectly matches the three elements which constitute an economic analysis of law. Cooter and Ulen formulated these elements as follows:

> The first step is to assume that the individuals or institutions who make decisions are maximizing well-known and clearly specified economic objectives, for example, that businesses are maximizing profits, and that consumers are maximizing wealth and leisure. The second step is to show that the interaction among all relevant decision makers settles down into what economics call an equilibrium, a condition that does not spontaneously change. The third step is to judge the equilibrium on the criterion of economic efficiency.[31]

They point out that 'the rules created by law establish implicit prices for different kinds of behaviour, and the consequences of those rules can be analysed as the response to those implicit prices'.[32] Hence, the law and economics approach treats law as a constraint – that is, it is viewed as an exogenous variable in analytical terms. In such an approach, the agents – a host state and foreign investors – are considered as the 'law takers'. Thus, in general, the law and economics approach allows the concentration of analysis on the actual execution of property rights and behaviour of agents *within* the context of an FDI relationship.

At the same time, however, insights from the law and economics approach are not sufficient for understanding the logic of creation of law as a constraint, its variations or actual content. While there is no doubt that this approach is helpful in analysis where both agents – a host state and a foreign investor – interact within a stable or static (in the analytical sense) framework of rules, it becomes less helpful in situations when this framework itself undergoes a dramatic change – in particular, as a result of a continuing mismatch (of information environments or pursued goals) between the users of property rights. Finally, the application of this method is also limited because the state is not only a 'law taker', but also a 'law giver' in relation to FDI. These shortcomings inherent to the law and economics school approach mean that we must shift our focus to the nexus between the host state and transition, the main underlying process in the former Soviet Union.

1.6 The neo-institutionalist approach

In relation to present reforms in Eastern Europe and the former USSR, Przeworski notes that in the realms of both politics and economics there have been attempts to make a radical break with the past; in fact, in both realms the word 'transitions' best describes the processes launched in a number of countries. These are transitions from several varieties of authoritarianism to democracy and from state-administered, monopolistic, and protected economic systems (again of several varieties) to a reliance on markets. Both of these transitions are radical, and they are interdependent.[33] In other words, 'transition' is a broad term in political science, which means the interval between an authoritarian political regime and a democratic one. At the same time account should be taken of the fact that that is only one way of considering transition. However, in this study we do not use transition in such a deterministic sense. There has been a transition from Communism, but it need not be a transition to democracy – it can be transition to a different form of authoritarian rule. Nonetheless, Bova recognizes that transitions involve two analytically distinct, but empirically interrelated phenomena: on the one hand, the dismantling of the pre-existing structures of authoritarian rule and, on the other, the task of creating new structures to take their place.[34] Thus, we will view transition as a process of the building of institutions and consequently our focus can be further narrowed in the sense that the interaction between the host state and foreign investors should be viewed as one which evolves within this broader process of institution-building. In turn, this explains the necessity of the application of the institutionalist approach, along with the law and economics approach. This helps us to expand the analytical borders of the study and to approach the research issue in a different dimension – that is, as a relationship between institutions and behaviour – while treating law as an endogenous phenomenon.

It has been correctly observed elsewhere that the study of institutions is experiencing a renaissance throughout the social sciences.[35] This has led to the development of different meanings for the term 'institutionalism' across the disciplines. For the sake of this analysis, we should admit that all these 'institutionalisms are united by little but a common scepticism towards atomistic accounts of social processes and a common conviction that institutional arrangements and social processes matter'.[36] Powell and DiMaggio encapsulate this point:

> The key thrust of institutional analysis is neither to expose the inefficiency of organizational practices nor to celebrate the non-optimality of institutional arrangements. We are skeptical of arguments that assume that surviving institutions represent efficient solutions because we recognize that rates of environmental change frequently outpace rates of organizational adaptation. The point is not to discern whether institutions are efficient, but to develop robust explanations of the ways in which institutions incorporate historical experiences into their rules and organizing logics.[37]

In this study, a basic definition of 'institutions' to be employed is that suggested by Ruttan and Hayami:

> Institutions are the rules of a society or of organizations that facilitate coordination among people by helping them form expectations which each person can reasonably hold in dealings with others. They reflect the conventions that have evolved in different societies regarding the behaviour of individuals and groups relative to their own behaviour and the behaviour of others. In the area of economic relations they have a crucial role in establishing expectations about the rights to use resources in economic activities and about the

> partitioning of income streams resulting from economic activity – institutions provide assurance respecting the actions of others, and give order and stability to expectations in the complex and uncertain world of economic relations.[38]

It seems also that this concept matches the legal nature of this study inasmuch as it corresponds well with the definition of property rights defined as sanctioned behavioural relations and, thus, allows for treatment of law as an endogenous variable. This is especially important for our study which deals with the newly emerging legislation on foreign direct investment in a country which was previously completely closed to FDI. Therefore, we are required to focus on the state of the legal regulation 'as is', but it is equally necessary to shed light on how the new institutions emerge and how they change. Bromley, for instance, believes that institutions change because of income streams. Given the present institutional environment, there is a constant flux of preferences, resource endowments, and technologies. Old income streams (economic opportunities) may dry up and promising new ones may fail because of a lack of suitable institutions.[39] If a change in the institutional environment is expected to yield a positive income stream, such an investment will be made. Posner, in turn, also admits that institutional change is based upon efficiency rationales and is modelled as a rational choice. However, these authors neglect the *process* of change in their analyses.

The institutionalist approach provides us with other useful insights which could be helpful in our further analysis. Brennan and Buchanan define a distinction between two kinds of choices: the choice of constraints and the choices made within constraints. Buchanan says:

> It is essential to acknowledge ... that individuals choose to impose constraints or limits on their own behaviour primarily, even if not exclusively, as a part of an exchange in which the restrictions on their own actions are sacrificed in return for the benefits that are anticipated from the reciprocally extended restrictions on the actions of others with whom they interact along the boundaries of private spaces and within the confines of acknowledged public spaces.[40]

The aim of this exchange of restrictions is to achieve efficiency. In this context, Bush, Buchanan and Schmidt-Trenz formulated a game-theoretic model which consists of three parts: a 'natural' game, sanctions matrices, and an 'effective' game. If a society remains within a Hobbesian state of nature, it then follows that it does not realize its productive potential. This leads to an elementary and low-productive *natural equilibrium*, which is characterized by lack of transactional security and vulnerability of possession. Trade, for instance, does not take place because of unavoidable asimultaneity of exchange activities: no one can be sure of getting a return for what he gives up. To overcome the inefficient natural equilibrium in anarchy, certain legal constraints upon actions, called sanctions-matrices, are required. This was mainly done by setting up a protective state that uses two kind of sanctions: sanctions defining property law and sanctions defining contract law. The sanctions-matrices being superimposed on the pay-off matrix of the 'natural' game thus results in an 'effective' game that describes the basics of civil society. This focuses our attention on the mutual nature of constraints that are imposed by parties on proprietary relationships in order to achieve higher pay-offs. We will keep this point in mind when analysing the state–foreign investors relationship.

Equally important to note is that the institutionalist approach presupposes a study of the relationship between foreign investors and a host state in such a way that the latter is also looked at as a 'law giver' or, even more importantly, as a 'law creator'. In analysis *vis-à-vis* property rights this is particularly important because, in fact, most of the restrictions are those imposed by the state. Change in the content of the property right means a change in the allocation of resources to which legal support is given by the state. Therefore, the theory of property rights is viewed as being incomplete without the state:

> ... opportunities for gain, whether pecuniary profit or other advantage, accrue to those who can use the government ... If income distribution and risk allocation is a partial function of law of property then the law is an object of control for economic or other gain ... whether the instances be tariff protection, oil subsidies, real estate agents' attempts to ban 'for sale' signs on private homes or any other type of property rights.[41]

Such a focus on the state becomes even more important in the context of studies of the former USSR, which was a highly *etatistic* society throughout its whole history.

Furthermore, in applying the institutionalist approach we use the insights accumulated by its 'neo-institutionalist' stream, which has become widely accepted in studies of law, politics and economics.[42] The new institutionalism is not a completely new school. March and Olsen define it as 'blending elements of an old institutionalism into the non-institutionalist styles of recent theories of politics'.[43] More pointedly, they express this point as follows:

> new institutionalism insists on a more autonomous role for political institutions. The state is not only affected by society but also affects it ... Political outcomes [are] a function of three primary factors: the distribution of preferences (interests) among political actors, the distribution of resources (powers), and the constraints imposed by the rules of the game (constitutions).[44]

North, an economist, in turn, says:

> What is different about the new institutional economics approach from the traditional economist's account? After all both accounts use neoclassical price theory. The difference is that the former abandons a crucial assumption of neoclassical theory, and incorporates a crucial feature about the characteristics of institutions. Abandoned is instrumental rationality; incorporated are the characteristics of institutions that produce path dependence.[45]

These analytical insights are echoed in the legal field. For instance, according to 'old' institutionalism, legal scholars assumed that actors construct institutions that achieve the outcomes they desire, rarely asking where preferences come from or considering feedback mechanisms between interests and institutions. The neo-institutionalist approach fills this gap, for if law does indeed matter inasmuch as 'institutions do not merely reflect the preferences and power of the units constituting them; the institutions themselves shape those preferences and that power'.[46] Furthermore, in this more process-oriented view, institutions define the scope of the constraints on political actors, and interests emerge within particular normative and historical contexts. Institutions do not just constrain options: they establish the very criteria by which people discover their preferences. In other words, we should assume that some of the most important sunk costs are cognitive. This assumption will be helpful in our analysis of the interaction between the political and the legal aspects of FDI.

1.7 Summary

The above discussion provided explanations of reasons and definitions of those methodological tools which form the theoretical framework of this book. The following chapter will determine the subject of this research in that it will split the issue in question into several units of analysis on the basis of the methodological approach applicable to each of them. By so doing it will also delimit the scope of certain concepts to be applied to the units of analysis that are defined in the following chapter.

2
Units of Analysis

2.1 Introduction

Having defined the relevance to the present study of the methodological techniques advanced by scholars in recent years, it is necessary to define the subject of research. In order to achieve this goal, we need to break it down into its component units: foreign direct investment (FDI), transition, the state, and, finally, legal regulation.

2.2 Foreign direct investment

Economists have been dealing with capital movements, as well as those of labour and trade, since the time of Ricardo. Efforts to explain why firms engage in FDI have provided the starting point for a large number of studies.[1] Earlier theories focused on international trading patterns and on macroeconomic determinants. As noted above, this reflected the fact that FDI was not then as common as it is today. In contrast, more recent theories have focused on the determinants within individual businesses and industries; they have also focused on FDI as part of a process of multi-stage international growth. These shifts in the understanding of FDI reveal not only a deepening of the scope of the examination of FDI, but also emphasize how the phenomenon of FDI has been affected by changes in the economic, social and political framework. Equally importantly, this process of transformation sometimes results in the disappearance of certain concepts of FDI that had previously been in existence. Such studies have also displayed how significant non-economic determinants affecting FDI can be – pure economic reasons do not fully explain the multifaceted nature of FDI. This becomes even more important when we examine the legal regulation of FDI in the context of an unsettled society where institutions and the rules of their interaction are either not clearly defined or have yet to emerge. Therefore, an understanding of these various determinants is a methodological starting point for our study, which can assist us in formulating research questions which will be relevant to our aims.

An analysis of the existing economic literature shows that it offers an inadequate analytical basis for understanding the nature of FDI. This is particularly true for the study of legal regulation of FDI in the conditions of a transitional society such as Kazakhstan. Seemingly, the approach based on economic grounds omits entirely the sociopolitical context which is more fluid in conditions of transition and affects the law-making process more directly. On this point, Johnston commented: '[A]s an instrument of analysis which inevitably shapes the legal world it analyses, the economic model alone is not enough: It must be enriched by a broader understanding of the social and cultural context within which law and economics operates.'[2] Nonetheless, the economic ingredient in the legal analysis of FDI cannot be ignored. The primary reason – that is, profit maximization – which stands behind any FDI presupposes consideration of the existing economic theories on FDI as an inalienable cornerstone of legal analysis.

Although the willingness of the post-Soviet states to allow foreign investment in their domestic economies clearly displays the economic rationale that lies behind FDI, the review of economic theories on FDI that follows is not merely an acknowledgement of the economic contents of the existing or emerging legal norms. For the purpose of this study, it is more important that any economic analysis of the law on FDI helps us to achieve several methodological objectives. First, it should allow us to assess how the newly emerging law on FDI corresponds with the economic rationale inherent in the international flow of direct investment. Secondly, an understanding of current economic theories on FDI should allow us to better understand how the legal arrangements established by a host government meet the objectives of the emerging domestic market economic system, how far-reaching in terms of time these objectives are, how they affect the actual execution of the emerging system of property rights and, accordingly, how they affect the decision-making process of private economic actors, particularly foreign investors. Obviously, the second task can be achieved if one considers the issue through lenses other than economic ones, particularly using the neo-institutionalist tools of political science.

In sum, the goals of this section are as follows. We will first outline the contours of the economic analytical framework within which our legal phenomena will be studied. This is necessary in order to define and then to assess the peculiarities of the domestic economic rationale for FDI. This will help us to identify the underlying conditions from which the institutional formation takes place and in particular how this domestic rationale is reflected in the host government's legal arrangements. Secondly, we consider the existing legal regulatory framework from the point of view of certain economic objectives that are being pursued by the law-maker. This will begin with an outlining of certain basic theoretical propositions that are provided by international economic scholarship.

Generally, most authors see FDI as being a response to market imperfections, which vary significantly from country to country. Hymer, one of the first scholars to examine FDI, considered multinational corporations (MNCs) from the point of view of their internal nature and suggested that firms invest overseas in order to gain higher profits from the competitive advantage afforded by these activities. To achieve this advantage, these firms had to organize an integrated international operation so as to retain control over their advantage, and to avoid the uncertainties of operating at arm's length in an open market.[3]

Vernon, in turn, emphasized the importance of new product technology as a determinant for international investment and suggested a theory of 'product cycle' which was the first attempt to integrate both the firm- and the location-specific factors of MNCs. According to this theory, as the product matures, demand in the domestic market becomes saturated. This leads to the seeking of new opportunities for profit in outside markets which, in turn, makes firms expand their operations overseas. As the lifecycle of a product nears its end, the only way to remain competitive may be to reduce production costs still further. This explains why MNCs use less developed countries as locations for FDI.[4]

Another aspect of the market imperfections approach to FDI focuses on the internalization of transactions within multinational firms because the transaction costs associated with trade and/or licensing are more expensive than those associated with FDI. For instance, Buckley and Casson assert that the internalization of markets across national boundaries generates MNCs.[5] They further argue that of the various markets in intermediate products the market in productive knowledge is considered to carry the strongest incentive for internalization. From this observation they conclude that the pattern of growth of MNCs since the Second World War is a by-product of the internalization of markets in knowledge.[6] The shift towards the internalization of markets in knowledge also explains why MNCs have tended to invest more in developed countries since the Second World War. The cost[7] of adapting such knowledge to different markets makes developing countries less attractive than locations for investments based on high-technology knowledge.[8]

Other economic theories treat FDI as a stage in the process of internationalization. In particular, one such approach is associated with differences between the strategic objectives of different types of FDI: market-seeking, production cost-minimizing, and raw material-seeking. If resource-seeking is considered to be a special subset of production cost-reducing, then there are two fundamental types of FDI projects – those that are primarily designed to serve the foreign markets where they are located, and those that are primarily designed to provide low-cost production facilities for exports (of raw materials, intermediate goods or finished products) to other markets or to production facilities in foreign countries (including, in some cases, the home markets).[9]

The studies of Dunning provide fertile material for examining the evolution of theorizing on this subject.[10] In his 'eclectic approach' he accepts that, although it is not possible to formulate a single, operationally testable theory that can explain all forms of foreign-owned production, nevertheless, it is possible to formulate a general paradigm of MNC activity. According to Dunning, this paradigm may set out a conceptual framework and seek to identify clusters of variables relevant to all kinds of foreign-owned output.[11] Dunning's 'eclectic paradigm' is based on the complementary nature of theories based on firm or ownership-specific, location-specific and internalization factors. In particular, Dunning's recent findings are based on an analysis of FDI in the context of the process of *globalization*. This approach refines and partially puts in logical tune previous theories related to FDI.

In a concise form an 'eclectic paradigm' was initially formulated by Dunning in 1993.[12] At this time, he argued that the pace and direction of technological, political and institutional change, especially as it has affected the extent and character of international transactions, demands a systemic recasting of the traditional role of national governments as custodians of the economic welfare of citizens within their jurisdictions. Central to his thesis was the premise that, as a result of the dramatic growth in the number of cross-border linkages forged by

MNCs, the latitude for autonomous and purely domestic-oriented actions on the part of the governments of nation states is being severely curtailed.[13] In light of the present 'almost universal trend towards the deeper internationalization of economic activity', he defined globalization as 'a process towards the widening of the extent and form of cross-border transactions; and of the deepening of the economic interdependence between the actions of globalizing entities – be they private or public institutions or governments'.[14] There are three substantial features related to globalization. First is a dramatic increase in the significance and scope of all kinds of cross-border transactions.[15] Second, the value of production financed by FDI now considerably exceeds that of trade.[16] Third, the organization of international transactions, particularly among the largest MNCs, has become both more systemic and geographically integrated.

Dunning concludes that the movement towards globalization is essentially technologically driven and that the most critical distinction between the globalizing economy of the 1990s and the international economy of the 1980s rests in the nature of income-generating assets. He notes that a century ago the international division of labour was primarily based on the spatial distribution of natural resources. Today, the capacity of a country to produce wealth rests increasingly on the extent to which it can create new resources or assets – such as information, technological capacity, management techniques and organizational competence.[17] This means that FDI in less developed countries, which as a rule cannot contribute to the creation of substantial new knowledge or other intangible assets, is mainly caused by final-product marketing reasons (the theory of 'product cycle') or FDI is aimed at the performance of functions supplementing product manufacturing or marketing (the internalization of transaction costs).

Furthermore, Dunning points out that the key wealth-creating actor in his scenario is the MNC, which is also the main determining institution of the spatial distribution of created assets. Such a distribution depends upon certain conditions faced by an MNC in a particular host country. Accordingly, the qualitative characteristics of FDI, its aim, scope, and specific role in the strategy of MNCs' growth, will vary depending upon peculiarities of location. It is obvious from the theoretical overview above that the agenda of a multinational corporation in a developed country is different from that in a less developed country. This is because in conditions of an established market economy an MNC carrying out FDI is more hard-pressed by competition, which requires from it more research and development (R&D)

capital expenses directed at the creation and updating of its intangible assets (knowledge, technology, and so on) or both. This contiguity with a developed market results in the creation of new intangible assets which, according to Dunning, are the principal engines of globalization and which drive the whole process of present international production.[18]

Given this new international division of labour, what strategy is likely to be developed by MNCs towards transitional states of the former USSR? More specifically, how dependent are host nations on the strategies of multinational corporations? Is their relationship a two-way process? Finally, how are the answers on these questions likely to affect the emerging laws on FDI?

According to Dunning, globalization is indeed the first and foremost expression of a new international division of labour, which is based increasingly on the way in which countries and firms are able to engineer the production of new income-generating assets, and to combine these with location-bound natural resources – the quantity and quality of which, itself, is influenced by the policies and strategies adopted by governments.[19]

In turn, in a comparison of four East Asian and two Latin American newly industrializing countries, Haggard concludes that it is a country's choice of a particular development strategy that determines the nature of its links to the international economy, not the other way around.[20] Evans states that 'the opportunities for transforming dependency may be structurally given, but local political action determines whether the international opportunities result in local change'.[21] In other words, the link between external and internal forces is no longer as mechanical as previously portrayed. Therefore, our central concern here is that if law on FDI is a manifestation of such a connection, what makes different transitional states choose different legal designs for the treatment of foreign investment?

Indeed, international economic transactions have become increasingly internalized within MNC-controlled intra-group and intra-firm production networks.[22] Many commentators suggest that transnational forces have marginalized the state as an agent of development and have rendered national industrial strategies far less effective, if not altogether obsolete.[23] Nevertheless, although the changing MNCs' strategies did indeed decisively alter the strategic options available to late-industrializing countries, the national policies and institutions of the latter still influence industrial growth patterns, even in the context of internationally integrated production chains. An examination of the countries that have liberalized foreign investment laws over the past decade shows that each individual host state has managed FDI in a different way.

Furthermore, as the practice of South East Asian states indicates, these countries have exchanged their prior efforts to build integrated industries under national control for new policies aimed at harnessing MNCs' international strategies to the tasks of domestic industrial change. Legal tools have played an important facilitating role in this shift of policies. Different legislative approaches to the arrangement of links between the international and domestic economies among otherwise similar countries offer important clues to the interplay of political interests and institutional constraints which undergird developmental orientations. The outcomes of this interplay may well be the driving force behind, and a key for, understanding the nature of the emerging law on FDI in the transitional states of the former USSR. What makes the impact of these outcomes for the creation and implementation of property rights in the developed world different from that in the developing one? More pointedly, why is the nexus between these outcomes and the legal regulation of FDI so crucial for studies of the latter in conditions of transition?

2.3 Transition

What makes a study of legal regulation of FDI in transitional countries different from one focused on the 'settled' countries? The following may be the answer. The newly emerging sociopolitical and economic realms are potentially capable of making an impact on the formation of law and its implementation. The degree of such an impact, however, is unforeseeable. This is partly because definitive borders between the realms of politics, economics and law are yet to be formed and the rules of interaction between the three realms are also in the process of formation. In other words, transition is a process of institution formation. Therefore, the focus of this study in general can be described as the relationship between 'old' institutions and the process of the formation of new ones and their efficiency, as well as the extent to which models of institution formation allow us to believe that the institutions which will emerge will be efficient.

The primary aim of this section is to narrow down the phenomenon of transition to certain analytical terms which may accordingly form a framework that integrates a number of factors underlying the existence and effects of the legal regulation that are often omitted or treated separately in the relevant literature. In order to achieve this objective we employ here the relevant findings and methodologies applied by political scientists, bearing in mind that legal regulation is part of the broader process of social regulation which is indisputably a political process. It exhibits one of the defining features of any such process – the contest for power, the study of which, as such, lies at the heart of the interests of political scientists. In the legal regulation of FDI in conditions of a highly fluid process of competition for a new balance of power and, accordingly, for access to the law-making process, therefore, lies an important opportunity for reconciliation between the long-divorced disciplines of law and political science. At the same time, the purpose of applying political science methods here differs from the purpose commonly pursued by students of the politics of transition. The application of a political perspective to these matters is not only to achieve an understanding of power per se or to understand what kind of sociopolitical organization is likely to be achieved in Kazakhstan, given the present characteristics of transition, but, more importantly, is to find out why and how certain kinds of sociopolitical organization lead to the establishment of a particular model of legal regulation of FDI.

The current socioeconomic changes, generally referred to as the 'transition', are considered by many political scholars as the culmination of the 'third wave' of a democratic transition. According to Huntington, this 'wave' started in 1974 and continued up to the beginning of the 1990s. As he noted, within this period democratic regimes replaced authoritarian ones in approximately thirty countries of Europe, Asia and Latin America.[24] Socioeconomic processes which began in the mid-1980s are still a controversial subject which has captured the continuing interest of scholars in many fields. The sudden disintegration of the USSR itself and the subsequent independence of the 15 newly emerged states have shifted the academic debate onto a level of even greater complexity. Undoubtedly, one needs to prevent overreliance on the previous knowledge generated with regard to transition because, in the end, this transition from socialism to capitalism is the first of its kind. Thus, a real challenge in analysis of post-Soviet transition is to rely on previously said words to express, rather than to restrain, thoughts.

The theory of transition first defines modes of transitions, which are usually distinguished according to the process through which authoritarian power-holders are replaced by oppositions. There are transitions from above (transformation/transaction/reform), transitions from below (transformation/breakdown/rupture), and transitions where the regime and the opposition have an equal role in system transformation (trans-placement/extrication).[25] In practice, the mode of transition has important implications for the stability of an emerging democracy and it is 'a principal determinant of whether democracy will emerge'.[26] Accordingly, the Kazakh case is one which can hardly be fitted into any of the above models. Some commentors have assested that transition in Kazakhstan is a case of transformation when, following the disintegration of the USSR, the previous power-holders were replaced by republican ones. Further, it is assumed that the Kazakh case is a case of transformation of the system. It seems, however, that the actual case fits none of the above models. In reality, it was a case of mere replacement of one group of power-holders by another, similar group. What was different though was the new quality of external pressures which affected the actions of the newly emerged power-holders, as well as a new agenda which emerged before them (as, it will further be argued, this agenda is just for their self-survival) and a weak demand to allow an embryonic civil society to develop.

The demarcation of stages within the transition process is another component of modern theory. According to Rustow, there are three phases in the transition process.[27] The preparatory phase features the polarization of the main political actors, followed by a decision phase in which some crucial elements of democratic procedure are institutionalized. The third phase is the period during which politicians and the electorate are 'habituated' to the new political rules. Given the facts that the Kazakh power-holders have made an effort to prevent the emergence of any social forces to offer a feasible alternative to the state as well as presiding over a gradual decrease of national economic wealth (and thus decreasing the underlying potential of power in resource allocation), one may conclude that the country has not even entered the first stage of transition. Rather, the above reality will first result in formation of certain social forces from below. Presently, the opposition is a by-product of the ruling elite itself – that is, people who have been excluded from access to resources.

Transition varies from country to country and there may be many roads to democracy.[28] There are also variations with regard to the speed, methods and players involved in transition. At the same time, there are a number of features in common. In particular, Welsh emphasizes the following.[29]

First, transition periods are characterized by the need to address certain crucial key matters. After long periods during which major political, social, and economic changes have been postponed or blocked, there is a growing impatience among the population which intensifies the apparent need for change.[30] Second, transition periods are characterized by great uncertainty with regard to both progress and the results. In practical terms this means that democracy (as the final goal of a transition) is not the only possible outcome of transition: the collapse of authoritarian rule may result in a variety of outcomes. Third, previous authoritarian structures are altered during a transition period by the rapidly expanding range of political actors and the need for political communication among them. Fourth, transitions are elite-centred. The terms of transitions are settled by emerging elites, not by the public.[31] Last, but not least, transitions involve bargaining between various political actors (namely, rulers and opposition).

The transition process, its timing, modality, type and final success depend upon the nature of the previous authoritarian regime. This issue has also been widely discussed by scholars throughout the 1990s. Their arguments, made on the basis of historical facts, point to major differences between the transitions in Eastern Europe and those in Latin American and South Eastern Asian countries. As Linz stresses, totalitarianism in Eastern Europe had 'succeeded in changing societies and largely destroying the bases of the socio-cultural pluralism of civil society ... [and] the independence of economic actors'.[32] By contrast, on South America and Southern Europe authoritarian regimes did not change society in this extreme way: non-political groups were allowed a degree of autonomy that could potentially be used as a power base from which to oppose the regimes.[33] While the transitions in Southern Europe and South America were accompanied by what O'Donnell and Schmitter refer to as the 'resurrection of civil society', in Eastern Europe it is more accurate to talk of 'a re-inventing' rather than 'a resurrection' of civil society.[34] In the Kazakh case, the country has not experienced classical industrialization, but rather entered the stage of socialism from the stage of feudalism. Hence, one may assume that a Kazakh civil society has yet to emerge.

The central and universal question concerning transitions is whether they lead to a consolidated democracy. The processes of transition from authoritarian rule and of democratic consolidation are quite distinct, moreover – 'the actors, strategies, and conditions that facilitate transitions do not necessarily overlap with those that make democratic consolidation likely'.[35] Democracy is consolidated when most conflicts are processed through democratic institutions, when nobody can control the outcomes ex post and the results are not predetermined ex ante, they matter within some predictable limits, and they evoke the compliance of the relevant political forces.[36] In other words, consolidated democracy is the institutionalization of a new set of rules for the political game on the basis of the construction of a new type of regime.[37]

In contrast to the transition, democratic consolidation is a more complex process. As Valenzuela argues, democratic consolidation involves both the elimination of residues of the old system that are incompatible with the workings of a democratic regime' and the building of new institutions that reinforce the democratic rules of the game.[38] The literature on the consolidation of democracy is rather broad and sometimes includes diametrically opposed opinions. It is worthwhile outlining some of the main ideas they embody in order to then apply these to the case of Kazakhstan. A first area of inquiry concerns the correlation between the preceding type of authoritarian regime and the problems of democratic consolidation. The debate is centred here on the role of historical legacies. Przeworski, for instance, considers that a country's destination, rather than where it is coming from, is the key. In contrast, Huntington argues that the nature of the rulers under the preceding regime makes a difference in the process of democratic consolidation. To back up his approach, he compares transitions in Latin America, where the military's retreat to the barracks entails a full withdrawal from the political scene, and Eastern Europe, where the Communist Party remains a political actor. He then concludes that transition from a one-party system to democracy is likely to be more difficult than the transition from a military regime to democracy, but that it is also likely to be a more permanent change.[39] Another approach is represented by O'Donnell, who argues that cases in which the authoritarian regime was economically successful and relatively less repressive are more prone to an authoritarian regression, given that the people's memories of the authoritarian period are less likely to focus solely on the regime's repressive policies.[40]

Another area of inquiry concerns the differential effect of modes of transitions on the prospects for democratic consolidation. Przeworski sees either no, or a very limited, historical connection between the modality of transition and the features of the emerging regime.[41] Huntington, in contrast, argues that 'a consensual, less violent transition provides a better basis for consolidating democracy than do conflict and violence'.[42] O'Donnell supports the position of Huntington. He also believes that transition through transaction allows for too much continuity with the old regime, while the break introduced by a transition through regime defeat may militate against the exercise of restraint and, most fundamentally, the emergence of the consensus needed to shore up a nascent democracy. Hence, the prospects of democratic consolidation appear to be enhanced in those cases where the more or less balanced power between the authoritarian leaders and emerging opposition groups makes compromise on both sides an essential ingredient of the transition.[43]

The next area of debate in relation to democratic consolidation is focused on the effect of economic factors. Huntington states that a country's level of economic development both helps to trigger a transition and assists the process of democratic consolidation.[44] Przeworski presents an even more fundamental study, using the presence of economic crisis and the necessity of dealing with it as the driving force of his argument. He underlines that what matters in terms of the process of democratic consolidation is the decision-making style adopted to deal with an economic crisis. He considers the political dynamics of economic reforms in terms of the attitudes of three groups of actors – politicians in office, technocrats and the voters. As practice shows, the political consequences of economic reforms are far from beneficial. As governments 'vacillate between the technocratic political style inherent in market-oriented reforms and the participatory style required to maintain consensus, representative institutions are undermined and democracy is weakened'.[45] To solve this problem, Przeworski suggests 'widespread consultations channelled through representative institutions and ratified by elections', which would avoid the destabilizing consequences of market reforms and assist emerging democracies to consolidate.[46] At the same time, he acknowledges that such an economic policy-making style does not appear to be present in most new democracies. How does the Kazakhstani reality fit the above opinions, given the fact that most earlier transitions took place, as a rule, in countries at a lower level of socioeconomic and industrial development, at stages when both privatization and a change of development strategy are far easier to implement? How relevant to the above discussion is the fact that industrialization in Kazakhstan happened in conditions of almost complete isolation from the outside world?

The basic underlying questions provided by this section can be formulated as follows: Do we presently have transition in Kazakhstan in the sense outlined by the earlier authors? Is a post-independence period a continuation of the transition which seemingly started during the Soviet period under Gorbachev or is it, perhaps, a 'new' kind of transition? Is it possible that transition conceived by *perestroika* died with the collapse of the USSR? What do we have now? Even if we assume that there is transition, what implications arise from the fact that the main impetus for the breakdown of the old order came from outside Kazakhstan and not from a powerful democratic or nationalistic movement within the country which brought down the Communist regime? How independent are the new institutions from the old ones, and how, eventually, will they affect the implementation of property rights provided to foreign investors? Furthermore, one must note the absence of embryonic forms of civil society in the pre-Communist history of Kazakhstan.[47] How is this historical factor likely to affect the seemingly emerging new democratic and market institutions?

The next question is relevant to the previous one. Given the absence of civil society, how does the fact of the preservation of the elite of the *ancien régime* affect its likelihood to react to the idea of building democracy? Is it able to conduct itself in the same way as the state elite in conditions of established democracy would behave? Undoubtedly, the above discussion sets up a fertile ground for an analytical approach to transition in Kazakhstan.

2.4 Transition as it affects property rights

The previous discussion provided a basic theoretical framework to evaluate the behaviour of parties in relation to property rights. This section seeks to explain how the search for efficiency in the legal regulation of foreign direct investment can be matched with the outcomes of transitional political processes and behaviour of the state. It should be first noted that political science has addressed the issue of economic efficiency. For instance, political scholars agree that two principal goals are commonly pursued by all transitional countries: economic growth and political democratization. Further, the notion of development also in principle has to do with efficiency. Yet, there is less consent with regard to the analysis of the modes of interaction between the above two objectives.

One should also note that this debate is not a recent phenomenon. A few decades ago, Hayek and Friedman and a number of other scholars suggested that political and economic liberties should be viewed as interconnected and mutually complementary phenomena.[48] Their key argument was that democracy is the only guarantor of a limited state and hence of free enterprise. Lindblom stresses that historically the effort of early merchants in Europe to protect their property from an absolutist state coincided with the emergence of democratic political institutions.[49] Accordingly, early liberal theorists considered the establishment of an orderly system of exchange among proprietors as the main function of the popular government.[50]

Still, political scholars sometimes arrive at controversial outcomes. One group of scholars tend to believe that transitional countries cannot simultaneously pursue democracy and economic growth. Hence, they argue that authoritarianism at earlier stages of development facilitates material growth. Accordingly, they view premature democratization as a factor which brings instability and thus discourages economic growth and foreign investment.[51] Similar views are implicitly echoed in recent works by legal scholars. In particular, Waelde and Gunderson note:

> While legislation in the Western market economies has generally evolved through the socio-economic and political processes in each country, the legislative and regulatory development in the transition economies must keep pace with, or anticipate, the unprecedented rate of political, economic and social change taking place. In fact, the type of legislative and regulatory perfectionism appropriate to fully developed market economies could actually impede the dynamism of emerging economic forces so essential to the transition economies chances for success.[52]

In opposition to this view is a proposition made by another group of scholars. Shepsle, for instance, argues that political institutions can be the '*ex ante* agreements about a structure of co-operation' that accordingly 'economize on transaction costs, reduce opportunism and other forms of agency "slippage", and thereby enhance the prospects of gains through co-operation'.[53] This group of scholars also suggests that a democratic political system makes investors believe in the durability and sustainability of a country and thus encourages material growth and long-term foreign investment.[54] Several studies, in turn, tested both notions and arrived at divergent outcomes. In some cases, it was concluded that popular governments failed to boost economic development and to attract foreign investment. The conclusion was that this showed quite the opposite to what might have been expected because it suggested that authoritarian regimes would promote a country's material improvement. Hence, the process of democratization may include certain variables which can hamper economic growth. Likewise, a dictatorial regime may provide conditions able to boost foreign investment and improve a country's economic performance.[55]

Having elaborated upon his earlier views, Olson revealed the link between democratic institutions and legal mechanisms of property rights enforcement and the growth of a country's output.[56] He argues that more democratic political systems are likely to perform better economically because they restrain their respective states from infringing property rights. In turn, Goldsmith suggested in his study that representative government institutions and secure systems of property each have a positive association with the rate of production growth.[57] Based on his empirical findings, he proves that there exists a causal, not just a correlational, relationship between democratic and property-oriented regimes, on one hand, and the better growth record, on another. He notes that:

> The more democratic countries in the sample grow faster, perhaps because political competition is a check on predatory rulers. The more democratic countries also appear to offer greater protection of property. The reason may be that business interests can wield disproportionate influence on representative government. With motivation and resources, producers can lobby for secure ownership and contract rights. Such economic prerogatives, in turn, are conducive to private sector investment and growth.[58]

The above discussion allows us to suggest that private-property rights should have no a priori special status among institutions that promote efficiency. Furthermore, it requires focusing on the notion of power, more specifically for our case the state – the 'fittest' institution surviving after the collapse of the USSR – as a unit of analysis. Further, in our next section we should split this unit inasmuch as viewing it as a unitary and monolithic entity will yield little insight into a host government's development policies and the true nature of its legal regulatory arrangements for FDI.

2.5 The state

One of the arguments of this thesis is that the mechanism which provides the link between efficiency and institutional formation is not similar, as suggested by some authors, to evolutionary models in biology, in which the fittest institutions survive, and the inefficient ones are weeded out. To ensure efficiency, it is not enough that individuals are wealth-maximizers; they must also be exchanging within a well-specified framework which channels individual self-seeking activity towards collective ends. When considering institution formation, individuals are functioning within an incomplete institutional framework. Therefore, the mere possibility of cooperative gains in institution formation will not ensure that institutions evolve optimally as the result of interaction among self-centred individuals. In other words, our argument is that in a pre-market (that is a pre-institution) environment there is no structure that will align individual and social benefits and costs.

At the same time, even if the institutional framework had already evolved, a certain degree of enforcement is required to guarantee the functionality of the whole system. In the words of Umbeck:

> Ownership rights to property can exist only as long as other people agree to respect them or as long as the owner can forcefully exclude those who do not agree. If the individuals agree to respect each other's ownership rights, they may do so either implicitly, in which case they are usually called customs or traditions, or explicitly through contract, in which case they are called laws or rules ... However, even if all individuals enter into an explicit agreement to assign and respect each other's ownership rights, some force or threat of force will still be required. This follows from the postulate of individual maximization. If one person can violate the terms of the agreement and deprive another of his assigned rights he will do so if the gains exceed the costs. Therefore, the contracting group must agree to impose costs upon anyone who would take someone else's property. This would involve the forceful exclusion of would-be violators. Ultimately all ownership rights are based on the abilities of individuals, or groups of individuals, to forcefully maintain exclusivity. Force also underlies all allocative systems.[59]

In other words, the property rights are based on the underlying distribution of power. It is a commonplace that there is a direct correspondence between the structure of power and resource allocation. Hence, allocation is dependent on a distribution of force prior to entitlements and, by its nature, unalterable without cost. If entitlement systems are grounded on some underlying structure of force, then there are clear limitations as to how entitlements can be varied to alter allocations. The cost of enforcing entitlement systems will depend on this underlying structure of force. Consequently, the issues for this study are: What makes the state in conditions of transition exercise its power to enforce the rules in such a way as to try and align individual and social benefits and costs? Or, accordingly, what prevents it from doing so? Further, what exactly prevents the state from altering its underlying structure of power which then affects the allocative system within society, even though the latter is obviously inefficient?

The behaviour of the state is a result of the interaction of multiple factors. In his study, Putnam presented a set of plausible arguments about the ways in which foreign policy-makers play two-level games which fuse together domestic and international calculations.[60] Similarly, in its relationships with foreign investors, the state's behaviour is also the result of such a fusion. It is more important to note that the content of actual policy towards FDI is a continuation of the state's domestic policy considerations. This means that, given the state's ability to create institutional constraints, first of all, via the property rights assignment, the content of interaction between a foreign investor and a host state may vary depending on the latter's adherence to long-term efficiency.

The state, as with any political actor, is indeed rational in most of its actions. A few theories have emerged to explain the rationale behind the state's and its officials' behaviour. For instance, according to the public interest theory, state officials seek to promulgate and enforce laws in a welfare-enhancing fashion because it is their job to do so. On the other hand, according to public choice theorists, it is naïve to expect officials to work selflessly to promote laudable social goals. They argue instead that the lawmakers and individuals who administer and enforce the legal rules act in a manner designed to maximize their own welfare. Hence, government officials and civil servants are primarily interested in accumulating power and perks, while legislators are motivated by a desire to be re-elected.[61] In turn, Cheffins and other legal scholars correctly observe that public choice theory does not explain all political behaviour and, in fact, 'people in government do not appear to act in a self-interested fashion at all times'.[62]

It is clear that politics is a complex social phenomenon inasmuch as it almost invariably involves a large number of interconnected problems that impinge simultaneously on a political actor's calculations. Actors seldom play any one game in isolation from many others; they rarely have complete information; games are iterated; and players in any one game are simultaneously concerned about the information they reveal at any one time to their opponent through their choices of strategies.[63] Hence, Tsebelis comes to the conclusion that:

> Instead of the concept of rationality as a model of human behaviour, I propose the concept of rationality as a subset of human behaviour. The change in perspective is important; I do not claim that rational choice can explain every phenomenon and that there is no room for other explanations, but I do claim that rational choice is a better approach to situations in which the actors' identity and goals are established and the rules of the interaction are precise and known to the interacting agents. As the actors' goals become fuzzy, or as the rules of the interaction become more fluid and imprecise, rational-choice explanations will become less applicable.[64]

This observation confirms the postulations of rational choice theory which, in general, assigns a fairly important role to the interaction among the players in determining which equilibrium they will end up playing. More importantly, the above statement emphasizes the importance of the goals and the rules of the interaction because they determine the initial expectations of participants. Hence, it is the designer who makes the choice of a particular equilibrium by creating certain institutional structures.[65]

Economic policy is always a political process. State elites inevitably view it in terms of its impact on their political authority and base of support. The numerous examples of authoritarian regimes whose economic policies have been dominated by patronage interests, however, suggest that the issue runs far deeper than the formal political institutions which identify a given regime. In particular, one of the crucial conclusions of recent studies is that the degree of elite cohesion is the key to determining whether leaders can adopt a long-term view of the political consequences of economic policies, such as their impact on regime legitimacy, or must instead use economic decisions to mobilize support in order to secure their short-term political survival. When heterogeneous elite factions struggle to capture and hold state power, they almost always seek to mobilize support from broader constituencies by granting favours. In such cases, economic policies are likely to be used exclusively for political mobilization and fund-raising rather than developmental guidance. In turn, as Geddes notes, elite unity and cohesive political authority allow leaders to build and sustain strong bureaucracies. Conversely, when a country's political elite is fragmented, and elite factions mobilize support to compete for or retain power, they will eventually undermine and politicize even the most well-organized bureaucratic systems.[66] When different institutions such as militaries, political parties, regional ties and the like foster elite cohesion and lend the state coherence as a corporate actor, policy-making will be insulated from short-term political imperatives.

At the same time, policy strategies still reflect the state elite's fundamental need to maintain political support. Thus, even 'autonomous' states must engage society in an ongoing negotiation for cooperation and support, which circumscribes policy strategies in specific ways. For instance, in capitalist states, private business interests exert a unique structural power through their control over the crucial investment resources needed to stimulate growth and employment.[67] This means that the state autonomy explanation, offered by some scholars as an explanation of the phenomenon of late industrialization, is a problematic explanation of efficacy. It seems likely that a fuller explanation lies in the patterns of interaction between the state and society, which, in turn, results in the efficient behaviour of the former. As Doner and Howes and Okimoto observed, the superior economic performance of the newly industrialized states stemmed neither from unilateral state guidance nor from unassisted market forces. Rather, their structural dynamism came from a unique ability to harmonize public policies and private decisions to encourage and guide *long-term* investments.[68] One clear strength of this proposition is that it is far more plausible in terms of the information requirements for successful industrial policy. Here, strategies are not the fully preconceived master plans of elite bureaucrats but, instead, emerge through ongoing negotiations between state authorities and private business. The state serves not as a far-seeing guide, but as a broker for consensus and a catalyst for private-sector or public–private collective action to invest in public goods or otherwise overcome market failures. This also corresponds with North's observation that 'institutional change is an incremental process in which the short-run profitable opportunities cumulatively create the long-run path of change'.[69] Accordingly, as Doner further notes, the shared goals shape specific institutional mechanisms which play developmental, long-term investment role, rather than being directed towards short-term rent-seeking.[70] But why should certain types of relations between the state and society (or state and business) produce more effective growth policies rather than rent-seeking?

Neo-institutionalism provides a framework for approaching this question. It emphasizes the ways in which the institutional setting – formal legal rules, organizations and informal social norms – restrain actors' self-interested behaviour and facilitate collective action to overcome market failures. In this view, as Doner and Howes argue, state–business interaction results in coherent policies instead of rent-seeking when it occurs within well-designed institutions rather than clientelist networks:

> Whatever the direction of [political] influence [from the state to the people or vice versa], the form and success with which a country undertakes economic adjustments are a function of at least two network dimensions: density and institutionalization. Density refers to the number of access points between public and private actors and is a function of the level of government and business concentration and the degree of differentiation between the two ... But even dense networks are likely to be inefficient in promoting economic adjustment if they are highly personalized or clientalist. Seen comparatively, the East Asian cases highlight the value of institutionalized, function based networks in providing dependability for the private sector and consistency in terms of outcomes. ... An ideal-type institutional structure for industrial policy, then might include a state with centralized policy authority, a highly organized private business community, and dense, organized, transparent linkages between the two.[71]

This approach resonates across other disciplines. In particular, the new institutionalism in economics recognizes the ubiquity of transaction costs and the need to create institutional frameworks to support ordinary market transactions.[72]

However, at the same time, the neo-institutionalist approach cannot explain everything. In their review of neo-institutionalism in political science, Thelen and Steinmo explicitly state that 'institutions constrain and refract politics, but they are never the only cause of outcomes'.[73] Thus, politics, viewed as the interaction of actors' power, interests, and strategies, does not fit as an object of analysis in the neo-institutionalists' approach. Rather, they emphasize that bargaining between the state and business is likely to produce a certain political outcome. However, they do not describe the content of this bargaining; they assume rather that explaining how efficient consensus will emerge as the outcome of this bargaining. In other words, the presence of well-institutionalized policy networks explains *how* the state and business might collaborate effectively for long-run growth, but not necessarily *why* they choose to do so. Inspired by the rational choice theory, instituionalists assume that the state and business share common interests in economic growth. Consequently, their main focus is on how to avoid rent-seeking, which is an activity that frustrates cooperation for the common good. Their belief is that the avoidance of rent-seeking is achieved by strong policy institutions. For example, March and Olsen suggest that institutions shape actors' goals through socialization, which fixes actors' assumptions about appropriate behaviour. Once established, strong policy networks 'create' actors' interests in a largely perpetuating way. But if the policy networks impose limits on self-interested or rent-seeking behaviour by the state and business actors, who monitors cooperation and punishes transgression of these limits? Naturally, if the state and private business share a mixture of common and diverging interests, institutions cannot make their cooperation fully self-enforcing. Who creates, then, institutions for coherence and why?

The above question appears to be crucial for a transitional economy whose primary struggle is precisely to replace clientelistic power structures with coherent and authoritative economic institutions. Seemingly, an exploration of the links between coherent institutions and economic outcomes is more politically contingent. The logic behind such a conclusion is that effective industrial policies require a minimum degree of public–private cooperation. States must coordinate such policies with private investors in order to be effective, no matter how much political autonomy they enjoy. By the same token, even a market-based policy stance requires coherent political authority to enforce property rights and protect against clientalist distortion.

Naturally, this economic interdependence between the state and the private business actor is reinforced by politics. The need to secure political rule forces state elites to maintain social support and inevitably shapes economic policies. In turn, state–business interaction can be made coherent through the presence of strong institutions – the Weberian-style bureaucracy on the side of the state, the well-organized business sectors, and the transparent policy networks that link them. The most important point to be addressed in the subsequent chapter is that a broader and long-term view of the political consequences of policy decisions can be achieved only through elite cohesion.

To sum up this section of the analysis, we should state that in this study we will assume that the actual cause of externality is not the lack of institutions.[74] On the contrary, multiple equilibrium points in the models may exist – that is, many possible institutions can evolve. Equilibrium points may or may not contain Pareto-optimal points:

suboptimal institutions may perpetuate because the system of enforcement will punish any deviant behaviour once regularity has been established. An optimal allocation of resources requires an optimal set of institutions. An optimal set of institutions requires an optimal system of interaction which will ensure the formation of optimal institutions. Further, to make a case that institution formation is efficient one has to provide a framework, conceptually similar to the general-equilibrium framework, that is able to forge a link between individual behaviour and collective action. Finally, if one assumes that institutions are formed by a direct maximization of net social benefits by some governing institution, one needs to focus on how the government body is formed, and how it actually arrives at the correct decisions about which institutions should be implemented. These will display the basic reasons for efficient institutions to evolve.

2.6 Legal regulation

As with any other commercial transaction, a relationship which occurs as a result of FDI involves two parties – a foreign investor and the state. However, fundamental differences exist in a relationship between an investor and the state as private parties, on the one hand, and a relationship between them as a governmental entity and a private party, on the other. Therefore, due to the dual nature and the unique powers of the state, the legal regulation of FDI can be analysed from an institutional perspective in which the unique roles of the state and its effects on private foreign investors are addressed.

Given the special characteristics of FDI, which make them highly vulnerable to administrative interference, a wide range of regulatory procedures can be considered to be compatible with sustained private investment. Levy and Spiller provide a comparative assessment of the impact of core political and social institutions on the telecommunications regulatory structures and utility performance in five countries: Argentina, Chile, Jamaica, the Philippines, and the United Kingdom.[75] They argue that the credibility and effectiveness of a regulatory framework, and thus its ability to facilitate private investment, varies with a country's political and social institutions. In their analysis of the legal aspects of the regulation of the telecommunications industry, they come to the conclusion that three complementary mechanisms restraining arbitrary administrative action must be in place: (i) there must be substantive restraints on the discretion of the regulator; (ii) there must be informal or formal constraints on changing the regulatory system; and (iii) there must be institutions that enforce the above formal, substantive or procedural constraints. Thus, the critical methodological starting point in dealing with the legal regulation of FDI is that the focus must be directly placed on restraining arbitrary governmental power – not only maximizing efficiency – so that, through such restraint, investment will be encouraged and sustainable over time. In this way, long-run dynamic efficiency – but not necessarily short-run efficiency – will be served. Such an approach provides insights into how the domestic regulatory regimes provide a suitable environment for investment, both by domestic and foreign parties.

This broadens the entire framework within which we should look at the issue of the legal regulation of FDI. More specifically, we need to answer the question about how, given its existing political and social institutions, a host nation's restraints on arbitrary government action are being addressed. In other words, an assessment of legal regulatory regimes, especially in the conditions of transition, must be addressed through an adequate consideration of the unique aspects of government power, not simply the market power of the state and a foreign investor as private parties involved in FDI relationships.

Further, regulation can be viewed as a design problem with two components: regulatory governance and regulatory incentives. The governance structure of regulation consists of mechanisms that society uses to regulate discretion and to resolve conflicts that arise in relation to these constraints. The regulatory incentive structure consists of the rules directly affecting private entity behaviour. Similarly, the neo-institutionalist law and economics school suggests that the analysis of regulation should proceed at two different levels: one macro-oriented, and the other micro-oriented. In particular, Davis and North draw a distinction between the institutional environment (macro) and institutional arrangements (micro). Williamson provides the following definitions:

> The *institutional environment* is the set of fundamental political, social and legal ground rules that establishes the basis for production, exchange and distribution. Rules governing elections, property rights, and the right of contract are examples ...
>
> An *institutional arrangement* is an arrangement between economic units that governs the ways in which these units can cooperate and/or compete. It ... [can] provide a structure within which its members can cooperate ... or [it can] provide a mechanism that can effect a change in laws or property rights.[76]

In practice, the institutional environment and institutional arrangements are interactive in that the institutional environment sets the general framework within which institutional arrangements take place; in turn, institutional arrangements, their effects, or the difficulties in devising them may effect pressures for change in the institutional environment.

To date, most theoretical work on legal regulation in both industrialized and transitional societies has been focused on the structure of regulatory incentives. The reasons for this are different for transitional and settled countries, and will be explained in the final part of this section. However, Levy and Spiller make a point which can be relevant to industrialized and transitional states. They observe that 'although we find that regulatory incentives indeed affect performance, their impact (positive or negative) comes to the forefront only if regulatory governance has successfully been put into place'.[77] Furthermore, although policy- and law-makers do have a choice of both governance and incentives rules, at the same time each is constrained by the specific institutional endowment of the nation.

It seems that, because of the depth of the ongoing process of institution formation, an approach which focuses exclusively on the regulatory incentives in the case of transitional countries is inadequate and, consequently, the need to focus mainly on regulatory governance rules, rather than regulatory incentives, should be emphasized. Thus, another methodological point is that it is the nature of the institutional endowment itself, and the constraints or options that it does or does not provide, which need to be analysed here for the compatibility with FDI.

North defines the five elements of domestic institutional endowment.[78] These are: (i) the country's legislative and executive institutions; (ii) the country's judicial institutions; (iii) the customs and informal (but broadly accepted) norms that constrain the actions of individuals and institutions (iv) the character of contending social interests within a society and the balance between them, including ideology; and (v) the administrative capabilities of the nation. We will use these elements as a starting point for the analysis given in Chapter 7. What should be noted at this point is that no special institutional endowment is necessary to provide the crucial mechanisms that restrain the arbitrariness of the state. Regulation is likely to be far more credible and long-term in countries with political systems that constrain executive and legislative discretion and have a strong judiciary to limit administrative discretion. In this context, an important element of a host nation's endowment is its constitution because this defines the structure of the government and the rules of interactions, outlines the powers of the various state authorities and includes express limitations on government action. Through this structure the Kazakh Constitution places constraints on the rules of regulatory governance or the incentives that may be implemented by any unit of government in Kazakhstan with respect to FDI. In so doing, the Constitution provides the means by which critical mechanisms identified by Levy and Spiller can be achieved for sustainable investment from foreign parties. It is the nature and significance of these constraints on state action, and the reasons for their existence in the Constitution, which have not been adequately addressed in many of the works of commentators on FDI in the former USSR. Thus, another methodological proposition here is that if regulatory rules are adopted which ignore the important institutional function of Constitutional and other fundamental legislative provisions to restrain government action, then the desired capital inflows, and the overall long-term performance of FDI, will not occur.

The centre of gravity of analysis in the 'settled' countries has been geared mostly towards the analysis of regulatory incentives – that is, the micro-level. These industrialized nations are characterized by political systems in which constitutionalism and the rule of law are paramount features. In other words, even when regulation is not narrowly concerned with rules it is still shaped by the legal structures of public power. Another feature of the nature of the system of regulatory governance in industrialized nations is the 'embedded minimum rationality' which links the state and firms and helps to explain why a firm is a key unit of the economy which the state needs to work with. Accordingly, the underlying task for regulation here is to how to direct this pre-existing rationality in a firm's behaviour towards a consolidated and more efficient outcome. In turn, the state's actions can be viewed as exogenous actions with the purpose of correcting (or correcting for improving) the firm's behaviour. This explains the significance and centrality of the micro-level policies – the regulatory incentives rather than regulatory governance – in understanding and analysing legal regulation in the industrialized nations.

Quite the opposite is the case in post-Soviet transitional countries. Of course, here too, one can find the enterprises and the state as two actors in the emerging market. However, what is lacking in these circumstances is that 'minimum of embedded rationality' which links both of the agents and underpins the rationale behind their behaviour.

Due to the *etatistic* legacy, and thus the continuing strong domination of the state, the centre of gravity of analysis should shift towards the state, rather than a firm, as a driving force of regulation. Seemingly, the primary task for transitional countries is to produce a certain degree of common rationality in the behaviour of both the state and a firm. This, however, can be achieved only if a firm's (and the state's) behaviour is a response to market forces, not exclusively the orders of the irrational state. Thus, in the conditions of a transitional society the issue of legal regulation of FDI is more complex. In contrast to the settled systems, it includes two aspects in which the issue of the regulation of the behaviour of the firm per se is preceded by a more basic question associated with a macro-level – that is, the regulatory governance or institutional environment. More pointedly, the issue here is how the state facilitates the emergence of such a system of regulatory governance which will be truly conducive to the truly market-based behaviour of the firms.

The major difference in reform of the legal regulation in post-Soviet states is in the nature of transformation of the behaviour of the regulated. Under Soviet rule, the mode of behaviour was completely subordinated to the state's will and, consequently, the overall system was based on imposed constraints rather than the self-motivation of the regulated entities and incentives.[79] Therefore, a crucial starting point for the reforms was the privatization of the formerly state-owned enterprises.[80] Gray correctly observes that the main objective of privatization in ex-Communist countries is not just a transfer of ownership titles.[81] Rather, she states, the privatization task goes beyond changing ownership of assets per se. Privatization programmes in transition economies should be evaluated on three broad dimensions: (i) the corporate governance mechanisms they create; (ii) the supporting institutions they foster; and (iii) the extent to which they create a self-sustaining economic and political reform process. As the current literature shows, however, the process of privatization already undertaken by all post-Communist states, including Kazakhstan, has not achieved these objectives.[82]

Thus, it is important to note that corporate governance emergence through the privatization process is too slow to be effective. Accordingly, it is far too early to theorize about any meaningful effects of the regulatory incentives in Kazakhstan. In order to fully understand the nature of the legal regulation of FDI in transitional conditions, one needs to undertake the analysis at a deeper layer – that is, the regulatory governance which, as practice shows, plays a pivotal role in shaping the regulatory framework in transitional countries.

The final methodological proposition relevant to the legal regulation has to do with the domestic economic context. In particular, one needs to look at legal regulation from the perspective of the transitional host state's economic objectives – namely the achievement of growth. The issue here is, what kind of regulatory regime causes growth? Does a host government conceive growth as a factor facilitating FDI or is FDI a precondition of growth? It is obvious that understanding of the above questions can shed light on the rationale behind a host state's choice of a certain model of legal regulation. In this section, we can briefly outline a starting point. One is provided by the institutionalist approach. North argues that the key to sustained economic growth is adaptive rather than just allocative efficiency.[83] He specifies that the notion of adaptive efficiency is concerned with the willingness of a society to acquire knowledge and learning, to induce innovation, to undertake risk and creative activity of all sorts, as well as to resolve problems and bottlenecks of the society through time. In a world of uncertainty, he emphasizes, no one knows the correct answer to the problems we confront. The society that permits the maximum generation of trials is the one that has the best likelihood of solving problems through time. Consequently, in an analysis of the legal regulation of FDI in transitional countries, we should focus not only on the static features of the rules directly relevant to FDI. We should also consider them within a framework of all rules which provide a consolidated flexibility and adaptation of the entire host nation's regulatory system towards international flows of FDI.

2.7 Summary

This chapter has identified and defined a number of multidisciplinary methodological tools for approaching the main issue. Its main concern was to answer the question as to why we need a multidisciplinary approach to the issue in question. Having answered it, we split the research subject into certain units of analysis, each having their own methodological approach. As a result, this approach has provided us with a working framework for the following chapters which will test the theoretical propositions in the context of the Kazakh practice.

3
The Legal Framework for FDI: Origins, Principles and Structure

3.1 Introduction

This chapter makes a retrospective analysis of FDI legislation. This is in part a response to the work of Gordley, who noted that the law of a single country cannot be an independent object of study. In order to understand law, even within a single country, one must look beyond its boundaries – indeed, beyond one's own time.[1] However, the purpose of this historical review is also to present a comparative historical sketch of the common and divergent features of Kazakh legislation relevant to FDI. In trying to understand what role the state does and should play, it is helpful to take into account the structure of law.[2] Further, because the rules have been aptly described as the 'skin' of a living policy,[3] it is equally important to identify correlations between FDI legislation and changes in sociopolitical structures, and to monitor shifts in the dominant state policy towards FDI. Furthermore, undoubtedly, the legislation, through its history, principles and structure, reflects the choice of the government. The following section will examine the evolution of the relevant legislation in order to assess the overall dynamics of the FDI-related legislation before and immediately after Kazakh independence.

3.2 The historical determinants of the legislation on FDI

Legislation on FDI is not a new phenomenon in Soviet and post-Soviet law – the first laws regulating foreign businesses were enacted in the early 1920s.[4] At that time, the new socialist state embarked on the New Economic Policy (NEP), which included the scaling-back of nationalization and the reintroduction of work incentives. These measures were the result of a severe economic crisis associated with a sharp decline in Soviet productivity. On 8 March 1923 the Decree on Concessions was passed.[5] This established the legal foundations for the transfer of nationalized enterprises to foreign entrepreneurs and established the Chief Committee on Concessions as a state organ authorized to negotiate with foreign investors. In this manner, outside investment was permitted within the Soviet economy.[6]

In Kazakhstan the development of concessions in the 1920–1930s had its origin in the tsarist period – that is, before the 1917 October revolution.[7] A cheap labour force and abundant natural resources facilitated the first inflows of substantial FDI into Kazakhstan at the end of the nineteenth and the beginning of the twentieth century. In the periods 1893–95 and 1901–05 two major railroads – the Siberian and the Orenburg–Tashkent – were built through the territory of Kazakhstan. Interestingly, not only Russian, but also German, French and British banks took part in the issuance of special bonds, secured by the Russian government, to finance the construction of the two above-mentioned railroads. As observed by Chulanov, the construction of these railroads facilitated inflows of Russian and foreign capital into the Kazakh steppes and contributed significantly to the process of breaking the isolation of the region.[8]

After the 1917 Socialist Revolution, the Kazakh economy was, in fact, largely based on the previous tsarist structure. This structure, however, stagnated after the change of political regime. In order to achieve the two major objectives of the NEP – to kick-start the economy and to modernize equipment – the Soviet government entered into negotiations with foreign investors.[9] In particular, trusts were adopted as the main vehicles for FDI. As a result of such a policy, the total sum of FDI in Kazakhstan amounted to more than 100 million roubles between 1923 and 1930. Four major territorial industrial complexes (TICs) which emerged on the eve of the 1917 revolution were restored within a short period of time: Vostochnyi (Ridderskii-Ekibazstuskii); Spasskii; Zhezkazkanskii; and Zapadno Uralo-Embenskii. The first TIC – Vostochnyi – produced zinc and lead as well as copper, gold, silver and other non-ferrous metals. The Ekibazstus zinc and lead plants, along with the Ridders' mines and the Ridders' refinery plant, were the core units of this territorial complex. The Spasskii and Zhezkazganskii TICs specialized in copper production.[10] The fourth conglomerate specialized in oil production. The archive materials indicate that foreign investment was present not only in the extracting industries. For instance, 'Ridderskoye

Gornorudnoye Obshestvo' produced a wide range of final products within Kazakhstan.[11]

At the same time, as pointed out by Sutton, in the 1920s the involvement of foreign investors was never viewed by the Soviet government as a long-term policy. It was a short-term expedient to ensure the industrial modernization of the Soviet economy. Accordingly, the Soviet legislature viewed FDI (namely concessions) as a temporary measure. Therefore, a concessionaire did not enjoy the complete ownership of factories and buildings, but merely a so-called 'concession ownership', which excluded the right of free disposal and mortgage.[12] In 1932, this period of limited openness of the Soviet Union to foreign investment was brought to an end.[13]

The Soviet economy was reopened to foreign capital in the second half of the 1980s, when Gorbachev launched his policy of *perestroika*. The first legal act to signal this policy was the Decree No. 49 of the Council of Ministers of the USSR of 17 January 1987 'On the Establishment in the Territory of the USSR and the Operation of Joint Enterprises with the Participation of Soviet Organizations and Firms of Capitalist and Developing Countries'.[14] This stated that joint enterprises were to be designed to 'more fully satisfy the country's demand for certain types of industrial goods ... to bring in advanced foreign equipment and methods ... and financial resources into the USSR economy, to develop the country's export base and to reduce inefficient imports'.[15] Thus, at the very beginning of the period of *perestroika* the Soviet government considered joint ventures as a means of ensuring more rapid modernization and ultimately a more stable state of self-sufficiency. In other words, pragmatic considerations were included to attract western investment, while other clauses were designed to uphold and strengthen the Soviet economic system.

Nevertheless, even during the short period between 1987 and 1991 the legislation on foreign investment underwent substantial changes. For instance, the aforementioned Decree No. 49 of the Council of Ministers of the USSR envisaged the establishment of joint ventures as the only possible form of foreign investment in the USSR. It also initially prohibited foreign investors from holding more than 50 per cent of a joint venture, and it required a majority of the management, including both the chairperson of the board and the director general, to be Soviet citizens. Later, when it became clear that such provisions restrained foreign investment, Gorbachev's Edict of 26 October 1990 allowed the establishment of enterprises wholly owned by foreign investors.[16]

The Council of Ministers also issued additional decrees which made it more lucrative for foreign investors to establish joint ventures with Soviet partners. In particular, these regulations eliminated the restrictions preventing foreign investors from holding more than 50 per cent ownership in a joint venture, and they also allowed foreign investors to exercise managerial and executive control over joint ventures.

On 5 July 1991 the USSR 'Fundamental Principles of Legislation on Foreign Investment' (hereafter referred to as the Fundamentals) were passed by the Congress of the People's Deputies, the supreme legislative body of the USSR.[17] The Fundamentals became the first federal law on FDI. They summarized the previous experience of the treatment of foreign investment in the Soviet Union, proclaimed guarantees for foreign investment activities and provided an avenue for constituent republican legislators.[18] In this way the consolidation of the first laws in the federal Fundamentals played an important role in digesting the investment legislation.[19]

Other federal laws introduced certain provisions that further developed the emerging investment legislation and gradually removed the obstacles which hampered foreign capital inflows.[20] At the republican level, paramount legislative activity directed at establishing special investment legislation was carried out at the end of 1990 and the beginning of 1991. The following laws were enacted in Kazakhstan: the Law on Foreign Investment, 7 December 1990;[21] the Law on Basic Principles of Foreign Economic Activity, 15 December 1990;[22] the Law on Free Economic Zones, 30 November 1990;[23] and the Law on Concessions, 23 December 1991.[24] These laws, presently rescinded, attempted for the first time to establish a legislative and institutional investment infrastructure in Kazakhstan The laws prohibited the interference of the state's organs and officials in the private businesses of foreign investors, as well as in the businesses of domestic participants in foreign economic activity. They also stated that all subjects of foreign economic activity, notwithstanding the forms of property and kinds of activity, were granted equal rights before the law. These subjects were allowed to determine freely the kinds and the scale of economic activities they wished to pursue. The law announced that the profits of participants in foreign economic activity had to remain with them in full. The republic formally guaranteed the interests of the subjects of foreign economic activity and stated that losses incurred as a result of the interference of state organs and officials would be reimbursed.

Other laws contributed to the process of establishing a pro-market environment in order to facilitate the emergence of business attitudes and to increase the attractiveness of Kazakhstan's investment climate. In particular, the Law on Freedom of Economic Activity and the Development of Entrepreneurship, effective as of 15 January 1991, provided a legal definition of 'entrepreneurship' for the first time.[25] It stated that 'entrepreneurship' is an economic or other activity of an individual or individuals at the expense of his own or borrowed kinds of property and means with the purpose of achieving mutually beneficial results for all participants in the activity. According to Article 2, foreign legal entities and individuals, registered to conduct business activity according to the legislation of their country of origin, were recognized as the subjects of entrepreneurship. This law declared the freedom of entrepreneurship and stipulated that entrepreneurs have the right to conduct their business in any form, provided that they register their activity in a special registrar agency. The registration in legal terms was not of a permissive character, as in the Soviet-era legislation. Rather, it was simply a formal, bureaucratic confirmation of the correctness of the filing of the founding documents and the issuance of a special certificate of registration.

On 1 April 1991 another statute – the Law on Enterprises – was enacted.[26] This defined the legal bases of the organization and functioning of enterprises in conditions of a pluralism of forms of property. In general, this law established the rules for enterprises as independent from the state entities, including their rights, obligations, liabilities, and their relationship with other legal entities and individuals as well as with the state organs. Article 3 of this law, which enumerated possible types of enterprises, in Item 5 included joint ventures and defined them as 'enterprises established by uniting the property of its founders, including foreign judicial persons and citizens'.

The Law on the Development of Competition and Limitation of Monopolistic Activity determined the area of the state monopoly where the entry of foreign investment was not allowed.[27] The defined areas were electricity, construction and railways, branches of the economy that serve defence, space activities and research, as well as oil and gas pipelines and telecommunications.

The Law on Lease granted foreign states, judicial persons and citizens the right to lease property, including land, buildings, constructions, and equipment, on the basis of the contract of lease.[28] Furthermore, this law provided the leaseholders (foreign states, foreign judicial persons, foreign citizens and joint ventures) with the right to establish associations, unions, consortiums, concerns and other conglomerates and to finance the activities of these entities.

Article 9 of the Land Code of 1990 included the right of foreign states, foreign judicial entities and foreign citizens and joint ventures to take land for temporary use on the basis of the contract of lease.[29] Article 33 of the Law on Taxation of 1991 established a rule of reciprocity in the taxation of foreign juridical persons and citizens, elimination of double taxation and the supremacy of tax clauses of international treaties over the domestic tax laws.

Article 6 of the Law on Circulation of Securities and Stock Exchange of 1991 stated that 'foreign juridical persons can be investors, i.e. subjects allowed to acquire securities on the securities market'.[30] In addition, Article 4 of the law allowed them to be members (stockholders) of the stock exchange. Article 1 of the Law on Currency Regulation stipulated that foreign juridical and natural persons and the enterprises with foreign participation could take part in the currency market of the republic.[31] Article 6 of the Law on Banks and Banking of 1991 allowed foreign and jointly owned banks to operate in the territory of the republic.[32]

Although the new provisions listed above were dispersed across different parts of the legislation, they clearly manifested, on the one hand, the growing assertion of economic and political independence and, on the other, the inability of the federal centre to deal with emerging economic hardships associated with the shortcomings of reforms. Equally, the process of liberalization of the republican legislation was partially a response of the republican leaders to the pressure to keep the negative effects of economic crisis away from the boundaries of their republics.

It would seem clear that the differences between the legislation on foreign investment in the 1920s and the laws of the late 1980s and early 1990s were more significant than the similarities between them. The legislation of the 1980s was part of an overall restructuring of the Soviet economic system and therefore, in contrast to the 1920s, this later investment legislation underwent a substantial change along with the whole system of economic legislation. In the 1920s foreign investment was regarded as a temporary phenomenon. As a result, the structure of the legislation was inflexible, in particular, the relevant rules and doctrines restricted private ordering. By contrast, the legislation of the late 1980s and early 1990s increasingly recognized foreign investment as a component of the domestic economy and an integral part of the new pro-market legislation. Structurally, the legislation on FDI was not an isolated 'island' in the overall system of domestic laws. The FDI-related clauses appeared in other parts of legislation; the state displayed a gradual shift in its approach and increasingly adopted a facilitative approach. This change of approach also ensured the emergence of a sense of permanence that the earlier legislation lacked. Furthermore, where each concession contract had varying terms, Soviet legislation of the 1980s included uniform standards which gave it a coherence that the earlier situation had lacked. All investors were subject to the same rules. Thus, the first difference was the place of laws on direct investment in the system of Soviet law and their interaction with other parts of the legislation.

Other differences are also apparent. For instance, the evolution of investment legislation in the 1980s displayed a gradual shift in the Soviet economic system towards a more open model and reflected a willingness to accept market principles which had previously been rejected by Soviet economic legislation. In particular, the 1920s concession contracts imposed an increasingly stringent tax on excess profits. By contrast, the 1980s legislation did not hinder profits with restrictive tax provisions but provided a uniform rate for all profits. Furthermore, Soviet legislation protected the foreign partner's investment by returning its contribution for the residual value at liquidation, instead of merely confiscating all buildings and fixtures when a concession ends. This acknowledged that joint production was not simply joint exploitation of an industrial opportunity whose effects end when the concession terminates. Rather, joint production was expected to leave a legacy of infrastructure or technology which would continue to benefit the Soviet economy, even after the foreign partner left. The legislative logic was that since foreign resources have continuing beneficial effects, these should be compensated. Finally, the 1980s' laws removed some elements of inflexibility. Both a prearranged production schedule and a hard-currency importation requirement, which was imposed upon foreign investors by the legislation in 1920s, was no longer required. This reflected better Soviet understanding of supply and demand pressures and the need to give investors some financial independence.

The difference in the state ideologies underpinning legislation on foreign investment in the 1920s and 1980s is also noteworthy. The 1920s' laws show that retaining strict control over the economy was more important to the Soviet government at this time than was the attraction of foreign capital. This was most clearly expressed in the provisions taxing excess profits heavily, which would allow the Soviet authorities to regulate their internal price structure. In the 1980s, by contrast, the continued liberalization of foreign investment rules indicated that attracting hard currency into the Soviet economy was becoming increasingly important. Furthermore, the Soviet government in the late stages of *perestroika* explicitly indicated its willingness to see the USSR as part of the world economy. This may be explained by the fact that legislation on foreign investment of the Gorbachev era was but one part of an overriding restructuring of Soviet economic and sociopolitical systems. In the second half of the 1980s the entire Soviet system was involved in this process of transformation, where formerly the concession contracts were an exception to the established legislation and, as such, they attempted to comply with the existing structure without coming into conflict with it. The foreign investment laws of the 1980s mirrored the fundamental changes occurring within the Soviet economy as a whole. Thus, over a period of approximately 65 years, the USSR had become increasingly, yet cautiously, pragmatic. Under these conditions the legal system reflected a slow movement of the economic policy towards rationalization.

3.3 The post-independence period

An abortive coup in August 1991, followed by the reincarnation of the former Soviet republics as independent states, concluded the historical stage (1985–1991) during which attempts were undertaken to adapt the whole Communist system to market forces. Huge progress was made in moves towards democratization. Because fully-fledged democracy was not achieved overnight, this does not mean that the democratization process achieved nothing. What was unsuccessful was the limited extent of economic reforms and attempt to hold the Soviet state together. Indeed, an attempt to combine the diverging 'essences' was the major obstacle on the way to more decisive and radical reforms because every new, more or less radical, step was assessed on the basis of how it complied with the principles of Communist ideology. The position of the Communist Party in Soviet society was such that it was indeed very difficult for any impetus towards far-reaching reforms to get emerge from any other social group.[33]

The disintegration of the Soviet Union, however, did not immediately invalidate the laws of the Soviet era. These laws were also different and, depending upon the time of their enactment (whether at the beginning of *perestroika* or later, when more economic and less ideological considerations dominated the decision-making process), were more or less pro-market.[34] In other words it would be correct to differentiate among the models, by distinguishing between contingent and lasting models, between political macro-models which incorporate choices of economic policy and technical models that accompany those choices.

When they approved the Agreement on the Establishment of the Commonwealth of Independent States in December 1991, all republican supreme legislative bodies confirmed that the laws of the USSR would stay in power so long as they did not contradict the existing legislation of the republic and until proper new laws were enacted. In this way, the danger of a post-collapse legal vacuum was overcome. This decision, however, created significant restraints on growing pro-market economic and sociopolitical attitudes and institutions because the result was a clutter of late-Gorbachev era and post-independence laws regulating commercial activity, often with contradictions that even the lawyers could not fully understand. To tackle these problems, in early 1994 the president of Kazakhstan approved the State Programme of Legal Reform which outlined the priorities and a time schedule for the implementation of the new post-independence laws. More importantly, this programme suggested a first attempt to form a comprehensive and clear concept of legal reform as well as the basic principles of every branch of post-Communist law. It would be wrong, however, to think that post-independence legislation has emerged from nowhere. On the contrary, the process of building the new corpus of laws has had a peculiar combination of sources.

Kazakhstan, part of the Russian Empire since the eighteenth century, historically belongs to the Romano-Germanic legal tradition, as does its former metropole Russia. Nevertheless, the disintegration of the USSR and Kazakhstan's subsequent ideological emancipation did not mean an automatic return to the Romano-Germanic legal tradition. Unlike other Eastern and Central European socialist countries, the successor states of the USSR have had a longer experience of socialism and therefore jurists in the newly emerged states have been less capable of reanimating pre-Socialist legal concepts. It seems that, as a result, borrowing from other legal codes has become a principal method of building a new corpus of post-independence legislation in Kazakhstan, where foreign legal concepts have not met with any meaningful cultural resistance and their incorporation into the domestic legal system has been comparatively smooth. Even the draft Civil Code was prepared in close cooperation with Dutch legal scholars from Leiden University. However, at the same time it is hard to accept the rather optimistic point made by some scholars who believe that the end of the old ideology does not mean merely a return to the models of Continental Europe, but also the adoption of a western legal tradition where geographical and cultural limits traditionally used in order to classify national legal systems into 'legal families' no longer matter.[35] The substance of recently adopted legislation, in particular, that relating to Pledge, Petroleum, Bankruptcy, and Company, indeed allows us to admit the fact of a significant reception of common law concepts. However, this does not necessarily entirely prove the observations of legal scholars cited above. Rather, it seems that a more precise reason is identified by Ajani, who noticed that this openness of the emerging legal systems of the former socialist states to the common law concepts

> was deeply connected with the widely accepted belief that with the introduction of the formal elements of democracy and of the legal pillars of market economies a 'happy end' to the transition would have followed. [Therefore] the second stage is marked by a more critical approach towards 'paper laws' and by a more conscious attitude towards the 'Anglo-American thinking' of legal advisers and of international financial institutions.[36]

A 1997 statement by the president of Kazakhstan to the effect that 'in previous years we actively followed the Anglo-Saxon model as the goal we set was rapid change' reinforces this assumption.[37] Yet there were other, more profound reasons for the rejection of 'Anglo-American' legal thinking by the Kazakh law-makers. These will be discussed in Chapters 6 and 7. Nevertheless, it would be a simplification to say that all of the former Soviet republics' characteristics in the first post-independence years held in common a delusion that the enactment of legal statutes would bring about a rapid transition to a market-type economy. Of course, the fallacy of this approach, as rightly observed by some scholars, was in thinking that legislation per se without economic policy backed by social and institutional change, can be a lever for change. In fact, laws become effective as a result of social forces and pressures interested in and working for implementation.[38] It seems, therefore, that a lack of such forces within the transitional societies of the former Soviet Union is a key reason for the emergence of the current model of the legal regulation of FDI. This topic will be considered in more detail in the subsequent chapters.

3.4 The post-independence sources of legal innovation

It is a widely held belief that in order to achieve the optimal equilibrium between a foreign investor and a host nation, the legislative framework of the latter should provide the grounds for matching the expectations of a foreign investor. More secure grounds lead to more long-term investment attitudes. Naturally, an issue arises over how the process of formation of the new laws relevant to FDI evolved after the disintegration of the USSR, when most of the previous ideological barriers were finally uprooted. If we argue that the problem of informational mismatch does exist, can it originate at the stage of convergence of a western rational and a seemingly rationalizing transitional Kazakh legal system?

The previous chapter discussed the overall movement of the late-Soviet legislation towards a more liberal model for the regulation of FDI. Indeed, an assertion of political sovereignty and economic independence has reinforced this process and removed most of the political and ideological obstacles to direct foreign investment, and has led to active legal innovations. The first source for borrowing was the legislation of the former European socialist states, some of which had experimented with a new, more liberal economic legislation since the late 1950s, even in some cases being open to foreign investment. This happened after the death of Joseph Stalin, when the ideological restraints that Moscow had imposed upon the legislators of these states were gradually relaxed. Later, it was these European socialist countries that became the initial sources of tested laws on foreign investment which were then incorporated into the late Soviet and post-independence legislation of Kazakhstan.[39] After the disintegration of the Soviet Union, the model laws from the formerly socialist European countries were more trusted and welcomed by the country's leadership and scholars. For instance, the drafting of the Law on Privatization in 1994, as well as a critical assessment of the results of the initial privatization programme, was conducted by a team led by Professor Balcerowisz, the architect of economic reform in Poland. The personal involvement of Balcerowisz in this process undoubtedly facilitated the openness of law-makers, officials, bureaucrats and the president to criticism and made them more responsive to the comments of his team.

Foreign investors, the majority of whom initially came mainly from the United States,[40] and their legal advisors have formed another source which also played a significant role in exporting the western, particularly common law concepts. For instance, the draft of the Law on Petroleum was drawn up over eight months in 1994 by a joint team of Kazakh, American and British legal scholars and petroleum advisors.[41] The Tax Code had been drafted by the International Tax and Investment Centre and the International Tax Foundation, two US nongovernmental organizations. The drafting process of the Land Code and the Law on Mortgage was sponsored by the US Agency for International Development which, in turn, was represented by a group of US legal experts.

Equally, the IMF and the IBRD, staffed mainly by Anglo-American legal experts, have played an important role in exporting Common Law concepts to Kazakhstan, because the membership of these organizations was accompanied by a formal requirement to draft new economic legislation. Does this mean that offer of and demand for legal models in Kazakhstan has been ruled not only by the techniques of legal expertise, but, more significantly, by the political and economical considerations aimed to expedite the formation of the fundamentals of national independence? Have the western-sponsored rational models put down roots into the Kazakh soil? If so, should the entire system of the legislation designed by or in close cooperation with foreign experts for regulation of FDI evolve in a western direction – that is towards an optimal model?

This study argues that the process of 'rationalization' was a result of momentum carried over from the liberal reforms of Gorbachev, which was reinforced at the last stage of the existence of the USSR by the constituent republics, who were looking to maintain their economic autonomy. Further, since the collapse of the Soviet Union, when the process of disintegration became irreversible, the remaining system of laws has gradually moved into the opposite direction, after a short period of inertia, while the effects of the laws produced during the latter part of the Gorbachev era were offset by certain clauses in other parts of the new legislation. Accordingly, one may conclude that the problem of transplanting the western model here is associated with certain domestic factors that prevent these transplants from putting down roots into the Kazakh ground. What are these reasons? We will test the above proposition by looking at the legislation, and, in particular, those provisions specifically designed to regulate the economic and FDI-related relationships. First we need to consider the post-independence structure of the evolving legislation.

3.5 The structure of the legislation

The most significant structural change in post-independence legislation in Kazakhstan is that the system of laws on foreign direct investment has evolved in a legal framework which aimed to promote at least four of the basic economic functions in an emerging market-type economy: (i) to define the universe of property rights in the system; (ii) to set a framework for exchanging those rights; (iii) to set the rules for the entry and exit of actors into and out of productive activities; and, finally, (iv) to oversee market structure and behaviour to promote competition. In this manner, the previous Soviet ideological underpinnings were formally removed.

In a manner similar to the systems of the industrialized nations, the above tasks of a legal system have been accordingly related to specific and well-recognized areas of law. Property rights are defined in the constitution of a country and in more specific laws dealing with real, intellectual and other kinds of property. Exchange is covered generally by sale, company and foreign investment laws, while bankruptcy and liquidation laws govern exit. Finally, anti-monopoly and unfair competition laws are intended to promote competition. These basic areas of law are joined by many other important ones – labour, taxation, and banking, to name but three.

In Kazakhstan, legislation is considered to be a combination of legal norms, constituted by the state by its supreme legislative (Parliament) and executive (president and government) bodies.[42] These norms are mandatory for all subjects to whom they are addressed. The mandatory character of the norms is ensured by the possible use of coercion on the part of the state. The content of legislation is constructed on a hierarchical basis with the Constitution at the top of this hierarchy.

A broad definition of the term 'legislation' includes legislative acts – that is, normative acts passed by the Parliament of the country as laws and resolutions. In their legal force these are equal to the decrees of the president that have been adopted in accordance with the Law of the Republic of Kazakhstan of 10 December 1993 'On the Temporary Delegation of Additional Authorities to the President of the Republic of Kazakhstan and the Heads of Regional Administrations', as well as in accordance with Articles 53 and 61 of the Constitution of the Republic of Kazakhstan of 1995. In contrast with the regular decrees of the president, such decrees are referred to as the decrees of the president *with the effect of law*.

The central legislative act regulating business activities is the Civil Code, which, in common with all other laws, has to comply with the constitution of the country. In turn, other legislative acts relevant to civil law (including those regulating FDI) must comply with the Civil Code. This requirement is included in the Civil Code.[43]

The term 'legislation' also includes, besides the legislative acts, the normative acts issued by the president and the government – that is, the Cabinet of Ministers. Legislative acts have a supremacy over presidential acts, and legislative acts and the acts of the president have precedence over the acts of the government, which is appointed by the president.

The clear limitation of the terms 'legislative act' and 'legislation' has an important practical implication. For instance, if the Civil Code says that a certain rule shall be described in detail in the 'legislative act' it means that a relevant clause must be enacted only by the Parliament or by the presidential edict, having the force of law (for instance, Item 2 of Article 18 of the Civil Code). If the Civil Code refers to the 'legislation', it means that the relevant clause can be either in the regular edict or decree of the president or in the decree of the government (for instance, Article 5 of the Civil Code).

Legislation, particularly civil, includes clauses that have a different effect. By their content they can be either strictly imperative or they can give certain room for discretion between the parties involved in a transaction. Imperative clauses (for instance, Items 5–7 of Article 15 of the Civil Code) are applied as mandatory and cannot be amended by other legislation or by agreement between parties. The discretionary norms of the Code (for example, Item 1 of Article 359) allow for the possibility of exception to a particular clause to be stipulated in another legislative act or in an agreement between the parties to a contract.

The current structure of the legislation relevant to foreign investment includes two main categories of laws. The first includes the statutes designed specifically for the purpose of regulation of foreign investment. These are: the Law on Foreign Investment of 27 December 1994 and the Law on State Support of Foreign Direct Investment of 28 February 1997. The second category includes the laws which contain, among others, certain provisions that are addressed to foreign investors. These are the Constitution (Basic Law), the Civil Code, the Petroleum Law, the Tax Law, the Land Code, the Subsoil Code, and so on. Within this category the Constitution and the Civil Code occupy the most important role inasmuch as they provide fundamental principles that are elaborated in emanating laws, including those which are specifically designed to regulate foreign investment. Let us have a closer look at these two pivotal elements of the Kazakh legislation, in particular at those clauses directly relevant to economic relationships.

3.6 The Constitution, Civil Code and FDI

In Kazakhstan, the body of legislation is constructed in a hierarchical order according to the organ from which it emanates. This means that the highest rule is binding on all of the authorities at any lower level. In assessing the legal framework which regulates foreign direct investment, it is therefore important to become acquainted with the nature of this hierarchy.

In countries with a codified legal system the Constitution plays the central role, forming the basic legal framework of a country. The general perception of this law is well characterized by Herbiet: 'The Constitution is the immediate expression of the fundamental legal values received by the political community it establishes the relationship between those governed and the government, between the power and those subject to it; it is the basis on which all legitimacy and lawfulness rests.'[44]

It is equally important to note that in the post-Soviet context the Constitution has played an even greater role, since the creation of an efficient market is complicated by the desire to transform the entire structure of society. Accordingly, one finds here that 'uprooted are all the old informal constraints built around the family, personal relationships, and repetitive individual exchanges'.[45] In this sense, it is difficult to overestimate the political significance of the new constitutions in the former Soviet republics. In fact, this new political substance of the post-Soviet constitutions has provided an initial impetus for the opening up of the countries of the former USSR and their legislative policies towards foreign investors.

Since independence two constitutions have been passed in Kazakhstan – in 1993 and 1995. The present Constitution, enacted by the national referendum of 30 August 1995, provides the general principles of a new economic order as well as certain guarantees for entrepreneurial activities, which include the activities of foreign investors operating in Kazakhstan. These provisions, particularly those which are different from the provisions of the Soviet-era Constitution, need to be commented upon.

The most significant aspect of the 1995 Constitution is that it proclaims basic principles on which the whole system of economic legislation is to be built. These principles, which are taken for granted in countries with established market economies, display a formal departure from the principles that shaped Soviet-era legislation. They are as follows: a presumption in favour of individual freedom, protection against non-state interference, protection against state interference, the promotion of the exercise of freedoms through law, the tempering of market forces, the protection of the public interest, the social rectification of market inequalities, and, last but not least, the promotion of international trade and investment.

Several constitutional clauses include provisions relating to the equality of state and private property. Such an assumption is reinforced by Part 2 of Article 26 which proclaims: 'property shall be guaranteed by law' and 'no one may be deprived of his property unless otherwise stipulated by a court decision'. Furthermore, this article proclaims the principle of equal compensation in cases of the compulsory alienation of property for the public use in emergency cases that must be explicitly defined by law. This provision is of particular importance for foreign investors because it clearly formulates a guarantee that a property can be alienated *only* for the public use and *only* in exceptional cases that *must be* explicitly and exhaustively enumerated in the law. In addition, the Constitution includes a limitation with regard to the property right by saying: 'Property obliges, and its use must simultaneously benefit the society'. For a foreign investor this means that the enjoyment of property rights cannot be limitless. As an owner he is entitled to perform in relation to his property only those transactions that are not prohibited by law and, as follows from the cited clause, he must also undertake certain measures to prevent any harm potentially emanating from his property, for instance, affecting the health of people and the environment.

Furthermore, Part 4 of Article 26 states that 'everyone shall have the right to freedom of entrepreneurial activity, and free use of his property for any legal entrepreneurial activity'. At the same time, the following two sentences impose an explicit limitation by stating that: 'monopolistic activity shall be regulated and limited by law. Unfair competition shall be prohibited'. Another constitutional limitation relevant to business activities can be found in Article 39 which states that 'rights and freedoms of an individual and citizen may be limited *only* by laws and *only* to the extent necessary for protection of the constitutional system, defence of the public order, human rights and freedoms, health and morality of the population'.

It has to be mentioned that in contrast to the Soviet Constitution of 1977, the post-independence Basic Law proclaims its direct effect. Article 4 stipulates that 'the Constitution shall have the highest juridical force and a direct effect on the entire territory of the Republic'.[46]

Finally, an important provision of the Constitution relevant to foreign investment activity is included in Article 4 which stipulates the supremacy of the international treaties over the domestic: 'International treaties ratified by the Republic shall have priority over its laws and be directly implemented except in cases when the application of international treaty shall require the promulgation of a law.' Analysis of the FDI-related clauses of the 1995 Constitution allows one to conclude that post-independence Basic Law formally proclaims the fundamentals of the new economic order as diametrically opposed to that of the Soviet era. Let us examine the further elaboration of these new provisions in the new Civil Code of Kazakhstan.

Since the newly passed laws on FDI must conform with the principles of the recently enacted Civil Code, some explication of these principles as well as the manner in which they relate to the FDI regime must be undertaken. This is particularly prescient because both the enactment of the Civil Code and the passage of FDI laws are relatively recent events in the states of the former Soviet Union. For this reason, among others which will be elucidated below, both theoreticians and practitioners of FDI must understand the nature of and significance of this interrelationship.

Immediately after the collapse of the Soviet Union, each newly independent member of the Commonwealth of Independent States embarked on the process of drafting its own new Civil Code, which was rightfully characterized by Russian President Boris Yeltsin as the 'economic Constitution'.[47] The Code occupies a second position, after the Constitution, in the hierarchy of domestic laws regulating economic relationships which, accordingly, have to comply with its provisions. In cases of conflict between the Civil Code and other laws, the clause of the Civil Code has precedence. If Parliament decides to amend a certain rule, it has to amend simultaneously the corresponding clause in the Civil Code, so as to ensure that the newly passed law does not contradict the Civil Code. It is noteworthy that not only the newly passed but also previously enacted legislative acts must comply with the new Civil Code. In cases of conflict between the 'old' laws and the present Civil Code, the clauses of the Code have to be applied, and measures to amend the old law also have to be undertaken.

Unlike construction of the Constitution, which was associated with the establishment of a completely new legal substance, the drafting of the new Civil Code could be considered as a process of developing a simplified Soviet version of the western-type codes. Obviously, even the last, most improved version of the USSR Fundamentals of the Civil

Legislation of 1991, would eventually become incapable of dealing with the evolving complexity of relationships inherent in an emerging market economy. Professor Rudden pointedly observed:

> In structure, general principles, and in many detailed provisions [Russian civil law] has since 1922 been largely a simplified copy of that found in Western Europe, especially in the German-speaking countries. There seems to be little in the Soviet statutes which expressed a particular ideology and even less that might be thought to be determined by a particular economic infrastructure. So a 'pandectist' system fashioned to deal with non-socialist societies is fundamentally quite capable of handling post-socialism. Banality can be a blessing.[48]

Such a notion is also reinforced by history. It will be recalled that in 1913, in accordance with the decree of the Russian Tsar Nicholas II, a group of Russian legal scholars presented a draft Civil Code to the Russian State Duma. This code included much civil law thought of that time and, from its contents and form, was designed in a way similar to the German Civil Code, the *Burgerliches Gesetzbuch*, and the French Napoleonic Code. The First World War and the October Socialist Revolution prevented this draft Civil Code from being enacted. Nevertheless, even after the 1917 October Socialist Revolution this draft Code was used as a reference by authors of the Civil Code of RSFSR (Russian Soviet Federative Socialist Republic) in 1922,[49] as well as by the drafters of the 1994 Civil Codes in Russia and Kazakhstan.

The first significant difference in the new Civil Code is displayed in Article 1 which defines the scope of the code. It includes the following provision: 'Commodity-monetary and other relationships which are based on the equality of involved parties, proprietary relationships, as well as personal non-proprietary relationship associated with proprietary relationships.' In other words, the civil legislation does not regulate all proprietary relationships, but only those that are based on the equality of the involved parties – that is, non-subordination to one another. This provision departs radically from the previous Code of 1964 which proclaimed that civil law relationships have to be subordinated to the mandatory orders of the state – in particular, those orders related to or derived from the State Economic Plan. Thus, the whole system of contractual relationships, with very little exception, was subordinated to the imperative acts of the state. The new code has excluded such a subordination and proclaimed that civil law proprietary relationships can emerge and develop on the basis of mutual consent and agreement between the parties. From now on, the same proprietary relationships, which are based on the necessity to follow the state prescriptions, are regulated by administrative, not civil, legislation.

The previous Civil Code proclaimed: (i) the supremacy of state property over other, non-state forms of property; (ii) mandatory subordination to the state plan defined the top of the administrative-command system, while entering, interpreting and executing a civil law contract; (iii) prohibition of competition. All these principles reflected the centrally planned system of regulation of the economy and disappeared along with the Soviet system. The new Civil Code has established new principles, namely: (i) equality between all subjects of civil law relationships; (ii) inviolability of property; (iii) freedom of civil law contract; (iv) non-interference of the state and any other third party in private matters and the lives of individuals; (v) protection of entrepreneurs that are explicitly considered from now on the main subjects of civil law relationships.

These principles are formally proclaimed and enumerated in Article 2 of the new Code, which is called 'Basic Fundamentals of the Civil Legislation'. These are indivisible, interconnected and mutually complementary principles from which the whole system of economic laws derives. Let us briefly consider the legal meaning of these principles since they also govern the activities of foreign investors in Kazakhstan and are reflected in legislation specifically designed for foreign investment.

The relationship which occurs when a foreign investor undertakes his activities in a foreign jurisdiction is defined as a civil law relationship because it is associated with acquisition, possession, use and transfer of property to other persons or legal entities. More precisely, the equality of the subjects means that the state or its organs, when entering into civil law relationships, do not have certain privileges or immunities before their civil law partners – either individuals or legal entities. It also implies that both legal entities,[50] in any organizational form,[51] and physical individuals can equally be subjects of civil law relationships. Finally, this principle means that foreign citizens and foreign legal entities are entitled to acquire the same civil law rights and to be subjects to civil law duties in the same way as Kazakhstani citizens and legal entities. In fact, the latter reinforces the equality of domestic and foreign subjects as provided for by the special Law on Foreign Investment and bilateral investment treaties of Kazakhstan with other countries.

The proclamation of another principle – *the inviolability of property* – once more highlights a departure from the previous rules, which had allowed the state to interfere in all relationships connected with non-state property. Therefore, the principle of the inviolability of property has also been included in the Constitution of the country, in particular in Articles 6 and 26. This principle means, first of all, the recognition of an owner's right freely to use his property according to his own consideration, with the purpose of achieving any goal, not prohibited by law (Article 188 of the Civil Code).[52] It also means that coercive termination of this right is prohibited, notwithstanding the compensation paid to an owner whose right was infringed. The rule must work in that the coercive termination of property rights is allowed only on bases explicitly stipulated by law (Article 249 of the Civil Code). It is not enough, therefore, to say that the termination of property rights is possible only by a court decision. A court's decision itself must be based on reasons precisely defined in law. In investment practice, this principle is especially important as it provides a foreign investor with a powerful tool in cases where his property rights are infringed on a basis not explicitly stipulated in the special laws regulating foreign investment.

Freedom of contract is included in Article 380 of the Code. It is particularly important when a foreign investor enters into agreement with a local entity – for instance, in a joint venture. Under the law, any individual on his own consideration and under no coercive influence from outside is entitled to: (i) decide whether to enter or not into a certain contractual relationship; (ii) freely choose a partner with whom he wishes to enter into agreement; (iii) determine the terms of a contract. Of course, the other party in the contract is equally entitled to the same set of rights. Therefore, only those contracts that are based on the free and mutual consent of parties will be considered civil law contracts. The principle of freedom of contract cannot be mixed with limitations that parties voluntarily impose upon themselves. Such self-imposed and mutually agreed limitations become the mandatory conditions of a contract and, thus, cannot be unilaterally refused by them, or revised or cancelled. The scope of this principle can also be limited by the legislation – for example, those constitutional provisions relating to the imperative prescriptions of laws. For example, if the law prohibits trade in arms or drugs, it means that such activities cannot be the subject of any contract, even though both parties are willing to enter into a contractual relationship and have reached a mutual consent with regard to specific terms of a contract. According to Article 158 of the Civil Code, such contracts are considered void from the date of their formation.

It has to be noticed that, although the Civil Code is based on the principle of the equality of parties involved in a transaction, it includes certain clauses that have an imperative character. These clauses particularly: provide additional protection for a party who could be, because of certain circumstances (relating to, for instance, physical or mental infirmity), in a weaker bargaining position; limit monopolism; prevent unfair competition; protect consumers, and so on. Conditions provided by such imperative clauses for certain types of contracts constitute a part of any concrete contract, even though the involved parties have not formally included them into the text of their particular contract. This principle means also that the parties are free to enter into any contracts, even though such types of contract are not directly mentioned or described in the Civil Code. Freedom of contract also allows parties to establish contracts that combine elements of several different types of contract (Articles 7 and 380 of the Civil Code). However, again, the terms of such contracts cannot ignore prohibitions and limitations, explicitly constituted by law.

The next principle is *non-interference of anyone in the private business and life of individuals.* This principle covers civil law relationships to the extent that they have a personal non-proprietary character. In the Soviet-era Civil Code this principle was reflected rather weakly and narrowly. It was limited to the protection of an individual's dignity and honour, privacy or personal correspondence, diaries and letters. Following the collapse of the USSR this principle is now proclaimed in the Constitution and thus its legal value has been upgraded by becoming a constitutional principle. In the new Civil Code it is reflected in broader terms – in particular, its implication for the investment legislation is that the state organs, civil servants and other representatives of the state cannot interfere in the use of property, in the distribution of profit or in the use of dividends. Unless it is explicitly stated in law, no one is entitled to demand confidential commercial information, permissions or consents to undertake certain action associated with investment activity from a foreign investor. Articles 115, 125, 144, 156 and several others also address such provisions.

It is often mistakenly assumed that the only protection afforded foreign investors is contained in the special Law on Foreign Investment. In the case of Kazakhstan, this is only partially true since the higher law – the Civil Code – proclaims the principle of *protection of entrepreneurs* – a category of people which includes foreign investors as well. Therefore, the Civil Code is the first legislative act which needs to be analysed in order to define a full spectrum of legal means for the protection of foreign investors' rights. For instance, Article 10 of the Civil Code provides entrepreneurs with effective protection against unjustified state inspections and total control, preservation of commercial secrets and fair taxation. Yet, at the same time, Item 7 of Article 58 of the Civil Code stipulates that the law prohibits referring to the principle of protection of commercial secrets, if a businessman hides information which has a significant public interest (for instance, if his investment project is a potential threat to the environment).

One important provision, from which a clause known in the legal literature on foreign investment as a '*stability clause*' derives, is included in Article 4 of the Civil Code. This states that acts of legislation have no retrospective power and can be applied only with regard to the relationships which occurred after their enactment. The practical meaning of the rule about the power of the civil legislation 'in time' includes several important points. First of all, if a new legal act creates, amends or terminates civil law rights and obligations, the law which was in effect on the day when a certain relationship occurred will be applied. Secondly, in legal terms, a change in the civil legislation does not automatically cause a change in the ongoing civil law relationships and they are maintained in the same way as they were prior to the enactment of the new civil legislative act. Finally, if a new law prohibits certain activities that were not prohibited by law prior to the enactment of the new civil law, such activities must be stopped. These points are elements of the general rule 'The law has no retrospective power'. However, a foreign investor should be aware that there are certain exceptions to this rule that are explicitly stipulated by law (but not by the parties of a contract):

(i) If the law was explicitly given retrospective power and was expanded to regulate certain relationships which occurred prior to its enactment. For example, Item 4 of the resolution of the Supreme Council (Parliament) of Kazakhstan of 27 December 1994 'On the Implementation into force the Civil Code of the Republic of Kazakhstan' envisages that organizational forms of business entities, established before the enactment of the Civil Code, must be transformed into the forms established by the new Civil Code by 1 January,

(ii) Sometimes the law stipulates that amendments in the civil legislation do not cover certain relationships, if such changes impair the position of a subject of the right. For example, such a clause is incorporated in Article 6 of the Law on Foreign Investment.

(iii) The establishment of a rule, which has an effect on relationships which occurred prior to the enactment of a new law, but the substance of these relationships has been changed. (For example, change of the fees for communal services.)

The Code has introduced new concepts that are central to business law in classical market economies: good faith, reasonableness and custom of business turnover. The latter is defined in Article 5 as 'a rule of behaviour which has been formed and extensively applied in any domain of entrepreneurial activity'. In the section which deals with Obligations, the new Code then proceeds to apply this concept. For example, Article 427 states: 'If the conditions of a contract have not been determined by the parties or by the dispositive norm, the respective conditions shall be determined by the customs of business turnover applicable to the relations of the parties.'

Similar to the common law system, particularly the US Uniform Commercial Code (UCC), good faith requires that parties to an agreement act 'honestly in fact in conduct or transaction concerned'.[53] Article 8 of the Kazakh Code includes a similar ethical principle as fairness and good faith. It stipulates that the 'rights and duties of the parties shall be determined by proceeding from the requirements of good faith'. Breach of good faith means conscious neglect of another's interest in favour of one's own personal gain. For instance, Article 262 of the Code defines that a buyer is considered to be in breach of good faith if he knowingly acquires property from a seller who was not entitled to alienate it.

The new Code has also revolutionized civil law theory by permitting reasoning by analogy to other laws in situations unregulated by law or contract or where no discernible business custom has yet developed. When this analogy of *lex* is inadequate, the Code enables the rights and duties of parties to be determined 'from the general principles and sense of civil legislation (analogy of *jus*) and the requirements of good faith, reasonableness and fairness'.

3.7 The Constitution and the legal regulation of FDI

In contrast to the post-independence constitutions, the Soviet-era Constitution did not consider the purpose of a property to be profit-making. Accordingly, it was inherent in the entire structure of pre-*perestroika* law that private citizens were not permitted to choose for themselves whether they treated their belongings as investments, and their ownership right was restricted to the things they needed and to things they had earned.[54] Both of the post-independence constitutions have emphasized this crucial distinction of the purpose of property, as will be shown in the following discussion.

At the same time, however, one may see an obvious evolution in constitutional legal terminology relevant to property even within the short period of time between the enactment of two constitutions. Article 6 of the present Constitution states that 'the Republic of Kazakhstan shall recognize and by the same token protect state and private property'. The wording of this formula differs from that of the previous Constitution of 1993, which stated in Article 45 that 'the economy of the Republic of Kazakhstan is based on a variety of forms of ownership'. The formulation of the previous Constitution was inseparable from ideas that existed in legal science and practice at the time of its enactment. A great significance was allocated to the emerging forms of property which composed an alternative to the totality of the state property. The Law on Property of 1990, which was in effect during that period, recognized three forms of ownership: state, collective and private. Accordingly, one could clearly see that the legislature tried to facilitate these newly emerging forms of property and each of these forms was granted its own legal regime with particular emphasis on what made them different from state property.[55]

Why is the concept of state ownership restored in the 1995 Constitution? Presumably, transition to a market-type economy, with the corresponding increased complexity of business relationships inherent in such a liberalizing economy, implies that the need for state ownership should decrease, mainly because the state, in order to boost internal investment institutions, should not have special privileges in transactions with other economic actors. Nevertheless, in 1995, after seventy years' domination of state-owned property in all the economies of the former Soviet republics, the law not only defined the property right on the ground of its relationship to the state – dividing into state-owned and non-state-owned – but in the second Constitution has reinforced if not expanded the perpetuation of this domination. It seems that to answer this question we need to undertake a different approach to the Constitution. In particular, we should not concentrate solely on the economic clauses of the Constitution.

The above analysis outlines the reception by the Constitution of the fundamental provisions proclaimed in democratic societies for the regulation of market-type relationships. We also displayed the elaboration of the economic clauses of the Constitution in the Civil Code, which is specifically designed to regulate the relationships between equal market agents. A question, however, arises in the context of this analysis – how significant and relevant are the other constitutional clauses to the legal regulation of FDI in conditions of transition? Are the specific economic clauses sufficient for understanding the legal regulation of FDI in Kazakhstan? If not, how should one approach them?

First, one should take into account the fact that the Kazakh post-independence constitutionalism derives from American sources. Both the 1993 and the 1995 post-independence constitutions use language similar to that of the US Constitution, and the principle of the separation of powers, with the corresponding idea of system of checks and balances, forms their cornerstones. Seemingly, one can approach the analysis of the Constitution in the context of US constitutionalism. In particular, a few accounts should be taken, which are relevant to this chapter.

It should be recalled that the US Constitution is a document which sets forth the governmental framework for the nation and which was designed for the limitations it provides on the exercise of arbitrary power, not for its promotion of economic efficiency.[56] These limitations are reflected in the structural design of the branches of the state as well as in provisions expressly limiting governmental power. Accordingly, from a transaction cost perspective, the US Constitution purposefully structured government so as to increase transaction costs in order to make the exercise of government power more difficult.[57] The direct and indirect limitations on government action under the US Constitution were designed to be respected and enforced, notwithstanding the inefficiencies of their effects on either the policy-making process itself or the policy goals desired to be implemented. In this respect, constitutional limitations are exogenous constraints on government actions, even those for which government – or the majority of the citizenry – may have expressly sought efficient outcomes. Thus, government action may only take considerations of efficiency into account subject to the constraints of what actions are constitutional.

Nevertheless, the focus on constraining government power does not necessarily mean that the effects of proper constitutional analysis are devoid of any efficiency properties. Indeed, government has to make credible commitments so that parties will continue to contract with it in the future.[58] It is precisely the role that the institutional endowment of a nation plays in constraining arbitrary government power that provides an environment conducive to credible commitments by government.

The theoretical sketch above provides an approach for treatment of the Kazakh Constitution from an institutional perspective. More importantly, it helps us to locate the constitutional clauses correctly into the framework of our analysis of the legal regulation of FDI. In particular, the above discussion emphasizes that it is essential that the institutional (the political, social and legal) environment provides sufficient constraints on arbitrary government action. Such constraints include constraints on changes in the regulatory system and institutions to enforce such constraints.

3.8 Summary

In an efficiency analysis of the Constitution of a transitional country, constraints on the abuse of power should be treated as exogenous constraints, rather than endogenous variables. As a result, if an analysis of the legal regulation of FDI is based on this institutional perspective, the state is best viewed as an entity which should be able to provide the credible commitments essential for private investment. A consideration of the Constitution from such an angle – that is, where a long-run efficiency is encouraged by the state, albeit at the expense of short-run efficiencies – should be undertaken. However, we first need to define the types of models of the legal regulation of FDI as well as the country-specific criteria which would predetermine an optimal model for Kazakhstan.

4
The Types and Choice of the Model for the Legal Regulation of FDI

4.1 Introduction

One of the main reasons for codifying laws regarding foreign investment is to send a positive signal to potential investors and to place on record a host country's newly formulated policy towards FDI. The passage of clear and supportive foreign investment legislation conveys the message that investment is welcome,[1] which explains the necessity for implementation and the importance of special legislation on FDI in the newly emerged post-Soviet states, and the absence of such legislation in most industrialized countries. However, an analysis of current laws regulating foreign investment, including those that are designed specifically for the regulation of foreign investment as well as those provisions that are dispersed throughout other parts of domestic legislation, is unlikely to be helpful if it lacks any clear understanding of the sociopolitical and economic underpinnings. Waelde has noticed that in this regard:

> In every country, but particularly in ex-Soviet countries like Kazakhstan, a qualified lawyer will have to look behind official documentation to see things as they are. A prospective businessman would be less interested in official data, and more concerned to look behind the veil: What are the issues and the rules of the game? There is almost no understanding and reporting of these very complex – and for an investor most significant – issues.[2]

This problem can be lessened if a legal student conducts his analysis within a certain framework which could combine all three elements – law, economics and politics – simultaneously. Such a multidisciplinary approach allows us to appreciate the link between the socioeconomic, political and legal dimensions of transition and its overall impact on the legal regulation of foreign direct investment in the region. The application of such an approach is particularly important in the case of the former Soviet Union because:

> It is crucial for Western investors in the former Soviet Union to exercise caution and to maintain vigilance in undertaking business ventures purely on reliance on the texts of the new legislative acts governing their rights and obligation ... The macro-economic and socio-political dimensions of western investment in Russia should be carefully examined in light of current historical trends.[3]

To achieve this objective we need to employ those two models of the legal regulation of foreign direct investment which have evolved in the world over the past few decades: (i) the open or free entry model and (ii) the negotiation model. Our study does concede that hybrid models can exist in certain countries. This, however, does not weaken the analytical utility of models. In such cases the evolution of such hybrid systems towards one of the above models should be taken into consideration. In essence, the notion of models of legal regulation includes an economic rationale, according to which each model results in certain possible economic outcomes. Consequently, a law or combination of laws relevant to FDI can be grouped into certain models of regulation depending on the final outcome sought by the law-maker. Furthermore, this approach also sheds light on the specific choice which a law-maker makes.

4.2 Models of legal regulation of FDI

By its very nature, the regulation of foreign direct investment presupposes an interaction between international and domestic laws. In the years since gaining its independence, the Republic of Kazakhstan has signed up to the major worldwide multilateral treaties and organizations and has also concluded bilateral investment treaties with more than 30 countries.[4] However, these actions neither automatically ensure active inflows of foreign capital into a host country nor do they guarantee a foreign investor untroubled business relations. Rather, they signal the willingness of a host country to engage in cross-border relationships with other states and to become a recipient of foreign investment. Thus, a compliance with international legal standards is an important component of a country's overall legal investment regime, but it cannot be the only one. Another crucial element which makes a national investment regime either functional or dysfunctional is the web of domestic laws which make up the specific model of a host country's investment regime and reflect its policy towards foreign direct investment. In the case of Kazakhstan, there has been active development of such a model in the post-independence years. An analysis of its genesis and evolution clearly depicts the gradual formation of the contours of a country-specific model.

Any sovereign state has the right to limit and control entry of foreign investment. Certain limitations and conditions can be imposed upon a foreign investor not only at the time of entry, but also in the course of his business activities in a country. A host state can determine the manner and scope of business to be undertaken by a foreign investor, be it an individual or a corporation. This right of a state is universally recognized by international law and arises from a rule relating to the power of exclusion of aliens which sovereign states possess by virtue of their sovereignty. At present, laws controlling foreign investment are on the increase, mainly due to the rapid changes that are taking place in the shape of foreign investment flows around the world. Furthermore, for various reasons the use of laws to scrutinize the entry of foreign investment will be increasingly resorted to by host states,[5] a trend that is equally apparent in developed and developing countries.[6]

The different regulatory frameworks for foreign direct investment provided by a host nation can be broadly grouped into three models. The *free entry model* of foreign investment attracts capital by allowing foreign investors to take advantage of lower production costs in the host country. It relies on market forces and international competition to stimulate investment in the host country. The model assumes that the host country holds some advantage that would lead to lower production costs within an industry. If there are no impediments to entry into the host country's market, the existence of such advantages attracts foreign investors by promising higher rates of return on capital. Once a significant number of producers within a given industry have taken advantage of the lower production costs of the host country, the supply curve shifts, and international competition forces down the price of the industry's final product. Market participants who have not taken advantage of the host country's relative advantages find that they are not competitive at the new lower price. In the long term such producers must either take advantage of the host country's lower costs or leave the industry.

The *negotiation model* of foreign investment attracts foreign investors by promising monopoly rents and other contractual rewards for participation. It also starts from the assumption that the host country holds out the promise of lower production costs. The theory behind the negotiation model is that, acting together, a host government and selected foreign investors can jointly exploit these same lower production costs. The host government grants rents to selected companies in selected sectors, then shares in these rents through a contract formula. The host government benefits directly from the resulting venture through its contractual share of rents.

The *combined model* is a model of foreign investment law which combines features of both the free entry and the negotiation models. According to this theory, the host country may adopt a foreign investment law that guarantees free entry, yet may also negotiate contracts with foreign investors in selected sectors of the economy. The principal feature of the combined model is that this model focuses on industries which *naturally* lack the element of competition essential to the free entry model. In these sectors, the implementation of the negotiation model can help host countries capture monopoly rents and set internationally optimal levels of production.

In designing a specific foreign investment regime, a country's lawmakers focus on four primary goals of foreign investment policy: technology transfer, transfer of management expertise, foreign capital inflow, and integration of the host country into the world economy. Theoretically, an effective foreign investment regime will secure these on a permanent basis. However, how these goals will be achieved is the matter of host governments' current agendas, policy preferences and, last but not least, certain domestic political pressures.[7]

Technology transfer. The process of transfer begins when a foreign company uses such technology in a host country. The next step occurs when the technology 'spills over' into the foreign company's industry, and to other industries in the host country.[8] A host country has reached the highest level of technology transfer when native companies are able to improve on the existing technology. Developing countries generally desire that technology spreads throughout the economy through 'spill-over'. In evaluating the alternative models, technology should be considered transferred only when this 'spill-over' process has begun.

The negotiation model offers a quick way to encourage the use of technology in the host country. The host country can target sectors that would immediately benefit from the advantages of technology, then share these benefits with the transferring corporation through economic rents. However, two factors limit transfer in the negotiation model after this initial stage. To understand the first of these limiting factors, it is necessary to look at the dynamics of the negotiation model.

The host nation's government and a foreign corporation each begin with a valuable asset. The former offers access to local resources while the latter offers valuable technology. After the initial deal is made, the host country can enforce the foreign corporation's contract compliance through the threat of taxation, or even nationalization.[9] In the negotiation model, when a foreign corporation transfers its valuable technology, it loses its main bargaining tool. In order to enforce its bargain, the foreign corporation must retain control of the technology by prolonging the process of transfer and by guarding against 'spill-over' within the host country. In the negotiation model, foreign corporations will be reluctant to train foreign employees since this will be likely to facilitate transfer of technology to the host country.

The negotiation model also fails to make use of competition as a means of technology transfer. Since the host country and foreign investors share in economic rents, other producers will remain in business using outdated technology. Instead of forcing the industry supply curve upwards, the negotiated production has no effect on market prices. The existence of economic rents also allows the foreign corporation to weigh the risks of dissemination against the marginal benefit of using 'state-of-the-art' technology. A multinational corporation may rationally choose to implement outmoded technology and sacrifice some of their economic rents rather than risk the dissemination of sensitive technology.

In contrast, the free entry model attracts technology slowly in its initial stages since the benefits of relocation are measured only by the marginal cost advantage of the host country. Whereas participants in the negotiation model can rely on guaranteed rents, free entry participants must carefully weigh the advantages of the host economy against the risks of capital involvement. However, as the advantages of the host country are exploited by a substantial number of foreign investors in an industry, the industry supply curve shifts upwards. This forces competitors to lower costs or leave the industry. The mechanism of competition ensures the transfer of technology for use in the host country through the price mechanism. In the competitive free entry model, firms cannot afford not to use the best technology in a particular industry because only the most efficient producers in a competitive industry will survive.

After technology is transferred for use in the host country, the free entry model facilitates the 'spill-over' of technology between industries. Unencumbered by a narrow contractual participation in the host economy, foreign investors 'branch out' in a manner that is not possible in an environment in which every new step into the host market must be negotiated. The free entry model also facilitates inter-industry 'spill-overs' that occur between foreign and domestic firms. A foreign venture can stimulate demand among local suppliers of the components it needs. New products introduced by foreign ventures into the local market may also increase the productivity of domestic firms that purchase the foreign venture's higher-technology products.

The selected sector model utilizes the negotiation process to ensure the influx of technology in sectors where competition would not force inefficient producers out of the market.

Management expertise takes the form of both written instructions and actual management. The existence of the human element of management expertise complicates its transfer and reinforces the need for a free entry model of foreign investment. Foreign companies have managers with expertise in the target industry as well as managers who specialize in the implementation of management systems in new locations. However, this physical transfer does not complete the process of transfer of management expertise since a manager's stay in the host country is likely to be of limited duration.

The host country benefits only when the foreign corporation takes two additional steps. Foreign managers actually need to adapt the management system of the MNC to the host country's culture and resources. MNCs will undertake this process as they seek to lower production costs and maximize strategic output. Another step of management expertise transfer occurs when management is indigenized to the host country. This involves the training of local personnel leading ultimately to their assumption of managerial positions formerly occupied by foreign managers. The benefits from managerial expertise increase greatly once they are transferred to native managers. The training of labour and management which takes place in MNCs may then be dispersed throughout the economy. Eventually, MNC-trained employees may choose to exploit the human capital that they have gained by moving to domestic corporations or by starting their own enterprises.

The free entry model accomplishes the transfer of managerial expertise more effectively than negotiation since it provides for the indigenization of such expertise. In a competitive equilibrium, foreign companies must train local managers to take advantage of lower salaries. In the negotiation model, the foreign firm faces no such market pressures. The negotiation model also hinders the transfer of management expertise by forcing foreign firms to protect against leaks of expertise to domestic firms. Native employees can prove commercially-threatening conduits of management expertise to domestic firms. Therefore, In the negotiation model an MNC has an incentive to withhold such expertise from native employees by denying managerial promotions. An alternative strategy may be to transfer native employees abroad once they have reached a certain managerial level. Either way, the negotiation process stifles the process of indigenization of management expertise.

The encouragement of long-term capital investment. The free entry model stimulates long-term investment more effectively because it does not rely on the limited ability of the host government to negotiate away special privileges. In light of the capital shortage in most developing countries, the negotiation model may be a reasonably effective short-term fix. The guarantee of monopoly profits through the process of negotiation can be an effective stimulus to large-scale capital investment. The free entry model of reform may be slow to produce such large capital investments, since at the initial stages of economic reform, after discounting for risk, the marginal cost of production in Kazakhstan could be greater than the world market price of goods in many industries. In such cases, foreign investors will simply choose not to participate until the level of risk falls.

The benefits of the negotiation model in terms of capital investment level off in the long run since there are only a limited number of rents that the host country can grant. The host government must revoke or renegotiate contracts with foreign investors in order to provide scope for economic growth. Yet such behaviour discourages other potential foreign investors. In addition, domestic investors will once again be forced to remove their money from the stagnant host economy in favour of higher foreign rates of return.

Under a free entry regime of foreign investment, if the host government is successful in reducing investment risks, more capital will become available on the domestic markets as local costs dip below those in competing countries. The free entry model also promises continued growth through the establishment of stable financial markets. The negotiation model deprives the local economy of stable financial markets since local financial firms can achieve only limited access to foreign ventures. In the negotiation model, host governments negotiate transactions with foreign firms and arrange financing through a central bank, or through foreign investment firms. In the free entry model, local investors negotiate their own deals with foreign entrepreneurs, and are free to make use of the local credit market, thereby developing the market's ability to promote such transactions.

Although the negotiation model may provide a host country with a rapid injection of foreign capital, the free entry model offers long-term capital growth that is not constrained by the state's power to grant economic rents. Foreign capital participation in the host country usually accounts for only a small percentage of total capital investment. Therefore, those industrializing countries that intend to develop their own financial markets and to ensure the long-term participation of foreign capital should choose a free entry model.

Integration into the world economy. Developing countries generally consider integration into the world economy to be a goal in and of itself. Apart from the political benefits, integration allows the host government to make internationally optimal use of its endowment of resources. The free entry model naturally achieves these advantages because at every step, foreign investors weigh opportunities in the host country against those in other countries. The negotiation model does not achieve this international optimality. Instead, it relies on central planners to determine the types and extent of foreign participation. Although such planners are aware of the relative scarcity of goods, the very preferences they bargain with distort international economic choices.

The selected sector combined model does not necessarily hinder integration since it makes use of negotiation only in those areas of the economy where the market would otherwise fail to achieve competitive equilibrium. By restraining production of natural resources, the host government can take advantage of international cartels and oligopolies to maximize its income.

4.3 The elements of the free entry model

Having outlined the basic advantages of the free entry model over the negotiation model, it is helpful to define in more detail what the free entry model entails for the foreign investment legislation of a host country. There are five major characteristics of the free entry model. First, foreign investors must be able to establish wholly owned companies or subsidiaries and to maintain complete control of their operation. Foreign investors are willing to take calculated risks, but seldom will they do so without having control of their own enterprise. Host country laws that require a local joint venturer or partial host government ownership drive away foreign investment and inhibit the ability of existing foreign ventures to compete internationally.

Second, foreign investors must be treated identically with their domestic counterparts. Discrimination against foreign investors, either directly or indirectly, raises the cost of their capital participation in the host country. At higher marginal costs, fewer foreign investors will find the advantage of participation great enough to outweigh its inherent risks.

Third, foreign investors must have the right to repatriate their earnings without interference or delay. The right of foreigners to invest in a developing country loses its meaning without a corresponding right to retrieve its investment and earnings. For everyday business reasons, investors must constantly shift the form and location of their business investments. Laws that restrict this natural movement of capital only serve to inhibit capital flow into the host country. Foreign investors find the right of repatriation especially important in the developing countries because of the higher level of political risk. Foreign investors can discount for such risks, but they must be able to react to exogenous problems in order to protect their investments. Host governments that seek to control capital flow from their countries through restrictions on repatriation can expect to dampen foreign investors' enthusiasm. Given the virtual impossibility of stopping capital outflow by governmental decree, such provisions pay a high price for little effect.

Fourth, foreign investors must have the right to unrestricted use of the local currency and freedom of banking. By controlling a foreign investor's use of local currency, a host government imposes increased transaction costs for firms that import or export goods. Currency restrictions can also slow down transactions to such a rate that they are no longer economically feasible.

Fifth, the host government must guarantee a system of legal protection to foreign investors against other entities and also against the government itself. Legal protection against other entities requires a framework of commercial law that offers remedies for contract breach, and wrongful business practices. International and especially bilateral investment treaties, along with the domestic legislation of a host state, play an important role in securing the system of guarantees against a host state's government.[10]

To sum up, an efficient foreign investment regime utilizing the free entry model requires adherence to the five basic requirements outlined above. Ignoring this requirement diminishes the likelihood of the emergence of an optimal model for the legal regulation of FDI.

4.4 Country-specific criteria and the choice of a regulatory model

What model should be chosen by the government of a transitional country? More specifically, what are the criteria for the choice of an appropriate model? The choice will be dictated by two factors: (i) economic pressures, both domestic and international, upon a transitional country and (ii) the specific objectives pursued by its government and interpreted into policy. Correspondingly, that model is optimal which presents a more precise match between the objective economic constraints and opportunities on the one hand, and the chosen state's strategy, on the other. Therefore, in analysing the selection of an appropriate model of legal regulation for FDI one needs first to have a clear picture of the economic imperatives pressing upon the government of a transitional host country.

A brief historical overview allows us to highlight certain factors that have affected the contours of the Kazakh model. First, one needs to look back to see the source of the 1980s' *perestroika* which eventually caused transformations in the USSR, and, especially, the introduction of a policy which aimed to attract foreign investment. An examination of the causal relationship between the present system and the late-Soviet-era environment helps to give us a clear picture of post-independence reality. Several fundamental studies have been undertaken by western scholars to uncover the most essential sources of *perestroika*. Their findings emphasize the fact that the Gorbachev reforms which started in the mid-1980s were the direct result of the previous poor economic performance. In particular, analysis undertaken by western and formerly Soviet economists who have been involved in the implementation of the policy of *perestroika* clearly indicates that it was a negative total factor productivity which exacerbated politico-economic tension within the late-Soviet society and was the most substantial reason for economic decline in the late-Soviet period.[11] This, in turn, explains the necessity of outlining a post-independence economic environment within which FDI occurs.

It is noteworthy that one of the key factors behind Gorbachev's reforms appeared in the mid-1970s, when the rate of growth of investment was sharply curtailed in the midst of a mounting severe labour shortage which arose as a result of the loss of 25 million Soviet human lives in the Second World War. Instead of utilizing capital to alleviate the mounting labour shortage through accelerated replacement, mechanization and modernization, the government aggravated the problems associated with this shortage by cutting back sharply on the rate of growth of investment. A notion that the economy would function more efficiently at a lower rate of growth of investment was accepted by the leadership of that period, which, in turn, was pressed to find the resources required mainly to maintain strategic parity with the United States. Available statistical data show that the average decrease of investment during the period 1975–1985 was accompanied by severe reductions in the rate of growth of such important economic indicators as national income and industrial output. According to Soviet official statistics, the average service life of Soviet machinery and equipment in industry increased from 24 years in 1971 to 27.9 years in 1985, an increase of about 16 per cent.[12] It is no coincidence that the period from 1970 to 1985 was referred to in Soviet historiography as 'a period of stagnation'.

This policy was reversed after Gorbachev came to power. At the XXVIIth Congress of the Communist Party, held in March 1986, Gorbachev described the cutback in investment from one five-year plan to another as 'completely unjustified'.[13] According to this view, the 12th five-year plan (1986–1990) called for a 23 per cent rise in investment in the economy as a whole, which compares with a 15 per cent realized increase in the 1981–1985 period.[14] In late 1988, however, Gorbachev seemed to revert to the previous leaders' short-sighted policy of seeking to raise living standards immediately at the expense of investment – with its well-known adverse effects on the economy. This shift in Gorbachev's position forced the government, led by Nikolai Ryzhkov, to reassess and revise its economic policies. This change in course involved the redirection of investment away from productive projects provided for in the 12th five-year plan (1986–1990) to non-productive projects of a social overhead character not provided for in the 12th five-year plan. Investment was also reallocated away from heavy industry to consumer-oriented industries. This redirection of investment in some cases caused the cancellation of the financing of expensive productive projects, thereby seriously disrupting supply relationships between enterprises. Again, the Communist Party tried to solve economic problems by uneconomic measures such as increasing labour discipline, decreasing the rate of absenteeism among employees, and prosecuting alcoholism by legal punitive measures instead of uncovering its socioeconomic sources. As a result, negative effects spread throughout the Soviet economy. Supply problems were further compounded in 1989 and 1990 by strikes, by enterprises asserting their rights and refusing to fulfil contractual obligations, and by ethnic conflicts. The upshot of all this was a significant faltering of the economy in general.

In other words, the initial crisis, which *perestroika* was designed to solve, was, in principle, a systemic crisis of the centrally planned economy, and, more specifically, it was a *crisis of the internal investment system* – the pivotal element which ensures the functioning of any economy. In the Soviet case this system was completely thrown out of tune by the system's fundamental problem, which was far deeper, in the inherent input–output relationships built into the structure of production and exchange developed over decades. *Perestroika* has not accomplished the task of profound restructuring of the internal investment system. The depth of the problem was much more serious than expected at the beginning of *perestroika* in 1985. Therefore, political considerations took over from economic imperatives. This in turn meant that the newly independent states have had to deal again with the problem of restructuring the domestic system of investment generation. Professor Pyatkin, head of the Directorate for Economic Projects of the International Fund for Promotion of Privatization and Foreign Investment, has observed that:

> In these conditions the conclusion is obvious: the economy of the post-Soviet states needs major and aimed investment, as well as the new technical means and modern technologies. Another conclusion is also obvious: at present, Russia and Commonwealth (of Independent States) not only do not have these possibilities, but also are forced to reduce their internal investment.[15]

The deep depression of the Soviet and post-Soviet economy resulted in a dramatic drop in the levels of investment.[16] Only Turkmenistan avoided such a drop by concentrating upon the development and export of its natural resources (namely energy resources) while avoiding the disruption caused by economic, and in particular structural, reform. Other states which have hesitated on and/or delayed reform have faced a smaller fall in output, but have suffered an equally serious drop in investment activity as those that have pursued reform measures. The extent of the collapse can be seen in levels of gross capital formation in 1993 as a percentage of those in 1990. There are two observations to be made here, which are relevant to this study. First, the collapse in the investment system at this time indicates the fundamental and irreversible decline of the centrally planned economy. Accordingly, such a process should create the necessary macroeconomic preconditions for a market-type rationalization of investment policy. Second, such a collapse has naturally led to a reduction of state investment and, therefore, should facilitate the creation of more opportunities for private investors, both domestic and, mainly, foreign (given the lack of domestic capital). Furthermore, in conditions when domestic technology is significantly under-financed, FDI becomes the sole vehicle for introduction of modern technologies and equipment.

The next factor is the *break-up of the previously unified economic system into 15 parts (the 15 newly independent states) which are not self-sustainable.* The present economic crisis is worsened by the fact that many ties had been formed within the former Soviet Union. A unified fixed system had been developed, covering the supply of raw materials, machines and equipment, the distribution of products and the allocation of resources, and an integral, indivisible economic system had come into existence. The sudden disintegration of the Union, and the subsequent independence of the republics, put an abrupt end to the close and stable economic ties that had been cemented over many decades. Because the new economic ties, and in particular the new economic structure, could not possibly be set up overnight, the result has naturally been an entire or partial stoppage of work in enterprises, abnormal operation of production, chaos in economic order and semi-paralysis of economic life. Obviously, FDI could play a revitalizing role in curing this problem and thus rationalizing the structure of the country's economy in the way of linking and modernizing the backward domestic economy through contact with the international economy.

The Soviet pattern of economy and domestic investment has left a *sectoral structure of production which is unable to cope with the needs of a modern society*. This is the fourth factor which shapes the contours of the Kazakh regulatory model. The heavy industrial, natural resource extraction and agricultural sectors were hypertrophic, while business and consumer services, domestic trade and financial intermediation were underdeveloped.[17] Therefore, in conditions of a general lack of government investment, overcoming both technological and structural deformations will require a massive infusion of investment resources and substantial shifts in the patterns of resource use. An overconcentration on heavy industry and a heritage of the centrally planned economy is another serious problem of a structural nature with which Kazakhstan is beset. For example, in 1988 the USSR produced 17 times more steel per dollar of GDP than did the United States. In developing industry, the Soviet emphasis was always laid on heavy industry, especially the mining, metallurgical, non-ferrous, chemical and related machinery-building industries; the production of consumer goods had never been given its due attention. Correspondingly, the imperative to promote more sophisticated industries requires a model which is more conducive to knowledge-based investment.

Sectoral imbalance caused a sectoral allocation of the labour force that was peculiar to the FSU. At the start of the reforms, the vast bulk of the labour force in the FSU worked in industry and related services, while in Asian transitional countries, the majority of the labour force was in agriculture. Pomphret observes:

> A major reason why reform processes develop their own momentum is that they create vested interests in favour of reform, which outweigh original vested interests opposed to change. In China and Vietnam a crucial early reform was in agriculture, giving a stake in the reform process to a large part of the population. Through the 1980s the rural population, still the vast majority, provided solid support for continued economic reform.[18]

In China on the eve of economic reform the agricultural sector was the largest sector of the labour force. In the late 1970s more than three-quarters of the economically active population worked in agriculture, while in all the countries of Eastern Europe the comparable figure in 1989 was below one-quarter; in the USSR it was 14 per cent.[19] In other words,

> the key components of post-1979 growth in China were to raise agricultural productivity and to transfer labour from agriculture to higher productivity jobs in other sectors. Eastern European and the former Soviet Union countries faced the more quintessential transition problem of relocating labour from inefficient activities promoted by the central planners to more productive activities. Chinese agricultural workers had almost nothing to lose from reforms, while in the former USSR much of the labour force fears that it will suffer during the reform process.[20]

All of the FSU governments, while carrying out economic reform, are overburdened by *the previous Communist governments' commitments to universal social protection.* By contrast, in China and the South East Asian newly industrialized countries, the population has not been spoiled by such commitments and, therefore, in political terms, reforms have been much easier to implement in the Asian case, where people (used to the minimum of welfare, known as the 'iron rice bowl') are prepared for the sufferings of the transition period, while in the FSU, people disturbed by transition difficulties, more frequently appeal to the past.

Thus, it seems that the social protection commitments of the previous Communist governments, and the present uncertainties associated with structural adjustments undertaken by the new government of Kazakhstan, can generate major political tensions, even when a majority of the population stands to benefit ex ante from the reforms. In the Asian case, governments at the beginning of reforms have not been overburdened by such commitments and, therefore, the political costs of reforms were not as great as has been experienced by the FSU states. This emphasizes the fact that the legal regulation of FDI during transition is significantly affected by the political implications of transition. More importantly, it should, as it seems in the light of the above proposition, be tailored in such a way that it alleviates these tensions and is aimed at a more rapid economic recuperation.

The next imperative has to do with *the state of existing industrial and agricultural enterprises.* Although Kazakhstan is rich in mineral resources (mainly ferrous and non-ferrous metals), hydrocarbons (oil and natural gas) and produced a large share of former Soviet agro-industrial output, its plants, factories and farms are equipped with out-of-date machinery and technology. Earlier we discussed *why* this happened. To add to this discussion, we should say, by way of example, that the most attractive sectors for FDI – namely mineral deposits, oilfields and agricultural lands – have been exploited by outdated equipment and technologies due to the extensive, as opposed to intensive, nature of the Soviet economy. As a result, there are at present millions of tons of industrial tailings stockpiled by Soviet-era enterprises that, in the case of the utilization of modern technologies, can be reprocessed. A similar situation exists in the oil industry. Thus, the vast majority of existing enterprises in primary industry and agriculture, which can play the role of initial areas for FDI, need the introduction of high technologies to existing agro-industrial facilities. More importantly, the extensive approach to the development of the Soviet economy together with the administrative methods of management, resulted in disruption of market attitudes of enterprises' managers and in gross neglect of management and marketing skills as necessary requirements of economic planning. For present reforms to succeed, it will be critically important to change the system of corporate governance at the most basic level of the economy – enterprise. The emergence of links between domestic and foreign enterprises should also be addressed in the context of this problem.[21]

Dismantling the state-owned property system in Kazakhstan is likely to prove a more expensive and time-consuming process than has been the case, for example, in the transitional countries of Asia. In China, for instance, because of the much lower level of state-owned enterprises and the fact that most of the population is still to be found in rural areas, the process of establishment of private businesses and attraction of FDI was less expensive and less time-consuming for government. Such processes developed from the beginning of reforms, and have had more rapid and widescale dynamics. Because of this there was a quicker absorption of western ways of conduct of business and business culture by China as well as South East Asian states. Thus, in the Chinese context new enterprises have been far more important than reformed, that is, privatized state enterprises, as if the case in East European transitional economies. Because in the former Soviet Union state enterprises compose a much larger share of industrial activity, privatization plays a key role in the establishment of a market environment, which is, as experiences with other transitional states show, a necessary prerequisite for active FDI inflows into a country.

The geographical location of Kazakhstan, a landlocked country, also affects the decision about which model should be chosen. The country has transportation and telecommunications systems far below the international levels required to attract significant FDI. This factor is one of the major physical obstacles to FDI. The distant location of international markets and the high transportation costs associated with this, together with the poor technological state of existing enterprises, should force the Kazakh government to shape FDI regulation in order to promote the technological recuperation of industry and the processing of natural materials domestically so as to create added value within the domestic economy and for domestic or regional consumption.

Further, reforms in the former USSR started amidst rapidly changing (and not always in their favour) global economic conditions, which also influence the present currents of FDI into the former Soviet Union and, in turn, shape the policies adopted by the newly independent states. This notion requires further explication. After a stagnation which lasted until the mid-1980s, the volume of all FDI invested abroad increased from 5 per cent of global GDP in the mid-1980s to 8 per cent in 1990. The intensive movement of FDI at the end of the 1980s was followed by a slow deceleration in investment flows in the beginning of the 1990s. Inward FDI flows in developing countries became more active again and in the 1990s reached a level of US$32 billion with a growth rate of 22 per cent in the period 1986–1990 against 4 per cent during the period 1980–1985. At the same time, the share of developing countries in the total foreign direct capital pie was reduced, from 25 per cent at the beginning of the 1980s to 17 per cent at the end.[22]

At the time of writing, a decrease of FDI is apparent on the African continent, reflecting its deteriorating economic and political conditions. The share of Africa in FDI flows to developing countries declined steadily from 19.9 per cent in 1970 to 12.7 per cent in 1975 and 4.4 per cent in the second half of 1980s. From 1994 a decrease of inward FDI has also been seen in Latin America. While the vast majority of FDI occurs between the industrialized nations, inward flows have been slowly increasing into the developing regions of Asia, Central and Eastern Europe and the former Soviet Union. However, with regard to the Central and East Europe/Former Soviet Union (CEE/FSU) states, although the growth of investment there has been impressive, the absolute volume of the flows is still relatively small.[23]

An international debt crisis, following the inability of the borrowers to service or repay the capital lent by banks from 1970 to the early 1980s, caused this source of capital for developing countries to dry up. There was a dramatic decline in the capital available on the international financial market for lending to the developing countries, from US$44.5 billion in 1981 to US$4.1 billion in 1990. This considerable reduction increased competition between state-recipients for alternative sources of scarce capital, mainly for private (which presently composes up to three-quarters of total inward investment to developing countries), both direct and portfolio, investment. Presumably, this increased competition for much-needed FDI should press the Kazakh government to choose the most attractive model for MNCs – that is, the free entry model.

Another international factor influencing FDI in Kazakhstan may be defined as the 'neighbourhood factor'. The world can be said to consist of three poles generating international FDI flows: the North American pole (USA and Canada), the European pole (mainly France, the UK and Germany) and the Asian pole (Japan). The analysis of trends in Latin America and South East Asian transitional countries shows that FDI flows, their sectoral distribution, and market orientation are significantly influenced by the neighbouring FDI home countries. In the South East Asian case, such influence originates from Japan, which plays an increasingly dominant role and exhibits immense investment power in the whole Asia-Pacific region. In the Latin American case this role is performed by the United States. Accordingly, the decline in outward FDI activity in the USA partially explains the decline of FDI in Latin America, and, conversely, the increasing Japanese role in FDI generation explains the amazing capital inflows in countries of the Asian region during the last ten years. Until now the USA was much more active in FSU states than Japan, whose FDI was negligible. However, this situation is changing, especially in relation to the Central Asian republics and in particular Kazakhstan, which, as statistical data shows, is being firmly included into the orbit of Asian economic influence.[24] Furthermore, the recent signing of the US$6 billion deal with China to construct an oil pipeline indicates the strengthening of the eastern orientation of the Kazakh economic strategy.

Thus, post-independence Kazakhstan has emerged into a highly competitive global investment system. This entry will, in turn, draw each new country into a respective FDI-generating pole. Kazakhstan is likely to emerge into the orbit of Asian influence with Japan as a dominant source of influence. Taking into account the structure of Japanese investment, consisting mainly of technology-based and export-oriented manufacturing investment, one could assume that for the Kazakh model of FDI regulation to be most effective and to take advantage of the Japanese FDI, it should be a free entry model which provides better conditions for the introduction of knowledge-based investment. Political rationale could also reinforce this economic decision.

Kazakhstan, with its outdated post-Soviet technologies and equipment, subordinated for centuries to Moscow, should also actively seek an access to an advanced part of the world via the Asian direction which is less vulnerable to Russian caprice. Such aspiration will be dictated by the necessity to overcome the former and still remaining colonial pattern of its economy, to enhance economic self-sufficiency and its statehood, and also to secure economic and thus political independence in the future. Clearly, the former metropole, Russia, with her current economic and political problems, and her historical record of neglect of the constituent republics, is not the best partner for achieving this goal. Russia's current weakness and thus limited ability to control the former colonies could accordingly be used by Kazakhstan to make a historical breakthrough from the colonial past to true independence.

4.5 An optimal model for Kazakhstan

The above discussion allows us to conclude that the driving force behind economic reforms in Kazakhstan should clearly be a policy of *industrialization*. However, account should be taken of the fact that the post-Soviet context of industrial modernization has its own peculiar features. In the case of Britain, for instance, industrialization happened as a consequence of changing international opportunities and 'a "nightwatchman" state facilitated industrial transformation by permitting a domestic bourgeoisie to seize the economic opportunities provided by a successful colonialist policy'.[25] The state did not play an active role in restructuring British industry. On the other hand, the German example displays the crucial role which was accorded to the state in implementing industrialization in that case:

> National political forces were important in initiating and sustaining the industrialization process. Political cohesion was an essential prerequisite of economic recovery and industrial growth. The state played a crucial role in building an institutional network which consciously sought to relate financial and industrial developments. As time passed, German industry became competitive in a wide range of international markets. Protectionism became unnecessary.[26]

Soviet industrialization presents a further different approach. Because the USSR was a closed society which rejected private ownership and initiative,[27] industrialization here had an autarkic character – that is, there was concentration on the industrial branches at the expense of and with the exploitation of agricultural development. More importantly for this thesis is the fact that in the Soviet Union industrialization occurred in almost complete isolation from the outside world and international competition. As a result, Soviet industrial enterprises simply have not been adequately exposed to the ruthless competitive pressures of international product markets. The state was the main agent of industrial resource mobilization. Soviet industrialization remained geared to the expansion of domestic demand and to import-substitution. No attempt was made to promote manufacturing exports and Soviet exports remained dominated by farm products and mineral raw materials. As a result of this Soviet pattern of 'industrialization', which has left a heavy burden for the successor states, they have not only to restructure their economies and establish new domestic private sources of investment, but, more importantly, they must also tackle their emerging industries in the international division of labour and international market of products. In other words, the distinguishing feature of the post-Soviet industrialization is that it is technology-based.

It follows from the above analysis that FDI may play an increasingly prominent role in Kazakhstan's industrial take-off.[28] At the same time, the newly independent Kazakhstan has emerged in conditions of intense competition for scarce FDI. Therefore, account should be taken of one fundamental feature of this new situation for the Kazakh government environment – the dramatic quickening of the pace of technological change on a worldwide scale, which has concentrated power in the hands of multinational corporations (MNCs).[29] As the microelectronics revolution diffused across virtually the entire spectrum of economic activity, it revolutionized production techniques and product designs, even in manufacturing industries traditionally considered to be technologically mature. Instead of the economies of scale which defined the Fordist era, competition increasingly hinged either on compressing the product cycle to constantly introduce new products with advanced features, or on flexibly adapting production to sudden changes in market demands. The quickening pace of global technological change has thus made it difficult for aspiring industrializers to exclude multinationals, as Japan and Korea did during their industrial take-off, in hopes that local producers will soon be able to compete independently. Instead, attracting FDI has become virtually the sine qua non for technology access in the globalized manufacturing system.

Naturally, one pivotal effect of the 1990s' technological changes was to enhance MNCs' proprietary control over the key technologies necessary to be internationally competitive across a range of industries. The pressures of global oligopolistic competition compelled leading MNCs to seek a presence in all of the world's major markets, as well as to exploit the full production advantages of various locations around the globe. Improvements in international transport and telecommunications allowed MNCs to coordinate the functions of multiple overseas subsidiaries to produce a single final product, enabling them to transfer any part of the production chain – from research and development

(R&D), procurement, production, assembly, and marketing – to virtually any location in their worldwide networks. In contrast to the 1960s and 1970s, the motivations for FDI were now driven less by a host country's simple cost factors than by its broader advantages as a site for internationally linked production in terms of skills, infrastructure, and productivity growth. MNCs' international network structure began to be organized around the principles of 'complex integration'. At the global level, MNC networks moved from strictly hierarchical to more horizontal patterns. Parent companies decentralized production tasks and decision-making authority to regional subsidiaries in a search for greater flexibility and faster design-to-market cycle times. In order to capture more fully the production advantages of different locations, MNCs encouraged their subsidiaries to specialize in specific products or subsystems and to develop deeper, more integrated production, procurement, and design capabilities. MNC affiliates began to exchange information, components, and final products in reciprocal patterns throughout the parent company's regional or global networks.

While decentralizing functions from the parent company to overseas subsidiaries, however, MNCs also sought to rationalize their off-shore production by creating vertically integrated production chains within individual regions. Global decentralization made off-shore production more integrated and self-contained within given zones or regions, but individual subsidiaries became more specialized in particular components or assembly tasks in order to achieve scale economies. Thus, a flattening of MNCs' hierarchies at the global level often meant the creation of new hierarchical relationships within regions. Such intra-group networks, usually entailing much closer managerial and functional coordination across borders, implied less autonomy in key functions like components procurement at the level of the individual subsidiary, even while greater autonomy and a deeper array of functions developed to regional operations as a whole.

To sum up, MNCs' newly formulated complex integration strategies may hold potentially far-reaching implications for Kazakhstan. Foreign firms' willingness to move beyond final stage assembly to deeper production activities, in some cases extending even to design and adaptive R&D, holds out the possibility that Kazakhstan could use FDI to upgrade and integrate its presently shallow industrial base. At the same time, the threat of losing their technological competitive advantage forces MNCs to implement closer managerial and functional coordination. It is no coincidence that those countries that have imposed less strict requirements for indigenization over the foreign companies have been most successful in upgrading their national industries.

In short, for industrializing states the terms of access to technology had suddenly narrowed. Their ability to bargain with MNCs to separate technology from foreign ownership was undercut by the lack of alternative means of technology acquisitions, such as arm's-length licensing or 'reverse engineering'. Instead of 'unloading the multinationals', developing countries who hoped to advance into advanced manufacturing industries were now compelled to invite them in. Seen in this light, the entrance of FDI today should be seen, regardless of the regions, as an adaptation to the new global realities. Thus, the crucial feature of this stage of globalization is that the newly emerged transitional states, besides finding themselves faced by stiff competition for FDI, are forced to adapt their domestic policies and institutions to meet foreign companies' requirements, rather than the reverse.

Nevertheless, although the growth of MNCs' international production networks has constrained the ability of transitional states to pursue autonomous infant-industry policies, it has also created new possibilities for host-country states to influence MNCs' locational decisions as a basic element of national industrialization strategy. In other words, a country's comparative advantage is not exogenously fixed by factor endowments, but neither can a developmental state shape it by promoting infant domestic industries to achieve international competitiveness. Advancing in the international division of labour requires close linkages to MNCs who control a growing share of international production and trade. Insofar as a country's position in the international division of labour is created by MNCs' production strategies, however, a host country may attempt to influence those strategies to shape the local economy's role in integrated production networks. Thus, the more optimal model of a legal framework for FDI will be that which allows Kazakhstan to secure more advantageous positions within MNC-orchestrated international divisions of labour.

The assumption that the optimal model of legal regulation of FDI for Kazakhstan should be that which is designed to induce MNCs to upgrade into more technology-intensive activities is reinforced by another consideration. The concern that MNCs will operate as production enclaves without stimulating local technological development emphasizes the need for such a policy which will encourage technology indigenization. The hypothesis that MNCs' investment may lead to the creation of a dual economy in a host country was tested in previous studies.[30] Of course, in the case of Kazakhstan, legacies of the past system, discussed earlier, namely the overconcentration of industries and its previous social commitments, could create a dilemma for the Kazakh rule-makers – what policy to pursue, one aimed at the upgrading of the national industry within the MNCs' network or indigenization of those FDI which enter the country? One may argue that the pursuit of either of these two strategies would lead to the automatic achievement of the other. In practice, however, the pursuit of high-technology foreign investment always seems to be in tension with the desire to press for greater local control over technology. Therefore, faced with this trade-off, transitional states must choose to emphasize one or another goal in the hopes that progress towards the other would eventually follow. Indeed, the pressure on MNCs to indigenize technology by forming local linkages might act temporarily as a disincentive to new FDI. But if local technological capabilities were thereby improved, and capable local suppliers and subcontractors emerged, this industrial capacity would eventually attract new foreign partnerships on more favourable conditions. In the case of Kazakhstan, however, account should be taken of the low degree of readiness of the local infrastructure and of domestic suppliers and subcontractors. It follows from the above discussions that, despite its well-educated workforce and existing industrial base, Kazakhstan is still not ready to adopt indigenization as its principal economic strategy.[31]

4.6 Summary

This chapter defined the country-specific and international imperatives affecting the contours of the emerging legal regulatory framework for FDI in Kazakhstan. Indeed these factors can be viewed only as the basis for the formation of the optimal model by the Kazakh decision-makers. The actual choice of the optimal model of legal regulation of FDI is made not solely on the basis of unilateral preferences, be they of a host government or a foreign investor.[32] Rather, the increased complexity of economic relationships in the 1990s, along with dramatic technological developments, have affected the strategies employed by MNCs at earlier times. Accordingly, this has forced the governments of industrializing nations to change their methods for dealing with the MNCs.[33] This made the relationships between both parties – the state and a foreign investor – more interdependent, more risky and more vulnerable to changes in global economics. Sensitivities, on the side of

MNCs, associated with the transfer of technology and unavoidable necessity to share them with the host nations, in turn, put a major reciprocal responsibility on the host countries' regulators – namely, to ensure the long-term certainty of the MNCs' operations. As the practice of earlier transitions has shown, the most successful countries were those which were able not only to design their internal institutions to suit these developments, but also to ensure a coherent policy. The remaining parts of this study will define the actual model of legal regulation and then answer the questions on why, by whom and how the choice was made.

5
The Kazakh Model for the Legal Regulation of FDI

5.1 Introduction

This chapter deals with the Kazakh legislation on FDI. The purpose of this examination is to consider the evolution of the post-independence legislation in order to identify the existing model of legal regulation. It will be argued that since independence, the overall aim of Kazakh legislation has been to promote the free entry model. However, much of this was a result of the momentum carried forward from the period of *perestroika*, and the challenge of setting up a free entry model has not been achieved. The chapter will also demonstrate that after the collapse of the USSR the evolution of post-independence legislation in Kazakhstan has gradually shifted towards the negotiation model of legal regulation – that is, the less optimal model. The 1997 Law on State Support of Direct Investment[1] will be analysed as embodying the culmination of this shift to the present model. By stressing the fact that the shift occurred for other than economic reasons, this chapter will establish the framework for the discussion in subsequent chapters.

5.2 A Kazakh model, 1991–1995

Considering the late-Soviet and, particularly, the initial post-independence Kazakh legislation on foreign investment, one may conclude that, at first, post-independence Kazakhstan attempted to implement a free entry model of regulation. The adherence to the free entry model, however, during the first period of independence – that is, in the period 1991–1995 – was mainly, as argued earlier, due to the legacy of *perestroika*. The major liberalizing impetus which came from Moscow was in line with the interests of the constituent Soviet republics. Later, after the failure of economic reforms, this impetus was reinforced by the willingness of the union republics to bargain for as much independence as was necessary to keep their economies afloat.

As the following discussion will show,[2] despite the fact that the model adopted in the period 1991–1996 addressed the crucial features of the free entry model, there were also substantial elements in the system of legal regulation which undermined its effects. Of more significance is the point that these elements demonstrate a gradual regression of the Kazakh model towards the less optimal one.

An analysis of the relevant clauses of the 1994 Law on Foreign Investment of Kazakhstan confirms the above assumption.[3] The statute provides a national regime for the treatment of foreign investors; the latter can choose a most favoured regime, if his home country enters in a special bilateral agreement with Kazakhstan and if a foreign investor finds the terms of such an agreement more advantageous. The implementation of such a national treatment regime after gaining independence confirms the assumption that the initial model was focused on the regulation of structures, rather than conduct. Correspondingly, this means that the movement of the entire legislative system was geared towards a free entry model. Further, the 1994 law set up a system of guarantees which comply with the requirements of the free entry model. In particular, it includes the following provisions which are enumerated in the order they appear in the statute.

1. *Guarantee of the stability of legislation.* This is one of the most important clauses; it assures a foreign investor that his investment shall not be subject to changes in the host country's legislation.

2. *Guarantee against expropriation.* The national legislation presents a definition similar to that which can be found in the international treaties. Namely, that expropriation may be undertaken by the state only in cases explicitly defined in the statute and, if so, only in accordance with a certain legal procedure and with payment of adequate, prompt and effective compensation.

3. The law defines *the principles of compensation.* If damage was caused by the illegal actions of the state organs or by its officials full compensation shall be paid. If damage was caused by *force majeure*, a national regime for the compensation of such damages shall be applied to foreign investors.

4. *Guarantee against interference by the state organs* and its officials in the activities of foreign investors. The normative acts which are issued by the state and by its officials which do not comply with the law and which worsen the conditions of foreign investment shall be considered

void. Discrimination on the basis of the nationality of foreign investors is prohibited. This guarantee also includes the *guarantee during state inspections*, which means that any state organ or agency or official can inspect foreign investors' activities only within the scope of authority vested upon them by law. The law explicitly states that a foreign investor has a right not to respond to orders which were issued by the state organ or an official beyond their duties as well as to refuse to present information to them that is outside the scope of their authority.

5. *Guarantee of the free use of dividends* earned in the territory of the republic means that a foreign investor is entitled to freely reinvest his dividends either for acquisition or for any other objectives which are not prohibited by the national legislation of the country.

6. *Guarantee of the free transfer of currency abroad.* All transfers, after tax and other payments stipulated by law, can be freely undertaken by a foreign investor. Furthermore, a foreign investor is entitled to use hard currency in order to make payments for transactions occurring in the territory of the republic, as well as to paying salaries to his employees.

7. *Transparency of investment activity.* Foreign investors are guaranteed open access to all statutes and regulations, as well as court decisions, relevant to foreign investment. The law specifies that foreign investors have free access to information on registration of juridical persons, on their charters, on the registration of real estate transactions, on issued licences, except to the information which may constitute a commercial secret of another business entity or an individual. For instance, Article 4 of the Decree of the President with the effect of law provides additional reassurances with respect to petroleum transactions. All interested persons are allowed to have access to information on the procedures of investment tenders, on the results of a tender and of a contract which was concluded between the state licensing authority and a winner of a tender, except information which was agreed by a winner of a tender and a state organ to be confidential.

The proclamation of the national regime of treatment of FDI along with the above guarantees demonstrates Kazakhstan's willingness to adhere to an open, and thus optimal model of regulation. The focus of the regulator on structural, rather than on conduct, regulation, undoubtedly sets up a facilitative institutional environment in which a foreign investor anticipates a longer commitment on the part of the state and is more willing to put down deeper roots in the host country's soil. Accordingly, an anticipated 'spill-over' effect is likely to be deeper in the sense of quality and spread of knowledge-based assets to be diffused in the local economy. Nevertheless, further examination of the above clauses leads to the opposite conclusion.

As stated, the legislature of Kazakhstan proclaims a national regime for the treatment of foreign natural and juridical persons. This means that foreign legal entities and individuals are granted a regime which is no less favourable than that given to the host country's legal entities and citizens. The rule on the national regime is presently contained in the Constitution of the Republic of Kazakhstan[4] (Item 4 of Article 12), in the Law on Citizenship of 20 December 1991[5] (Article 6), and in the Law on Legal Status of Foreign Citizens of 19 June 1995[6] (Part I of Article 3). The Law on Foreign Investment of 27 December 1994 (Article 4) defines this regime with respect to foreign juridical persons. However, the most precise definition of this rule is included in Item 7 of Article 3 of the Civil Code,[7] which states:

> Foreign physical and legal persons, as well as stateless persons, shall be entitled to acquire the same rights and shall be obliged to fulfil the same obligations that are envisaged by civil legislation for citizens and juridical persons of the Republic of Kazakhstan, if the legislative acts shall not envisage otherwise.

This clause is reproduced in other laws; however, from the legal point of view it is not necessary in as much as if a law does not contain a similar explicit rule, the aforementioned clause of the Civil Code will be applied anyway.

Furthermore, the national legislation provides another, so-called 'most favoured' regime. It is usually defined in the bilateral inter-state investment treaties that are concluded between the republic and another state. For instance, such a regime was established by the Treaty on Trade Relationships between the Republic of Kazakhstan and the United States of America signed on 19 May 1993. The law provides that the Kazakh type of regulatory regime can be chosen by a foreign investor himself. This in turn facilitates the achievement of an optimal regulation. Article 4 of the 1995 Law on Foreign Investment explicitly states in this regard:

> Any forms of foreign investments and activity connected therewith not prohibited by prevailing legislation of the Republic of Kazakhstan shall be effectuated on conditions no less favourable than those which are granted in a similar situation to the investments of physical and juridical persons of the Republic of

Kazakhstan or any other foreign physical and juridical persons, depending upon which conditions are most favourable.

Yet, even though an introduction of the national regime in the host country's legislation is an important step, the operation of such a regime to the benefit of a foreign investor can be achieved only in conditions of interaction of all the laws related to businesses of the foreign investors. Let us, therefore, examine the current status of these laws. In an assessment of the national regime of treatment, one needs to look first at the business forms provided to foreign investors by a host nation's legislation. According to Item 1 of Article 1152 of the Civil Code, the legal capacity of a foreign juridical person is defined according to the country of the origin of this legal entity. This means that if a juridical person is registered in the territory of the Republic of Kazakhstan, his rights and duties shall be determined according to the domestic legislation of Kazakhstan.

The definition of juridical persons of the Republic of Kazakhstan includes, among other things, enterprises with foreign participation which, in turn, are classified as joint enterprises (sometimes referred to as joint ventures) and enterprises with 100 per cent foreign participation (referred to as wholly foreign-owned enterprises). A clear distinction between two definitions – foreign juridical person and foreign enterprise – is important for the purpose of defining a particular regime applicable to a foreign investor's business. A 'foreign enterprise' is a Kazakhstani juridical person incorporated in accordance with the legislation of Kazakhstan. By its legal nature a foreign enterprise does not differ from any other domestic juridical person and is therefore regulated by the laws of Kazakhstan. By contrast, a 'foreign juridical person' is an entity established in accordance with the legislation of a foreign country – that is, one that lies outside the jurisdiction of Kazakhstan. In Kazakhstan, a foreign enterprise may conduct its activity through a representative office, an affiliate or an enterprise with foreign participation.

In turn, the business activities of a foreign investor in Kazakhstan can be classified into two types. First, a foreign investor may conduct his business activity either by establishing a juridical person (that is, an enterprise with foreign participation) or without establishing a juridical person (that is, through the use of affiliates or representative offices). Second, a foreign investor may choose to conduct his business without establishing any of these legal entities for his business, but act directly by means of foreign economic contracts.

A foreign investor is entitled to establish a juridical person for the purpose of a profit-making activity only in the form of an enterprise with foreign participation. The principal source regulating the process of establishment and activity of juridical persons with foreign participation in the territory of the Republic of Kazakhstan is the Law on Foreign Investment. Article 1 of the law provides the following definitions:

> 'Enterprise with foreign participation' is a juridical person established in accordance with the legislation of the Republic of Kazakhstan in the territory of the Republic of Kazakhstan and acting in the form of foreign enterprise or a joint enterprise.
>
> 'Foreign enterprise' is an enterprise with foreign participation established in accordance with the legislation of the Republic of Kazakhstan in the territory of the Republic of Kazakhstan which wholly belongs to the foreign investor.
>
> 'Joint enterprise' is an enterprise with foreign participation established in accordance with the legislation of the Republic of Kazakhstan in the territory of the Republic of Kazakhstan in which part of the property (stocks or participatory shares) belongs to the foreign investor.

At the same time, the national legislation stipulates one exception in the regulation of joint ventures provided by the Civil Code. The fact of the matter is that a joint venture is usually established on the basis of an agreement on the foundation of a juridical person. Contractual relationships are governed by the Civil Code. Accordingly, the Civil Code entitles the parties to an agreement freely to choose an applicable law which will regulate their relationship. During the process of drafting this article of the Civil Code, some foreign experts insisted that this general rule towards contracts should remain valid in relation to an agreement on the foundation of a joint enterprise.

However, the final draft of the Civil Code presented to Parliament included a rule which stipulated that, in relation to the founding agreement of a juridical person with foreign participation, the law of Kazakhstan shall be applied. Yet, such an exception had raised a significant question: namely whether this rule is relevant only to the founding agreement of an entity with foreign participation or to all issues emanating from that founding agreement, including those which regulate internal relationships of parties to the joint venture (for instance, reorganization, liquidation, sale of shares of a company, and soon). What remains unclear is the question of whether this rule should be applicable in cases where issues like reorganization or dissolution of a company are included not in a founding agreement, but in a charter of a company or in another agreement concluded by the parties after the conclusion of a founding, agreement. The Civil Code has responded to these concerns by saying in Article 1165:

> 2. Relationships that are regulated by this article include the relationship on establishment and dissolution of a juridical person, transfer of equity and other relationships between parties of the juridical person, connected with their mutual rights and obligations (including those that are determined by the following [after establishment] agreements).
>
> 3. The provisions of this article shall be applied also in the case of the establishment of mutual rights and obligations of the parties of the juridical person with foreign participation by other founding agreements.

Thus, the current legislation provides that the national law of Kazakhstan shall be applied to relationships associated with the establishment, mutual rights and duties of the parties in an enterprise with foreign participation.

It is clear from the above analysis that the Kazakh law offers a clear legal concept of forms of business which can be utilized by potential foreign investors. This approach adheres to the national treatment regime proclaimed by the Constitution and the 1994 Law on Foreign Investment. Nevertheless, the following analysis indicates that through certain provisions the current legislation relating to foreign investment undermines the national treatment regime for foreign investors. Furthermore, a the shift in the centre of gravity of rule-making – from the legislator toward the executive – is clearly observed.

5.2.1 Failure to apply the national regime to all entities

In some instances, the 1994 Law on Foreign Investment itself contains provisions which contradict the legislation designed for domestic juridical persons and, by so doing, undermine the national treatment regime provided for foreign investors. For instance, Item 6 of Article 15 stipulates that if, a year after the registration of an enterprise with foreign participation, every participant of an enterprise fails to bring his equity into the charter fund (determined by the founding agreement), a joint enterprise shall be recognized as void. According to Item 2 of Article 39 and Item 2 of Article 57 of the Edict of the President of the Republic having the force of law 'On Economic Partnerships',[8] a different rule is determined with respect to the formation of a charter fund. These articles state that if a participant in such an enterprise fails to bring their share into the charter fund within a year of the registration of an enterprise, they shall be obliged to contribute their share and in addition to pay interest on the sum of the unpaid share. Thus, the Law on Foreign Investment establishes more strict rules for those enterprises which have foreign participation. Furthermore, the definition of the words 'to consider an enterprise void' is absent from the national legislation and, moreover, such a decision can be reached only by a court.

Also, as mentioned earlier, foreign juridical enterprise can conduct its investment activity through an enterprise with foreign participation as well as through representative offices and affiliates. However, Article 22 of the Law on Foreign Investment 'Customs Levy' provides that:

1. Property imported into the Republic of Kazakhstan as the contributions of a foreign enterprise to the charter fund of an enterprise with foreign participation shall be exempt from the payment of customs duty.

2. Such exemption shall be granted for property earmarked for the needs of an enterprise with foreign participation, and also for the personal property of the foreign personnel of such an enterprise.

3. In the event of the export of property specified in item one of this article, an enterprise with foreign participation shall be exempt from the payment of export customs duty.

Thus, the affiliates and representative offices of foreign investors are unjustifiably excluded from this rule.

Item 7 of Article 15 of the Law establishes a requirement to reincorporate the openly held stock-holding company into the enterprise with foreign participation in the case of a foreign investor acquiring the shares of such a company. Item 6 of Article 42 of the new Civil Code stipulates exhaustively the list of instances in which a company should be re-registered. The Code does not contain the case where the stock-holders of a company change; it only stipulates that a change of stock-holders should be registered in the company's list of its stock-holders. Thus, in fact, the clause of the Law on Foreign Investment worsens the position of foreign investors and again limits their right of national treatment.

The Edict of the President of the Republic having the force of law 'On Banks and Banking'[9] of 31 August 1995 provides a definition of the 'bank with foreign participation', which is in fact an enterprise with foreign participation. However, this decree determines a 50 per cent share of foreign participation as a criterion for recognition as 'a bank with foreign participation'. Thus, if a bank includes less than 50 per cent foreign participation it shall not be considered a bank with foreign participation and consequently neither shall it be considered an enterprise with foreign participation. This is a direct violation of the relevant clause of the Law on Foreign Investment.

Juridical persons with foreign participation may conduct any types of activity that are not explicitly prohibited by law. Certain types of activity, the list of which is exhaustive, may conduct such enterprises on the basis of a special permission-licence, which is issued by a special state organ. According to the Edict of the President of the Republic having the force of Law 'On Licensing' of 17 April 1995,[10] such licences can be of two kinds – general and special. General licences are issued for the conduct of those types of activity the licensing of which in accordance with the legislation of Kazakhstan is mandatory for all entities undertaking business activity. Special licences are issued for those kinds of activity the licensing of which is envisaged for enterprises with foreign participation. This provision, however, also infringes the national treatment regime as it explicitly limits the business capacity of foreign investors and creates the possibilities for additional administrative impediments (emanating from the process of issuing special licences) which are not faced by other domestic juridical persons.

Certain limitations of the regime of foreign treatment are established by the current land legislation. In particular, according to the Edict of the President of the Republic having the force of law 'On Land'[11] of 22 December 1995, foreign juridical and physical persons received a right to lease land for temporary use of up to 99 years (Item 1 of Article 41). As to private ownership, foreign persons received a right to acquire only the land on which buildings are already constructed for commercial purposes to be pursued by a foreign investor (Item 2 of Article 33).

Item 3 of Article 40 stipulates more pointedly that foreign persons are not allowed to acquire land for permanent use because this right is granted exclusively to domestic farmers, state enterprises, and non-state agricultural and forestry organizations.

According to the Edict of the President of the Republic having the force of law, of 23 December 1995 'On Privatization', no exceptions or reservations have been imposed upon foreign legal or natural persons. In Item 3 of Article 2 of the Decree it is determined that a buyer is a natural person, or a non-state judicial person, or a foreign juridical person which acquires property in the process of privatization. Nevertheless, the Regulation on Participation of Foreign Investment in the Process of Privatization, which was approved by the Decree of the Cabinet of Ministers of 20 July 1992 No. 633, contains a number of clauses that restrict the participation of foreign persons in privatization.[12]

5.2.2 Failure to provide clear legal mechanisms for compensation

Further, how the host country's legislation deals with the issue of nationalization is another important element in the free entry model of foreign investment law. According to Kazakh legislation, nationalization is a process of alienation of private property and its transfer to the state. Nationalization is a sovereign right of any state recognized by international law. Under the first post-independence Law on Foreign Investment of 7 December 1990, nationalization was completely prohibited. In the 1994 Law on Foreign Investment the legislature allowed for nationalization, although in such a way as to be accepted by international practice. The 1994 law stipulates:

> Foreign investment may not be nationalized, expropriated, or subjected to other measures having the same consequences as nationalization and expropriation (hereinafter: expropriation), except for cases when such expropriation is undertaken in the public interest in compliance with proper legal procedure and is done without discrimination and with payment of prompt, adequate and effective compensation.

The same clause is included in the bilateral investment treaties on support and mutual protection of foreign investment, as well as in the Treaty of European Energy Charter (Article 13). However, the legislation does not contain any specific definition for 'prompt, adequate and effective compensation'.

5.2.3 Infringement of the stability clause

Another provision which ensures the free entry model and the just national treatment regime is a guarantee of the stability of the legislation. It is included in Article 6 of the Law on Foreign Investment, which states:

1. In the event of a worsening of the situation of a foreign investor resulting from changes in legislation and/or the entry into force and/or change of conditions of international treaties, the legislation which was in force at the moment of implementation of the investment shall apply to foreign investment for 10 years, and with regard to investments effectuated under long-term (exceeding 10 years) contracts with agencies authorized by the state, until the period of operation of the contract ends unless provided otherwise by the contract.

2. In the event of an improvement of the situation of a foreign investor which resulted from the changes in legislation and/or entry into force and/or change of conditions of international treaties, the individual conditions of contracts between a foreign investor and an authorized state agency which represented the Republic may be changed by mutual consent of the parties for the purpose of achieving a balance of the economic interests of the participants.

These clauses were designed to respond to the concerns of foreign petroleum investors who were worried about the contracts they had concluded prior to the enactment of the Law on Foreign Investment.

Additional guarantees and reassurances associated with the stability of legislation have been included in the Presidential Edict having the force of law 'On Petroleum'.[13] Item 5 of Article 2 states that licences issued and contracts entered into effect prior to the effectuation of this Edict, as well as associated with these licences and contracts of the Republic of Kazakhstan, shall remain valid. This norm, however, relates only to the contracts concluded prior to the enactment of the law. As to the contracts concluded after the enactment of the Edict, clauses of Article 57 of the Edict 'On Petroleum' shall be applied, which state that revisions or amendments to legislation that serves to the disadvantage of a contractor shall apply neither to licences nor contracts issued or entered into effect prior to such revisions or amendments.

The above clauses are particularly important for foreign investors inasmuch as they affect the taxation of their activities. However, this clause also was infringed. In particular, Item 4 of Article 94 of the Edict of the President having the force of law 'On Taxes and Other Mandatory Payments to the Budget' of 24 April 1995[14] states that, in the event of the worsening of conditions [of concluded contracts] for the Republic or a subsoil-user resulting from changes in tax legislation of the Republic of Kazakhstan or the effectuation of an international tax treaty, amendments of the conditions of international tax treaties or their expiration, certain terms of an earlier concluded contract must be amended with the purpose of restoring the initial balance of economic interests between the state and the subsoil-user. Thus, the guarantee included in Article 6 of the Law on Foreign Investment has in fact been altered by the above clause of the Tax Law. In practice, there was a discussion as to whether this clause of the Tax Law should be applied to contracts concluded prior to the effectuation of the Tax Law – that is, 1 June 1995. The general theory of law and the fundamental legislation suggest there should be a clear answer. That is, 'no', inasmuch as the law does not have retrospective force. Nevertheless, this was a serious concern for foreign investors. Therefore, the Decree of the President with the effect of the law of 21 December 1995 amended Item 2 of Article 179 of the Tax Law.
Its new version states:

> 2. The conditions of taxation, defined in the contracts on the use of subsoil concluded between the Government of the Republic of Kazakhstan or an authorized state agency and national or foreign subsoil-users prior to June 1, 1995, shall remain valid during the period of the term of these contracts.

The above touched mainly on issues associated with investment in subsoil use. As to other kinds of foreign investment, the rule of Article 6 of the Law on Foreign Investment shall be also applied to investment which has been made before the enactment of the Decree on Taxes – that is, 1 June 1995. For instance, the same approach is taken with respect to the implementation of Article 6 of the Law on Foreign Investment. The Parliament of the Republic in its Decree 'On the Order of Implementation of the Law on Foreign Investment' of 27 December 1994 specifically pointed out that Article 6 of the new law shall be applied to those investments that were made before the enactment of the law – that is, 27 December 1995.[15]

However, another problem is associated with those investment relationships which were made after 1 June 1995. The issue in these cases is whether Article 6 is applicable in the context of the new Tax Edict, if this investment is made after 1 June 1995; for example, if a foreign investor established a joint enterprise in January 1996 on the basis of the conditions established by the new Tax Edict. A few years later, for instance in 2000, the Tax Decree is amended and accordingly worsens his conditions. The question is whether Article 6 shall be applied to this investor. The obvious answer is yes. However, the interpretation of legal norms and, more importantly, the provisions of the Tax Edict demonstrate that Article 6 of the Investment Law shall not be applied. Such a conclusion is based on the following reasoning. The Tax Decree prohibits introducing issues connected with taxation (Item 2 of Article 1 of the Edict), the Edict prohibits the introduction of tax benefits, including those designed for a specific case, by other legal acts and regulations (Item 3 of Article 2 of the Decree). Hence, because Article 6 of the 1994 Law on Foreign Investment establishes a tax benefit for foreign investors, after 1 June 1995 it shall not be applicable.

This example displays a diametric contradiction between the underlying ideology of the two laws. In fact, the main strength of the Law on Foreign Investment lay in its Article 6, which explicitly provided the foreign investors with assurances relating to the stability of the legal regime. More important is that this article has been mainly designed to respond to the tax concerns of foreign investors – the basic economic concern of any investor.

5.2.4 Lack of clarity of definitions

Another disputable issue in the context of the above discussion arises in connection with the interpretation of the words 'the moment of making an investment', which are included in the text of Article 6 of the Law on Foreign Investment. Some practitioners tend to believe that such a moment should be the time when capital is actually brought into a country. The argument of this group of experts is that presently there are many joint enterprises in Kazakhstan that are properly registered; however, these enterprises either have not yet started their operations, or their participants have still not contributed their part of capital in the charter fund of an enterprise. Therefore, it is unfair to extend to them the benefits of Article 6.

However, the intention of the drafters of the law was to bring as much clarity as possible into the process of regulation of foreign investment. This in fact was one of the ideologies of the Law on

Foreign Investment. If the above argument is followed, this objective cannot be achieved. Furthermore, there is no precise definition of the term 'making an investment' and a number of different interpretations have been put forward – the contribution of property or any other tangible or intangible asset in the charter fund of an enterprise, therefore, has been considered as 'the moment of making an investment'. Equally, the first dividend has been considered as 'making the investment' as well as the payment of the first tax on a dividend and so on. It seems, however, that the real definition of the term 'the moment of making an investment' can only be the date of incorporation of a juridical person. In the case of a contract, this moment should be the date of its conclusion.

Another problematic issue associated with Article 6 of the Law on Foreign Investment is its application to joint enterprises. In general, the law is undoubtedly applicable to joint enterprises. However, a clear differentiation must exist with regard to two terms: 'foreign investor' and 'an enterprise with foreign participation' (that is, a foreign or joint enterprise). The latter are the national juridical persons and as a result certain clauses of the Law on Foreign Investment do not apply to them.

At the same time, while dealing with guarantees enumerated at the beginning of this chapter, one needs to differentiate two further terms: 'foreign investment' and 'foreign investor'. In some cases the Law on Foreign Investment refers to 'foreign investment', and in other cases to 'foreign investor'. For instance, Chapter 2 of the Law on Foreign Investment is titled 'Guarantees of Foreign Investment'. There are two groups of articles in this chapter.

The first deals with the protection of a foreign investor (Article 5 'The Government Guarantees on the Contracts Associated with Foreign Investment'; Article 9 'Compensation and Reimbursement of Losses Caused to Foreign Investors'; Article 11 'Guarantees of Use of Own Currency Assets'). These articles are designed for and applicable only to foreign investors. They cannot be applied to joint enterprises. When the legislature wishes to extend certain benefits to joint enterprises it does so explicitly. For instance, Article 5 talks about contracts with foreign investors or enterprises with foreign participation – that is, the law talks specifically about enterprises with foreign participation as subjects with whom a separate legal relationship is being formed.

The second group deals with the protection of foreign investment. These articles provide an explicit protection not only for foreign investors, but also provide reinforced protection to foreign investors by protecting their investment. In such cases the objects of investment activity are being protected; for instance, Article 6 'Guarantee from the Changes of Legislation', Article 7 'Guarantees against Expropriation', Article 8 'Guarantee against Illegal Actions of the State Organs and Officials', Article 13 'Guarantees in the Event of the State Inspection'. It seems that protection provided through protection of investment is the best form in the cases contained in the aforementioned articles. Therefore, in cases where a foreign investor undertakes his investment through an enterprise with foreign participation, his protection is better achieved by protecting his investment.

The same approach can be seen in the application of Article 6 to enterprises with foreign participation. The drafters of the law believed that because joint ventures are the main vehicle of foreign investment, it is crucially important to secure the initial economic calculations of a foreign partner who intends to make a substantial contribution of capital or other assets. Therefore, according to this criterion, all articles of the Law on Foreign Investment were designed in such a way as to provide as much certainty and predictability as possible.

There is also a problem with the interpretation of the term 'worsening of conditions of investment'. Practice shows that worsening may include a variety of actions – ranging from a change in the tax regime to a change of attitude toward a foreign investor or his project. A practical problem is, therefore, who should decide whether the situation has worsened. It seems that the only subject who can decide this is the investor. However, in practice, this particular term of Article 6 caused a problem of which the following case is illustrative. The Chief Tax Inspectorate of the Ministry of Finance issued two instruction-letters 'On Taxation of Enterprises with Foreign Investment'. The first letter, No. 12–10–3–12/674 of 2 February 1996,[16] says that every enterprise with foreign participation which intends to enjoy the benefit of Article 6 must submit to the local inspectorate a documentary confirmation (with exact dates) that every participant in an enterprise contributed his share to the charter fund of the enterprise. In addition, such an enterprise has to submit the calculations which indicate the worsening of the tax regime in relation to every type of tax applicable to this enterprise. This example displays first of all an obvious limitation of the national treatment regime which any enterprise registered in the territory of Kazakhstan enjoys and, secondly, it demonstrates the fact that the inspectorate exceeded its authority inasmuch as according to Item 6 of Article 15 of the Law on Foreign Investment all issues relevant to the charter fund are in the competence of other state organs.

The second instruction-letter, No. 12–10–3–12/2174 of 24 April 1996,[17] imposes even more strict limitations on the application of Article 6. It states that the calculations indicating the worsening of the tax regime must be made on the basis of counting all taxes applied to an enterprise at the moment of making the investment (that is, at the very beginning of investment activity) and after the effectuation of the Presidential Edict 'On Taxes and Other Mandatory Payments to Budget' of 24 April 1995. In other words, unlike the previous instruction-letter, this letter requires calculations to be made with respect not to particular taxes, but to all taxes applied to an enterprise. After submitting such calculations to the local tax inspectorate, the latter has to double-check the submitted calculations, to confirm the fact of the worsening of the tax regime, and to prepare a brief letter which includes an economic description of an enterprise which is willing to apply Article 6. Finally, all of these documents have to be submitted to the Chief Tax Inspectorate which makes the final decision on granting the benefits of Article 6 of the Law on Foreign Investment. In reality, such a screen is almost impossible to overcome. Furthermore, these instruction-letters have created a fertile basis for corruption and arbitrariness at the local bureaucratic level.[18]

5.2.5 The expansion of executive discretion

Some laws enacted after the 1995 Constitutional reform reflect a tendency for the discretionary powers of the executive to be expanded. This is especially apparent in the legislation regulating the utilization of natural resources. On 16 August 1996 the Cabinet of Ministers passed the Decree on the Licensing of Subsoil Use.[19] It was designed to specify clauses of the Presidential Edicts having the force of law on Petroleum and on the Subsoil. Item 12 of this Decree contains a provision which includes requisites for the notification about a tender which is advertized for potential investors. However, the 1996 Decree does not include any further details relevant to the organization of tenders. In particular, neither of the normative acts includes provisions about the procedures to be followed in deciding a tender, especially from the moment when an application is submitted by a foreign investor to the state organ. Furthermore, none of the normative acts contains provisions about the refusal of a licence. Article 29 of the Edict on Subsoil and Article 14 of the Edict on Petroleum specify the grounds for refusal for participation in the tender, but neither of them mention (refusal to grant a licence. At the same time, Item 5 of Article 31 of the Edict on Subsoil states that the issuance of a licence on the basis of negotiations must be conducted with the *mandatory* study and assessment of the application. In practice, the licensing authority refuses to issue a licence if a foreign investor fails to prove that he has sufficient financial means to finance the project. Furthermore, one of the most important underpinnings of the legislation on minerals was to ensure a minimum discretion on the side of the executives who take part in the negotiations with foreign investors. Therefore a semi-licensing system was introduced which, in particular, included provisions about mandatory terms of a license which would establish a clear framework within which the host government negotiators could conduct negotiations. However, the 1996 Decree on the Licensing of Subsoil Use does not separate the mandatory terms of the license from those terms that can be established by the agreement of the parties.[20] This naturally entailed a lack of transparency in the investment decision-making process and resulted in an unjustified increase in the discretionary authorities of civil servants in their dealings with foreign investors.

5.3 The 1997 Law on State Support of FDI

On 28 February 1997 the Law on State Support of Direct Investment[21] was presented to the members of the Kazakh Parliament as yet another step towards 'improving the country's investment climate' and as a document which established a 'one-stop shop' for foreign investors.[22] Presenting the draft law on behalf of the executive, which was in charge of drafting activities, Serikzhan Kanapiyanov, the chairman of the State Committee for Foreign Investment, emphasized before the members of the lower chamber of the Parliament that the law had drawn on the previous positive experience of other transitional states – particularly Malaysia, one of the most successful recipients of FDI. The law was promulgated without any serious criticism by the legislature. Interestingly, unlike other laws relevant to FDI, a draft of this law was designed without the active involvement of the leading civil law academics and was thus a product mainly of the executive bureaucracy.

The idea of state support of FDI, particularly in relation to the targeted areas of the domestic economy, is common even in industrialized nations. It deserves approval for the cases in which a host country seeks to boost certain stagnating sectors of the domestic economy. A closer look, however, at the provisions of the Kazakh 1997 Law reveals that a different objective was being pursued by the host government in this case. In fact, the law can be viewed as a culmination of the shift in the ideology of the law-maker towards FDI. First, the design of the law displays the fact that its purpose is to ensure the interests of the State Committee on Investment, but not those of foreign investors.[23] The benefits, grants and preferences enumerated in the law are designed not for all the foreign investors but solely for those who are 'approved' – that is, those who have entered into a contractual relationship with the State Committee. The right to initiate such an agreement belongs solely to the State Committee: the Committee itself unilaterally selects a 'proper' foreign investor, defines the terms of a contract, controls its execution and applies sanctions where appropriate. Furthermore, the Committee defines who and what kind of preferences, grants or benefits will be given in every individual case.

Secondly, the law clearly departs from the ideology which underpinned the previous FDI legislation – namely, the granting of equal possibilities and preferences to all investors without exception. More importantly, these possibilities and preferences should be given to all investors automatically without a prior administrative approval or any other kind of blessing of the state. Therefore, if the legislature determines certain priority sectors of the domestic economy, the beneficiaries should be all investors undertaking investment in these specific sectors, not just those selected and approved by the State Committee. Otherwise, these sectors could be underinvested because of the restraining of competition.

Thirdly, the ideology behind previous tax legislation was to establish a universal approach to the taxation of all entrepreneurs. The 1997 law undermined this ideology and established the grounds for so-called 'contractual taxes' which can be established by the State Committee with regard to the individual investor. This, in turn, also undermined the Constitutional and Civil Code provisions which establish the national regime for foreign legal and physical persons.[24] In fact, one may conclude on the basis of Article 3 of the Civil Code that there was no need for an enactment of the Law on Foreign Investment or the Law on State Support of Direct Investment. Nevertheless, the reason behind the legislature's decision was to reassure foreign investors by spelling out their rights and guarantees in one particular law. Thus, it was assumed in 1994 that the Law on Foreign Investment of that year was designed as a temporary law to serve the interests of foreign investors during the transitional period and, equally, to invite the world business community to enter into the Kazakh market.

The enactment of the 1997 law entailed another serious problem – its correlation with the 1994 Law on Foreign Investment. There is no clear clause in the 1997 law on whether it acts independently or in connection with the 1994 law. Obviously, such a technical (albeit important) aspect could be avoided should the comments of the authors of the 1994 law be taken into consideration by the drafters of the 1997 law. A similar mismatch emerged after the enactment of the 1997 law with other laws regulating FDI – in particular, the Decrees with the effect of law on Petroleum, on Subsurface and Utilization of Minerals, on Licensing, on Privatization, and others.

Article 4 of the 1997 law states that direct investments are subject to the legislative guarantees of investment activity; this can be interpreted as meaning that not only are guarantees of the 1997 law implied, but also those guarantees included in other laws, first of all, in the 1994 Law on Foreign Investment. The 1997 law, however, does not include such a clear statement. Furthermore, certain important guarantees envisaged by the 1994 law are absent in the text of the 1997 law.

Lack of clarity in separation of the scopes of the 1994 and 1997 laws is another problem. In particular, three key clauses of the 1997 law have caused this problem. The first is connected with the definition of direct investment and the scope of the 1997 law; the law displays confusion in the legal definitions. In particular, it defines 'direct investment' as all investments, except those connected with the sovereign guarantee of the state and those that are part of the official foreign technical assistance programmes or non-commercial grants given to the Republic of Kazakhstan for developmental purposes.[25] Obviously this definition is meaningless because technical assistance or grants cannot be considered as an investment. As to another feature of the new definition – 'connected with the sovereign guarantees of the Republic of Kazakhstan' – in practice, the *sovereign* nature of the guarantee behind the investment does not constitute a crucial element of investment. Thus, in essence, the 1997 law deals with the same investment as does the 1994 law. Correspondingly, in legal terms, the scope and the title of the 1997 law does not exactly match the content of the law. The 1997 law should mainly deal with the investment in certain sectors of the economy specified by the host government. Accordingly, a more accurate title for the 1997 law would be that of the Law on State Support of Direct Investment in the Priority Sectors of the Economy. This would automatically exclude any of the above ambiguities.

Secondly, the 1997 law clearly displays the desire of its authors to monopolize the decision-making process towards FDI. In Item 1 of Article 14 the 1997 law states that 'the Committee is the only state organ, authorized to conduct the state policy of support of direct investment in the Republic of Kazakhstan'. One could assume that because the 1997 law deals with certain priority sectors of the economy the above clause should not cause any problems. However, Article 4, which defines only one state organ authorized to represent the Republic of Kazakhstan in relationships with the investors, does cause anxiety because it clearly contradicts the above provision of Item 1 of Article 14. In particular, it broadens the scope of the authorities of the Committee. This, in turn, undermines the scope of other laws related to the different areas associated with FDI. For instance, the Law on Licensing defines several state organs in charge of issuance of licences to foreign investors. Similarly, the Law on Petroleum, and others, stipulate that the relevant licences are issued on behalf of the Cabinet of Ministers (government) by special bodies – that is, different ministries. Should Article 4 be interpreted as it is formulated in the law, the relevant clauses of the above laws must be rescinded. This would inevitably cause a chaos in practice. The above emphasizes the intention of the authors of the 1997 law to monopolize the control over the flows of FDI. This assumption is further reinforced by another clause of the 1997 Law – Item 2 of Article 18. It stipulates that the moment the law enters into effect, the other legislation will remain valid unless it does not contradict the 1997 law. Correspondingly, all the inadequacies should be brought into accord with the 1997 law within two months of its enactment.

5.4 The 1997 Amendments to the 1994 Law on Foreign Investment[26]

One might assume that the above inconsistency of laws could be attributed to technical errors associated with the formation of a corpus of laws in an area of legislation previously unknown to the law-maker. Such an assumption is misleading, inasmuch as the inconsistency emanates clearly from the competing interests of multiple actors within the government involved in the drafting process. Furthermore, the substance of controversy displays a positive intent to impose an administrative restriction on foreign investment, even though such intervention does not comply with the letter and spirit of the statutes. It is equally important to note that different laws are drafted by different teams which in turn work within the three main subcentres of power – the Presidential office, the Cabinet of Ministers, and the Parliament.[27] Furthermore, these three sources of legislative initiative are divided into smaller interest groups, which sometimes compete over the substance of the emerging law.

The Amendments to the 1994 Law on Foreign Investment, enacted on 16 July 1997, confirm the above statement. The Amendments clearly show the dominant policy to amend the laws with the purpose of collecting quicker revenues, even though the country's legislation had earlier proclaimed stability as the cornerstone of its policy towards FDI. The changes illustrate the increasing adoption of a short-term attitude on the part of the law-makers, be they civil servants or politicians.

The 1997 Amendments undoubtedly introduced provisions which clarified the previous inconsistencies, mainly those concerned with the 1997 Law on State Support of Direct Investment. At the same time, certain newly introduced clauses display not the fact of bringing the two laws – of 1994 and of 1997 – into mutual accord, but rather the adjustment of the 1994 Law, which resembled more the free entry model, to the 1997 Law, which established a legislative framework for the negotiation model.

In particular, the 1997 Amendments changed the text of Item 4 of Article 6 of the 1994 Law. As a result, foreign investors were divided into two categories. The first includes those investors who import, produce or market excized products – alcoholic products, tobacco, luxuries, weapons, crude oil, automobiles and others – or import the products, without their consequent processing, for marketing in Kazakhstan – that is re-selling the commodities brought in from outside. The second group includes all the remaining foreign investors. Based on this new classification, the 1997 Amendments deprived the first group of investors of the guarantees provided by Item 1 of Article 6 of the 1994 Law. Furthermore, Article 2 of the 1997 Amendments stipulated that this new rule for the selective treatment of foreign investors would be applicable not only to future investors of the first group – that is, after the enactment of the 1997 Amendments. The Amendments stated that the new rule of treatment would be applied retrospectively. Thus, with regard to the first category of foreign investors, the law was clearly given a retrospective power. In practice, the above division of foreign investors into two categories caused yet another problem. In particular, the 1997 Amendments have not specified how those foreign investors who conduct activities which qualify them either for the first or second category should be treated – for instance, where a foreign investor is involved in a diversified business.

Furthermore, the 1997 Amendments worsened the position of foreign investors in terms of customs fees. Although the new rules of the Amendments apply to the first category of investors from the day of the enactment of the Amendments (16 July 1997), in practice, the Customs interpreted the new edition of Article 22 of the 1994 Law in such a way that the new rules were applicable to all investors. Furthermore, the 1997 Amendments exempted all the property of foreign investors brought into the host country for personal or company purposes. The new edition of this article provides such an exemption only for equipment and spare parts for this equipment brought into the country only as a foreign investor's share in the charter fund of the enterprise. This means that if the charter fund has been already formed, any newly brought equipment or spare parts will not be exempt from customs fees. The new amendments also nullified the item of Article 22 of the 1994 Law which allowed property to be taken out of the country without paying customs' fees if this property had been brought in earlier by a foreign investor for his personal or his enterprise's needs.

5.5 Summary

The previous discussion reflects the legislative changes in the Kazakh government's approach towards foreign investors. In particular, it is clear that these laws are focused on the collection of revenues. This is especially obvious in the 1997 Amendments.[28] The latter is also rather illustrative inasmuch as it emphasizes the tendency towards ignoring a fundamental principle of a free entry model – the stability of legislation. If one could say that before the enactment of the 1997 Amendment this principle was being violated because of technical inconsistencies in the newly emerging laws, the 1997 Amendments formally confirmed the state's departure from, and therefore neglect of, its adherence to the long-term approach to FDI. Current policy has been directed towards taking immediate advantage of foreign investment, even though the long-term perception of the country by investors is damaged as a result. In turn, the 1997 Law on State Support of Direct Investment fulfilled yet another purpose, in that it institutionalized the state's interference in the activities of foreign investors and made the whole decision-making process dependent on the discretion of the executive and not that of the law.[29] Finally, the analysis of the laws regulating FDI displays the lack of a clear state policy towards MNCs. One cannot see an effort on the side of the state either to indigenize incoming foreign investment or to upgrade the local industries within the MNCs' global networks. A short-term rent-seeking is the main *leitmotif* of the current legislation on FDI.

More importantly, the process of the drafting of FDI-related laws tends to be geared towards the executive. At the same time the above discussion indicates a growing lack of coordination between the legislature and the executive, as well as between the ministries composing the executive branch of power. This, in turn, emphasizes a weak inner-state cohesiveness which explains the absence of the definitive approach towards FDI which could be viewed as a part of the efforts of the transitional state to move towards the optimal model.

6
The Legal Regulation of FDI in the Context of Legal Reforms

6.1 Introduction

Professor Mattei has observed that any legal observation is lacking in analytical value unless the researcher is conscious of the layer of the legal system's structure at which he is conducting his studies.[1] Legal scholars who have undertaken a study specifically focused on the legislation on foreign investment in the former USSR expressed this succinctly:

> [i]t is crucial for western investors in the former Soviet Union to exercise caution and to maintain vigilance in undertaking business ventures purely on reliance on the texts of the new legislative acts governing their rights and obligations ... The macroeconomic and socio-political dimension of western investment in Russia should be carefully examined in light of current historical trends.[2]

In turn, in the course of an analysis of the process of development of commercial law in transitional states, Gray and Hendley stress that the transition in former socialist states is 'most fundamentally a change in the role of the state'.[3] They argue that the role of the state in the post-Communist context is vital because parties will have stronger incentives to take advantage of legal rights and abide by legal responsibilities primarily to the extent that they depend on the market, rather than the state, for survival.[4]

The above concerns also imply that a legal system cannot be regarded as operating in a vacuum. However, although it is a commonplace of legal and social science that the functioning of the state and its legal system are closely interwined, the nature of the relationship between a state and its legal system varies according to circumstances.[5]

An ignorance of these factors, as Siedman observed in his study of legal order and development, has led some modern writers on law to assume that law functions in the non-western world in exactly the same manner as it does in the West. Accordingly, because of this misconception, they begin with variables derived from studies of law and society in the western developed world – making reference to 'universalistic rules', 'the legal culture' or 'the autonomous legal system'.[6]

Perhaps this methodological observation is particularly applicable to the case of Kazakhstan due to the highly centralized nature of the state, which dominated the society; it is also clear that law was subordinated to the state and thus could not act in an autonomous fashion. Therefore, it may well be that the laws regulating foreign investment, enacted at different stages of the post-independence period, reflected the different equilibria which have been achieved within the domestic political arena.

Finally, it should be also noted that in practice the laws, tax incentives and other fiscal concessions in and of themselves are unlikely to provide all the security and comfort that foreign investors seek. Investors are more likely to look at the overall functionality of legal and institutional framework in a host state, rather than focusing solely on its investment laws and tax incentives.[7]

In the previous chapters we identified the optimal and actual models of legal regulation of FDI in Kazakhstan. The objective of this chapter is to understand why the free entry model, which facilitates the optimal equilibrium between a foreign investor and the state, is not currently employed by the host state. Having answered this issue, we can consider key factors which explain the actual functioning of the FDI laws in conditions of the post-Soviet transition.

6.2 Legal reform in Kazakhstan: a methodological approach

The relationship between law and society has always attracted the interest of academics in law and the social sciences. One group of scholars believed law to be only a response to social needs,[8] while another thought that the law embodies the story of a nation's development through many centuries[9] and that it reflects the nation's distinct legal culture.[10] Some scholars placed a great emphasis on the coercive characterist of law and thus considered it to be an instrument of social control. In particular, Soviet legal thought was based on the Marxist-Leninist notion of law, according to which law has been a part of the social superstructure which in turn was a reflection of particular economic structures. Accordingly, law was considered to be a tool for the suppression of the ruled by the rulers and thus was a reflection of class antagonisms. The above views have formed a wide spectrum of approaches in order to explain the nature of legal change. These approaches can be grouped into evolutionist, utilitarian, behavioural, intentionalist, and pluralistic schools of thought.

According to the evolutionist approach, legal change is said to be a movement from one stage of socioeconomic development to another, more advanced one.[11] This approach, inspired by a belief in the inevitability of any society's progress, has given an impetus to the notions of 'traditional' and 'modern' societies according to which the imposition of western legal institutions upon the less developed countries could bring about modernization and economic development.[12] Nonet and Selznick suggested another modification of the evolutionist approach which is based on three types of law – repressive, autonomous and responsive. Although they recognize that all three types of law may be present in one particular legal system, they state that 'the basic posture [of the legal system] may nevertheless approximate one type more closely than others'. Consequently, they argue that these are not only distinct types of law but, in some sense, 'stages of evolution in the relation of law to the political and social order'.[13] Feeley, in turn, provided a strong critique of this approach and argued that the evolutionist approach presents a overly simplistic and abstract explanation of legal change. Nonetheless, it seems that this approach emphasizes the dynamism of a legal system (by suggesting that any system passes from a primitive towards a more complex, differentiated, formal and rational law) and, more importantly, it singles out the economic or cultural conditions of a society as the prime driving forces of legal change. What this approach overstates is the predetermined direction of the evolution of a legal system, while avoiding the assumption that such an evolution can, in some instance, be regressive.

In contrast to the evolutionist approach, the utilitarian school suggests a more narrowly focused view. It goes to a lower level of abstraction in that it attempts to specify the mechanism of legal change. Although the proponents of this approach also admit the fact of legal progress is common with the proponents of the aforementioned evolutionist approach, they see the prime source of legal development in the particular ways in which legal innovations respond to social needs. One of the ramifications of this approach is an explanation of legal change as a search for efficiency.[14] For example, Clark suggests that there is a four-stage sequence involving changes in the economy and society that creates possibilities to reduce costs, followed by the emergence of legal principle that fixes the reduction of costs and so forth.[15] However, Clark is strongly convinced that the source of legal change lies outside the legal system and by taking this stance he undervalues the significance of legal professionals in carrying out innovations. Overall, both the evolutionist and the utilitarian approaches exclude the agents of legal change as a unit of analysis by placing an undue emphasis on either the notion of needs or progress and development.

Another strand of analysis of legal change is instrumentalistic, which considers legal change as a derivative of social change. In fact, this approach resembles to a certain degree and combines features of both the evolutionist and utilitarian explanations of legal change. According to this approach, law responds to changes in social structures and is shaped according to the prevailing opinions in a society. In such an approach the law is just a 'mirror of society' and it therefore cannot affect the social mores. What these approaches share with the evolutionist approach is that they both consider the law to have evolved out of the common understanding of people. The substantial difference, however, is that the latter approach does not accept social attitudes and ideas as forces affecting legal innovations. The utilitarian approach has a common feature with this approach in that social change can be viewed as a reflection of the new needs, and thus social change can be viewed as a basis for a legal response.

Another manifestation of this approach is the notion that law is an independent variable and that legislation is a vehicle through which a programmed social evolution can be brought about. Among Soviet legal scholars this notion was particularly strong.[16] Friedman, another proponent of this approach, points out four basic types of legal change by reference to the origins of the movement for change and its final point of impact.[17] It seems that these views represent the two extremes of a relationship between law and social change. Yet, essentially, as noted by Vago, the question is not: 'Does law change society?' or 'Does social change alter law?', because both contentions are likely to be correct. Instead, he accurately notes, it is more appropriate to ask under what specific circumstances can law bring about social change, at what level, and to what extent? Similarly, the conditions under which social change alters law also need to be specified.[18]

The behavioural approach attempts to respond to this call. For instance, Podgorecki tries to explain the functioning of law in the form of his hypothesis about 'the three levels of functioning law':

> An abstract legal precept enacted by the legislature influences social behaviour through a threefold connection. The first independent variable in the process is the content or meaning of the letter of the law in a given social and economic system where it is an element of the valid legal pattern. The second independent variable is the type of subculture functioning within the large social and economic system as a link between the directives of the lawmakers and the actual behaviour of people to whom the law is addressed. The third independent variable ... represents the personality types of those who are the ultimate agents carrying out the legal direction.[19]

In common with other commentators, Podgorecki believes that understanding the pre-existing legal culture is crucial to any analysis of the effectiveness of legal reforms.[20] Therefore, in his opinion, law can be an instrument of social engineering, but the policy-makers have to identify the conditions under which legal innovation is likely to be effective.[21] Equally important, according to Podgorecki, is the observation that the impact of law depends upon the extent and manner in which it is communicated to its recipients, as well as that the transmitters accept the legitimacy of these rules.

Watson, one of the most well-known proponents of the behavioural approach (sometimes referred to as the intentionalist approach), argues that legal professionals and their corporate culture predetermine the scale, speed and nature of legal reform. He admits that the impetus for a change may occur outside the legal system but for legal change to occur the adoption of innovations by professionals is necessary. Without this agency no change will take place. The main vehicle for such adoption, Watson says, is borrowing across legal systems. Such borrowing is likely to happen if the system from which legal statutes are to be borrowed is understandable to legal professionals from other countries, if it is more prestigious, and if it is culturally akin to their own system. Other proponents of the intentionalist approach place a greater emphasis on the political elite.[22] Accordingly, they view legal innovations as a result of the interaction between the politicians, who shape the contours of the legal system according to their own agendas and needs, and the legal profession. The change that emerges is, then, an amalgam of political preference and professional interest. This variant is different from Watson's view to the extent that it gives more weight to political, rather than only legal, agents of legal change. Nonetheless, all in all, for the purpose of this study Watson's conception of an intentionalist approach seems to be more applicable. This is because it presents a more balanced and complete scheme for understanding the nature and mechanism of legal change, inasmuch it includes both the agents of change and the content of legal development. The following section of the study allows us to evaluate the nature of the ongoing process of legal reform in Kazakhstan in the light of the aforementioned approaches.

6.3 Nature of the post-independence legal reforms in Kazakhstan

Although theorists differ as to the meaning of the term the 'rule of law', commentators seem to agree on a number of major institutional characteristics that go to the heart of investors' concerns. Some of the major institutional characteristics of the 'rule of law', especially in the transitional countries of Eastern Europe and the former Soviet Union, include government under the law, where the law precludes arbitrary actions, but includes certainty, generality and equality, access to the courts, and the judicial review of executive action. One of the arguments advanced by commentators is that the effectiveness of the emerging law on foreign investment in the post-Soviet transitional state can be achieved only in conditions of the actual rule of law. The importance of such an analysis is crucial for this study because, as some earlier studies have shown, the concerns of foreign investors can only be fully satisfied to the extent that the legislation creates a system of rule by law.[23] Therefore, to answer a question about the functionality of the emerging law on foreign investment one needs to look at the process of establishing this law from the angle of the ongoing legal change.

According to the theoretical overview of legal change given above, there is some evidence in the Kazakh materials for each of the three basic approaches to legal change. Consistent with evolutionist concepts, there is developmental change, manifested by the increased complexity of economic legislation and a growing sense of necessity of lawyers' law as opposed to the previous less formal versions. Consistent with utilitarian presuppositions, there is room to interpret at least some doctrinal changes in functionalist terms. The central theme of utilitarian approaches – cost reduction – is in evidence, particularly in the area of tax law, which implicitly proclaims this notion in its preamble. Consistent with social change approaches, some new rules have encountered resistance where opinion or practice is more traditional. Consistent with Watson's intentionalist views, the choice of specific rules and institutions is made by lawyers acting with some degree of autonomy. However, since lawyers are set in motion by politicians, there is also ground to apply other ramifications of the intentionalist approach. Thus, there is no necessary contradiction among the aforementioned approaches.

A starting point for an explanation of the complexity of approaches involved in our case may be offered by Mattei. Following Weber, Mattei argues that legal systems may be classified in a tripartite scheme according to the source of social behaviour that plays the leading role in them. Accordingly, legal systems may belong to the rule of professional law, the rule of political law, or the rule of traditional law. In any one legal system all three patterns can be at play. The only difference is in terms of quantity, acceptability and, most importantly, hegemony. Thus a legal change may be viewed as the outcome of the competition among them and, consequently, legal systems can be grouped in families according to the hegemony of one certain pattern. Undoubtedly, this approach responds to Schlesinger's concern about 'the layered complexity of the law'[24] inasmuch, as Mattei notes, as a legal system may follow the rule of professional law only in theory while allowing free rein to the rule of political law or to the rule of traditional law.[25] The rule of professional law is based on technical and legal merits as interpreted by a professional legal culture. In countries with the rule of professional law, referred to by Mattei as the western legal tradition family, the legal arena is clearly distinguishable from the political arena; and the legal process is largely secularized. Professional law, also referred to as 'lawyer's law', is related less to the social and economic philosophies and policies than to the rather autonomous legal culture and tradition, less responsive to and less contingent on pressing and varying societal concerns.[26] In the rule of political law, 'there is no such a thing as formal law binding on government'. Accordingly, the governments may make an effort to comply, but the surrounding circumstances and the need to keep power do justify the disregard for formal law.[27] Schlesinger defines this: 'when men rather than laws govern, people usually find it more prudent to seek a powerful human protector than to stand on legal rights against the State'.[28] Finally, Mattei suggests that in the rule of traditional law the hegemonic pattern of law is either religion or a transcendental philosophy in which the individual's internal dimension and the societal dimension are not separated.

The approach suggested by Mattei is not a comprehensive one. Nonetheless, it provides a new avenue for the classification and explanation of legal systems, particularly those emerging or undergoing profound transformations. More pointedly, his approach assists us in locating the pivotal links within the social system which explain the emergence, actual dynamics and, more importantly, the logic of legal reform in post-Soviet Kazakh society. In this manner, it connects a legal phenomenon with its underlying context.

Furthermore, account should be taken of the fact that Mattei's approach was conceived within the realm of the law and society school. Its intention was to grasp the individual social context within which the legal phenomena takes place. This is both Mattei's strongest and weakest point. It first allows three patterns to coexist in one legal system and, second, it captures the significance of process of interaction between them. The latter is a most important step forward from Rene's classification, whose approach was based on the statics of the most visible traits of the legal systems. His approach was focused on the architecture of legal buildings within the societies. Similar features in this legal architecture identified by Rene, allowed him to classify the countries into certain families of legal architecture. Mattei's approach is different. Although he deals with the legal architecture, his focus is not exclusively on the 'legal castles'. Rather, he discovers certain traits in 'city planning' of different countries, where the legal buildings are part of such a 'city planning'. Based on these traits he classifies these countries into one of his three patterns. Thus, he discovers the legal castles along with other creations of inner-societal architecture. His approach provides a different look at a legal system, while remaining at Rene's analytical level. He makes us think about the legal structures within a bigger architectural ensemble of societies.

One objective of the present book is to take an analytical step forward. Mattei's approach captures the significance of the nexus 'legal system–social context'. This study will attempt to explain why and how a certain pattern emerges. It will do so by translating Mattei's nexus into the language of institutionalism. Accordingly, it will be suggested that the rule of professional law can be viewed as an interaction of mature institutions able to defend their autonomy and to restrain other institutions, in particular, the discretion of the chief builder of formal institutions. The rule of political law can be viewed as an interaction of the dominant institution able to build new institutions, to reshape the institutional set-up of a society and to restrain other structures within society. Thus, it is suggested that the whole institutional system in such circumstances is driven by the self-interest of one institution-builder. The rule of religious law implies the imposition of norms by one dominant institution. This pattern is similar to the second. The difference is in the stronger influence of a country-specific context. The state here exploits (or is unable to ignore) the embedded local (historical or cultural) context which interweaves the existing inner-societal structures and institutions. Undoubtedly, the strength of Mattei's approach is in its focus on the interactive dynamics of the nexus 'legal system–social context'. Mattei's three patterns are three different city charts, displaying three possible combinations of the nexus 'legal system–social context'. Three patterns do not reflect the static portrayal of the institutions; rather, they focus more on the interaction of these institutions within a dynamic system. In developing Mattei's analysis we will make a closer examination of this nexus. It is 'unpacked' and treated as an endogenous phenomenon. The above theoretical explanation of the genesis of Mattei's pattern of the rule of political law is empirically tested in this work.

Despite the relatively rapid pace of development of the legislation on foreign investment in Kazakhstan, it is hard to say that its legal system, within which this legislation evolves, functions exactly as it does in those societies with established market economies, or, to borrow Mattei's expression, in the countries which are ruled by 'professional' law. Overall, as was demonstrated in the previous chapter, the laws are still limited by the discretion of the state. In this regard, the observation made by Professor Rudden is relevant to the present situation in post-Soviet society:

> To find the general rules of private law (on persons, property, obligations and liability), where does one look first, and to whom? Broadly speaking, in the countries of the civil law one looks in the Code and to the legislature. In the common-law world one turns to the cases and looks to the judiciary. In the Tsarist and Soviet tradition the residual normative source is the executive, and the material source the stream of edicts, decrees, dispositions, decisions, and the like.[29]

During the Soviet period this feature – that is, the power of the executive – was reinforced. After independence, a reincarnated bureaucracy became an impeding factor for FDI. In particular, a survey conducted

Table 6.1 Ranking of major barriers to foreign investment in the Republic of Kazakhstan (percentages)

Barriers to investment	*Major barrier (%)*	*Some barrier (%)*	*Not a barrier (%)*
Bureaucracy	54.2	41.7	0.0
Tax/fiscal regime	45.8	50.0	4.2
Legal infrastructure/ pace of legal change	45.8	45.8	4.2
Financial risk	37.5	50.0	8.3
Infrastructure	25.0	58.3	12.5
Local interference	20.8	58.3	16.7
Lack of distribution channels	20.8	16.7	50.0
Tariff barriers	12.5	45.8	33.3
Availability of local market/ commercial information	8.3	54.2	33.3
Exchange controls	4.2	54.2	37.5
Political instability	4.2	75.0	16.7
Language/culture	4.2	41.7	50.0
Identification of potential partners	4.2	29.2	62.5
Tax/fiscal regime in home country	8.3	16.7	75.0
Local currency inflation	4.2	50.0	41.7
Lack of clear privatization programme	4.2	58.3	33.3
Limits of inward investments	4.2	29.2	58.3
Patent/technology protection	4.2	29.2	58.3
Other	25.5	0.00	0.00

Source: *Kazakhstan Survey* (1997) Washington, DC: International Tax & Investment Centre, 5.

in 1996 among foreign companies operating in Kazakhstan by the International Tax and Investment Centre, a US nongovernmental organization, reinforces the above observation by listing bureaucracy as first among top five barriers to foreign investment in Kazakhstan, whereas legislation and the pace of legal change occupies the fourth place in the list.[30] The survey includes a few comments made by respondents (see Table 6.1). One of the respondents stated:

> There must be a change in attitude toward business and management to attract foreign participation. Bureaucracy inherent in every activity and stifles progress. The constant demand for foreigners to pay for everything and not have a voice will bring continual distrust from major investment sources.[31]

Another respondent reinforced this opinion more pointedly by stating that the authorities in Kazakhstan are much more keen on establishing a short-term cash stake in a company's investment than on endeavouring to safeguard the long-term integrity of the investment.[32] These survey results reveal a crucial point in understanding the legal regulation of FDI in Kazakhstan, namely that the practical outcome of implementation of the laws is embedded in a nexus between the law and power – that is, the state.

Watson's argument emphasizes that in order to succeed, any potential innovation needs to be screened and approved by the representatives of the legal profession. He believes that in legal change much depends on the identity of the carriers of change and the situation they confront. Therefore, the deliberative element in legal change – the matter of choice and decision – requires more emphasis than it has generally received.[33] Such observation, although made with regard to the countries with the rule of professional law, seems to be partially true in the case of Kazakhstan as well. It is partially true because the state is heavily involved in the law-making process and, more importantly, the bureaucratic elite performs a screening function in that it provides a final approval of any legal innovation suggested by the legal profession. This happens because, among other reasons to be discussed below, the Kazakh legal profession, in contrast to its counterparts in the countries governed by the rule of professional law, was for a long time subservient to the needs of power-holders during the Communist regime. In addition, of course, any lawyer maintains the imprinting received during his first year of legal education.[34] In the case of Kazakhstan, the majority of those currently active in the legal profession received their training under the old Soviet system. Therefore, due to this inherent internal corporate culture, the legal profession cannot stand out against the executive branch as it can do, for instance, in the United Kingdom or in the United States.[35]

At the same time, in Kazakhstan the involvement of bureaucracy varies from one branch of law to another, as does the closeness of the relationship between law and society, observed by Watson.[36] More pointedly, a degree of involvement depends upon the compliance of a new law with the behavioural setting of the bureaucracy. In the areas where legal innovation does not seem to present a conflict with their interests, the space for manoeuvre given to the legal profession is greater. As a result, the borrowing of new concepts in the non-politicized sectors of legislation has so far occurred without serious political obstacles.[37] To this end, an observation of Professor Kahn-Freund is particularly true. He classifies legal rules and institutions along a spectrum which ranges from the 'mechanical' laws (which are relatively easy to transplant) to the 'organic' (or 'home-grown') laws (which are not so easy to transplant):

> The degree to which any rule ... or institution ... can be transplanted, its distance from the organic and from the mechanical end of the spectrum still depends to some extent on the geographical and sociological factors mentioned by Montesquieu, but especially in the developed and industrialized world to a very greatly diminished extent. The question is in many cases no longer how deeply it is embedded ... but who has planted the roots and who cultivates the garden.[38]

The next section of this chapter seeks to answer this question.

6.4 The legal regulation of FDI in the context of legal reforms

Legal regulation of FDI in Kazakhstan should be understood in the context of the previous Russian colonial law. Under the colonial administration, law served two principal purposes: to facilitate the economic exploitation of the colony, and to conserve the power of the colonists.[39] In fact, the same objective was pursued by the Soviet system which was designed as an integral and indivisible entity, covering the supply of raw materials, machines and equipment, distribution and the allocation of resources from the centre of the metropole – Moscow. In one of his recent speeches, the Kazakh president stated that among the factors leading to the steady economic deterioration of his country, the sudden termination of those Soviet economic ties had caused as much as 80 per cent of the damage. This observation emphasizes the lack of self-sufficiency of the economies of the former Soviet constituent republics. Furthermore, the structure of the Soviet economy, with its strong emphasis on vertical (centre–republic) relationships, strongly resembled the structure inherent in the colonial systems – literally 'all roads, railway, and air routes led to Moscow'.[40]

The distribution of assets in the former USSR also helps to explain the weakness of the forces within Kazakh society in consolidating into the 'private interest', which can naturally emerge on the basis of certain material assets. Because the majority of the wealth of the USSR was concentrated in Russia, the process of formation of the non-state institutions able to articulate their agendas was undoubtedly much stronger there. This in turn explains the difference in the content of political processes in Russia and the other constituent republics of the USSR. This proposition is borne out by the evidence. Kazakhstan, being the Soviet Union's largest non-ferrous metal supplier, an important energy and iron-ore region and a major centre of marketable grains and animal husbandry, played a prominent role in the Soviet economy. In 1990, its industrial output value made up 3.5 per cent of the total, ranking it fourth among the 15 constituent republics. An examination of its economic structure, however, reveals that it was no more than an appendage for supplying industrial and agricultural raw materials and fuels. Mining is one of the core industries of a country. Among the 90 or so mineral resources whose reserves had been proven, the republic had between 30 and 70 per cent of the Soviet Union's copper, lead, zinc, chromium, and nickel. Its lead reserve was the largest in the USSR, its copper and zinc the second largest, and its coal the third largest. In terms of yield, its coal comprised 16 per cent of the USSR's yearly output, iron ore 10.5 per cent, chemical fertilizers 6.3 per cent and electric power 4.7 per cent. In the late 1970s, about 70 per cent of its iron ore was delivered to other parts of the USSR. The share of extracting industries in Kazakhstan at the beginning of the 1980s was 1.7 times higher than on average in other republics of the USSR. Total profit of all-union ministries made on Kazakhstan's natural resources amounted to around 15 billion roubles. At the same time their contribution to the republic's budget was 30 million roubles, or less than 1 per cent. The manufacture of machinery was also underdeveloped, composing only 17 per cent of all industrial activity, as opposed to the average level in the USSR of 27 per cent.[41]

Agriculture presented a similar picture. As the Soviet Union's eastern granary, the Kazakh Republic was a main source of marketable grains and animal husbandry and supplied the European part of the Soviet Union with large amounts of grains and ginned cotton. Though its per-hectare yield was rather low and an extensive method of cultivation was adopted, the commodity rate of grains was pretty high and its grain production came to 15 per cent of the country's total, as crops were grown over vast, thinly populated areas. The southern part of the republic was an important cotton-growing area. Yet, advantages and disadvantages went hand in hand. In spite of its rich resources, Kazakhstan had problems wrought by the traditional system of division of labour. Its machine-building and processing industries were comparatively backward; most of the means of production and subsistence it could not produce itself; 70 per cent of its daily necessities had to be supplied by other republics, especially those in Europe; and more than 40 per cent of the manufactured consumer goods also had to be imported. Most of its minerals, oil for instance, had to be transported to the European part of the Soviet Union for refining, and the finished products were then returned to it as commodities. Almost all of its trade was carried out with other republics of the Soviet Union, only 9 per cent of exports going to and 12 per cent of imports coming from other countries in the late 1980s. Most of its trade was with Russia: almost 60 per cent of its exports and a greater percentage of its imports, in terms of trade value, came out of its transactions with Russia in the late 1980s.

As practice shows, many of the features of colonial law prevail within post-independence Kazakhstan. In the case of decolonized states, Fitzpatrick explains this by the weakness of a new national ruling elite, which creates the need for protection against internal opposition.[42] The new ruling elite, although of native origin, becomes a de facto substitute for the former colonial power. In turn, Muchlinski argues that in order to achieve the above objectives law is used, inter alia, to control the local population.[43] This goal is achieved by maintaining the separation between the advanced and the traditional sectors of the economy. Such separation has the effect of limiting the involvement of the local population in the advanced economy, thereby preventing it from becoming a competitor against the colonial power. Muchlinski suggests that these features prevail in the postcolonial period. In particular, there is a division between those laws applicable to the advanced sector of the economy and society, and those that are applicable within the traditional sector. The former extends to the regulation of foreign investment and the domestic industrial sector. The latter seeks to preserve the traditional mode of production and social organization, for many of the same reasons as were applicable during the colonial period. Hence, there is some separation of those laws which are designed for the advanced sector, which is the main concern of foreign investors, and, on the other hand, of those laws applicable to the less advanced sector. In contrast to this view, the analysis provided in Chapter 4 has shown that the Kazakh regulator has chosen not to separate law in this way, but rather to offset the effects of the regime of national treatment of FDI. By so doing, it has created a de facto barrier between domestic and foreign investors. Furthermore, because the present regulatory regime does not provide the necessary conditions for stability of institutional behaviour, it thereby discourages mainly small and medium-sized companies from investing in the country's economy because of the increased risks and uncertainty that arise from the newly enacted laws. This in turn allows one to conclude that it will be the domestic enterprises which will suffer most. This is because, as experiences of the late industrializing countries have shown, the actual 'spill-over' effect of FDI occurs when they interact with domestic companies similar in size and scale to foreign companies. Given the present situation in Kazakhstan, these are in the vast majority small companies.

Further, in the case of Kazakhstan, the task for the newly emerged regulator is less challenging because there is no need to keep the advanced and less advanced sectors of the economy separate for political purposes. If one looks at the present structure of the economy, one may find a similarity with the colonial period, namely that the advanced sector – and, accordingly, the urban areas – are occupied by ethnic Russians and the less advanced, that is, the agrarian sector, by the native Kazakh population. For this reason, Russians are better organized, better educated and, therefore, can be more articulate in their political criticism of power-holders. By contrast, the native population, the Kazakhs, occupy mainly rural areas that are technologically backward, economically stagnant and, accordingly, are characterized by a traditional social structure and mind-set. This in turn explains the immense patience of the Kazakhs, who are presently less politicized and less organized. Prohibition of the private ownership of land, established by the legislation under the slogan of preserving the lands for the native population which had occupied it for centuries, in fact, produced the opposite effect. Most recent legislative actions aimed at the privatization of land, although allowing for the privatization of 30–45 million sq. hectares of land, at the same time prohibits its privatization to foreigners and to those who lack proper educational background in agriculture. In effect, this prevents the native population from moving to the urban areas and, in addition, it conserves the economic backwardness because other ethnic groups, who may be modernizing influences, are prevented from privatizing the land. Furthermore, even within the existing agricultural farms, the Kazakhs occupy the less fertile lands. This is because the Tsarist administration, in pursuing its policy of colonization, installed ethnic Russian peasantry on the better lands. Interestingly, the results of this unfair policy were never changed, even after the demise of the Russian empire and the emergence of the Soviet Union. This in turn means that the present farms allocated to the Kazakhs are unlikely to be commercially viable; hence, the less the likelihood for their modernization and, accordingly, for that of the social structure inherent in them. To sum up, the above factors emphasize the fact that a decrease in the number of ethnic Russians and the current situation with the native population, naturally dilutes the social bases needed for challenging the present executive.

Nevertheless, the Kazakh urban population is steadily growing, mainly due to the migration of the impoverished native population from rural areas.[44] This has happened despite the fact that the Kazakh president Nazarbayev did nothing to promote well-planned migration or, more importantly, to retrain the native population in order to prepare them for the move from the agricultural to the industrial sector. Assuming a certain level of economic development, undoubtedly, larger sectors of the population could eventually become involved in the modernization process. With growing numbers in the advanced sector the competing class formations typical of an industrial economy may develop. Even today, the unequal distribution of power and wealth has not only become more noticeable, but has come under increasing threat as the power and political sophistication of the poorer groups has grown with the spread of relative affluence.[45] Therefore, the present elite prefers to adopt a repressive policy which stunts the growth of an articulate opposition in the urban area in order to limit the social and political development of the majority.[46]

6.5 Summary

Because the executive branch in Kazakhstan has fought hard to maintain its privileged position in the new political conditions, it has commonly been overlooked that the economic goals of regulation have clearly been distorted in the process. Earlier analysis of the FDI legislation clearly confirms this point. No long-term efficiency objective is being pursued by the state as law-maker and regulator. Instead, the aim is usually to exploit the situation for short-term financial gain. This consequently causes the legal institutions to become weak and politicized, and results in an underperforming legal system which entails less efficient private capital accumulation and, hence, a higher cost of capital for private investment. Weak contract enforcement, partially resulting from the lack of inter-firm trust and the weak judiciary, leads to the inclusion of a risk premium in the pricing of goods and services, as well as to a lack of civic trust and corruption. Furthermore, the ruling elite is motivated by an overriding concern to consolidate their position against domestic rivals and, to this end, seeks to build up its power base through increased ties with foreign capital and foreign allies. Correspondingly, FDI is considered to be a crucial building block in the strengthening of what is, at present, the fragile legitimacy of the present elite.[47] FDI regulation plays a pivotal role in achieving this political objective, as Mattei notes:

> All these legal systems [of the states with the rule of political law] share a prominent political layer. The political target, be it free market and privatization, be it self-sufficiency, or be it development, determines, justifies and makes socially acceptable the outcome of most decision-making.[48]

Thus, the analysis of the law on FDI in the context of the current legal reform reveals the fact that the role of law is gradually changing, inasmuch as the new basic theme of a relationship between economic, social and legal imperatives has materialized. As the above analysis showed, the significance of sociolegal imperatives in the shift from the optimal model of regulation is crucial. This chapter has answered the question on why these imperatives affect the regulator. The task of the following chapter is to explain how this happens.

7
The State as the Regulator of FDI

7.1 Introduction

An important factor shaping the regulatory framework and influencing the effectiveness of legal regulation of FDI is the nature of the institutions which have the power to deal with the area in question.[1] An analysis of recent legal studies on foreign investment in the former USSR indicates that commentators perceive the ongoing process of transition to be a constant variable, in that they assume that the overall pattern of the present socioeconomic transformations – the transition – is a forward-oriented progressive process, one which presumably departs from the totalitarian past to a system which resembles western democracies. Furthermore, they tend to view the state in this process as a monolithic entity which is becoming, in a Weberian sense, 'rational'.[2] Thus, in the analysis of legal phenomena, this analytical unit – the state itself, which predetermines the overall direction of transition – is treated as an exogenous phenomenon. This chapter will employ an approach according to which this phenomenon will be treated as being endogenous. More specifically, we will suggest that the state – through processes of internal restructuring – can cause the regression of the transitional process and, accordingly, may impede the achievement of the optimal equlibrium of FDI regulation. The following specific issues emerge as the core of the following discussion – what are the institutions within Kazakh society that are involved in the formulation of the legal regulatory policy towards FDI, how are they organized, how do they interact and how does this interaction result in the choice of a certain model of the legal regulation of FDI.

7.2 The economic policy of the state: institutional implications

Earlier we suggested that economic reform in Kazakhstan should be directed to the promotion of industrial modernization. Correspondingly, on the basis of the analysis of current objective domestic and external imperatives, it was suggested in Chapter 4 that the optimal model of legal regulation of FDI for Kazakhstan should be that which is conducive to enabling MNCs to upgrade the country's industry to a more technology-intensive level. The transfer of technology as well as of any knowledge-based FDI, in turn, must be backed by a degree of certainty which will ensure the protection of transferred assets. Obviously, the long-term coherence in a host government's policy is a key factor here. Accordingly, the issue arises as to what would make a host government adhere to the sustainable and coherent long-term approach to FDI, as opposed to the short-sighted rent-seeking policy?

Previous empirical studies on FDI in transitional countries have emphasized the interaction of states and private capitalist groups as decisive in successful late industrialization. In this view, cross-country differences in economic performance are not a function of the extent of state intervention but rather reflect the quality of the state's economic role – more pointedly, the coherence of development policies and economic institutions. Coherent policies are those which harmonize public and private decisions to encourage long-term investment, and discourage the pursuit of short-term gains through non-productive activities like rent-seeking. But what restraints ensure the long-term policies? Some authors believe that state autonomy is a decisive factor here.[3] It seems, however, that such an approach cannot fully explain the issue. No matter how politically autonomous they are, bureaucratic decision-makers must depend upon certain information constraints – in particular, on the private sector for information on market conditions, industry performance and policy impacts. Another approach argues that the well-institutionalized state–business networks stand in contrast to patron–client linkages. Indeed, the well-disciplined institutions, including the regulatory regime for FDI, explain how the coherence is achieved. At the same time, the question remains as to why a transitional state, facing certain objective economic pressures, selects a policy that is less than optimal. Nor does institutional logic suggest what authority enforces institutional rules and holds cooperating economic actors accountable to their commitments to growth-enhancing, as opposed to clientelistic, behaviour. Clearly, to find the right answer one needs to go beyond the texts of statutes.

A number of studies have stressed the theoretical significance of this issue. Chu emphasized the importance (along with the structure of each state's bureaucracy) of 'the nature of the policy networks linking the state bureaucracy and the private sector ... ' as well as 'the nature of the broader relationship between state and society'.[4] Other scholars have stressed that the idea that policy networks, or institutionalized state–society links generally, exert a decisive influence on economic policies is not a new one. Katzenstein pioneered this approach in his comparative studies of trade and industrial adjustment policies in the advanced industrial countries.[5] Okimoto described Japan as 'a network state', in which coherent growth policies emerge from consensus developed through bargaining in multiple organizational channels between the Ministry for Industry and Trade and the private sector.[6] Fields argued that state–business networks in Korea and Taiwan facilitated coherent policy-making in those countries.[7] Evans similarly stressed the importance of institutionalized state–business linkages by propounding the concept of 'embedded autonomy', in which the state bureaucracy's Weberian internal characteristics are matched by dense networks with the private sectors.[8] All in all, their common point is that in those situations where strong public–private networks were lacking, industrial policies failed.

At the same time, it should be stressed that any state strategy may not be instrumentally rational. This is because it involves essentially non-cooperative bargaining games between state and inner-societal groups over the terms of coordination. Therefore, a coherent policy can be viewed as the outcome of the interaction of multiple actors who together 'entered' into the collective action efforts. Each actor evaluates potential cooperation not only in terms of likely economic gains, but also in view of its impact on her political autonomy and influence. Accordingly, economic institutions reflect the coalitional bargaining between the state and social groups (in our case, business groups which include foreign investors), and institutional change in this view is better understood as the product of coalitional bargaining. In game-theory language the state–business relationship can be defined as a coordination game. Thus, an economy's institutional make-up will tend to reflect state or business dominance. The collective action logic of the neo-institutionalistic approach suggests that, in functional terms, cohesive state authority and well-organized business sectors would complement each other in coordinating efforts to overcome market-failure obstacles to growth. Yet, the nature of authority in institutions infuses the state–business relationship with a tension that is never fully resolvable. A powerful state armed with discretionary authority is inherently a threat to private property rights, even when institutional commitments to respect them are given. A state might reduce market risk for business through developmental collaboration, remove greater threats to property emanating from other social classes, and even diminish the perceived threat of its own power by making credible commitments to respect private property. Yet, the power to create institutions, even self-restraining ones, is inescapably the power to undermine or destroy them. The next section will consider this proposition.

In contrast, politically powerful business actors, be they domestic or foreign, threaten state elites' freedom to manipulate social surplus to bolster support and maintain claims to rule. An influential business class might be the most important source of support for a country's political leaders. But its support always comes at a price and, precisely because its control of capital gives business unique structural leverage, this group imposes the greatest constraints on elites' ability to flexibly deploy economic policies in order to manage coalitions and shift resources to mollify a broad range of constituencies. State elites wish to control economic institutions to preserve maximum degrees of freedom in allocating resources and pre-emptively controlling or co-opting social forces for political advantage. Private business has a core collective interest in controlling economic institutions to protect property rights and secure the social conditions for capital accumulation. Cohesive state elites and powerful, well-organized business sectors tend to undermine or, more precisely, to pre-empt each other. To the extent that their internal cohesion allows, states and business elites seek to penetrate and weaken the corporate coherence of the opposite actor. Thus, state–business interrelationship in the conditions of a transitional society can be viewed as an unstable equilibrium, even when anchored by strong political institutions.

Account should be also taken of the external forces affecting the nexus between the state and private business. As noted in Chapter 4, the policy goal for Kazakhstan should be industrialization, which can be achieved by gaining access to the global production chains organized under MNCs' auspices. Today, it is the high-technology sector which concentrates the forces of dynamic change, which may bring an industrializing nation to rapid growth, but which may also raise the dangers of marginalization and failure to keep up with the advancing global technology frontier. However, breaking into and advancing within international knowledge-based networks is much more than a simple matter of opening up the domestic economy to foreign investment flows. Technology cannot be just transferred; it must always be learned or acquired through active effort.[9] The existing host country's institutional environment should therefore be conducive to such learning and acquiring processes. This, in turn, also explains why in conditions of a rent-seeking society, investors, both domestic and foreign, find it difficult to deepen and diversify their investments into new, risky growth sectors, especially in the face of competition from those MNCs better positioned either in the advanced countries or in one of those industrializing countries with a more optimal system of regulation.

To summarize, the choice of the economic strategy, which, in turn, shapes the legal regulatory framework for FDI, should be analysed through the 'state–society' nexus. The crucial methodological point is that this nexus should be approached not as a static phenomenon. Rather, in conditions of transition it should be considered to be a bargaining game reflecting political agency rather than simply in relation to structural characteristics. Coherent development policy thus involves state–business negotiation of policy priorities and the coordination of investment decisions through a range of public and private institutions; however, these mechanisms rest, in turn, on power and leadership. The earlier discussion shed light on the changes in the legislation, which reflect the changing priorities of the rule-maker. The following discussion will demonstrate that these changes, in turn, emanate from the change of the balance of power within the state. Finally, account should be taken of the fact that the interaction of state and business should also be viewed as a response to the challenges of globalization. Accordingly, the optimal model of regulation of FDI can be defined as that which reflects a host state's strategy which better fits into the global investment environment. The objective of the sections that follow is to apply the above approaches to the case of Kazakhstan, in particular, by looking at the dynamics of the post-independence institutional evolution at different levels: the state and society; the inter-branch, and the executive.

7.3 Post-independence evolution of the law-making institutions

A shift to a new political order in the former USSR, namely to one that resembles the western model, implies that effective law and its underlying legal culture must express the self-interest of the emerging classes and represent the aspirations of the whole community on its way to a new form of society.[10] However, mere forces and interests do not make law; what make law are forces and interest that express demand, which is channelled through the institutional framework of a society.[11] In this sense a legal system is viewed as a conduit, a medium, a kind of permeable membrane. Social demands flow in at one end; legal acts emerge at the other end, producing legal behaviour.[12] At the same time, a legal system is not just a tunnel for the transmission of certain interests. The law itself is conceived as a method of giving effect to 'interests'.[13] Therefore, its task is to classify these interests, to decide on the basis of certain criteria which interests should be given effect and to what extent and, if some interests conflict so that there has to be a choice made, to make this choice.[14] Is this proposition applicable in the case of Kazakhstan? If so, how can one define those certain criteria on the basis of which interests are actually realized? How can one define actual 'interests' in the analysis of legislation? Whose interests within the society (if any) and then, more narrowly, within the state do matter in the choice of the legal model of FDI regulation? How are these interests restrained and how are they motivated?

Any substantial social change presupposes changes in power structures, property relations and the ruling elite. It will be recalled that in Europe democracy emerged on the basis of a liberal system of property. By contrast, in the former USSR, political democracy has evolved in the absence of such socioeconomic foundations. As was shown in Chapter 3, laws originate mainly from the state because no significant interest groups have emerged. Relatedly, as shown earlier, the underlying property rights structure has not undergone a radical change; a new system of corporate governance has not emerged as a result of privatization. Furthermore, in the case of Kazakhstan, the changes in power structures and property were undertaken by the same ruling elite which had been in power during the Soviet period. Therefore, the majority of administrative structures, rules, customs, informal links and norms of behaviour have remained unchanged. Although the present system does not openly impose total control, which was the case during the previous system, and it has moved away from the command economy and a single-party system, it has nonetheless established a political order which resembles the previous regime in many ways. In large part, the remaining existence of these features helps to explains the lack of development of new social structures able to encourage consistency in institutional behaviours and thus to promote long-term stability. As a result, the optimal equilibrium which would resemble that which exists in the industrialized countries cannot be achieved. Yet, the elite itself has undergone certain metamorphoses too in order to adapt to the post-independence reality. As the following discussion will show, however, this metamorphosis has only been cosmetic and, even though basic freedoms, liberties and the fundamental principle of separation of powers were introduced in the Constitution, the actual control of polity over the government, which is necessary to ensure effective legal regulation, remains weak.

An examination of the law-making institutions is necessary not only in order to set out their formal powers, but, more importantly, in order to understand the dynamics of structure and the tensions and frictions it contains and which have had a significant impact on the rule-making process and the uses made of rules.[15] While undertaking such an approach, one can consider the case of Kazakhstan in the context of the failure of regulation. Accordingly, this allows one to assume that the reasons for the failure of regulation may include the following: (i) the regulator is not aware of or does not take into consideration determinants of effects of regulation on the regulated, (ii) the regulator is ignorant of firms' objectives and constraints, (iii) these are a lack of appropriate incentives facing regulators and, finally, (iv) these is a failure to consider disequilibrium behaviour. The purpose of the discussion in the subsequent sections is to look at how the existing institutional framework corresponds to the above criteria. The final aim of this exercise is not to assess the effectiveness of the framework. Rather, it is to see how well the institutional basis is prepared for the collaboration necessary for the formulation of the optimal model of legal regulation of FDI.

Further, in order to apply the above approach to an analysis of Kazakh regulatory practice, we also need to include the notion of the goal of regulation. This requires a brief explanation. If the effects of regulation that one desires are viewed as goals of regulation, the exact nature of these targets will vary considerably, depending on the objectives and constraints that confront different individuals and interest groups. In conditions of the present transitional society in Kazakhstan, which lacks well-established interest-groups, the issue of who formulates the targets of regulation becomes particularly important in understanding the nature of the emerging legal regulatory framework for FDI. Furthermore, this makes a legal student focus on the actual determinants of the behaviour of those individuals (or organizations) which form the regulatory framework for FDI. In view of the wide variety of regulatory targets that underlie the demands of different types of regulation, the general failure of regulation to achieve its optimal target (outlined in Chapter 4) suggests that the reasons for this failure may be much more fundamental than the nature of the individual targets themselves. This possibility implies, in turn, that an analysis of certain laws (say on FDI) focusing exclusively on written regulations that are aimed at a single target declared by the state may not reveal why that type of regulation has failed to achieve its intended objectives.

The present political order in Kazakhstan includes both the features of a primitive procedural democracy and the elements of an authoritarian style of governance. However, one crucial achievement of the Gorbachev era is that the post-Soviet elite permitted basic formal democratic procedures. In particular, a perception that legitimacy should come from the people became a widespread conviction which could no longer be ignored by the state. At the same time, in practice, the role of the Kazakh transitional state, namely to institutionalize the emergence of different interests and open democratic forms of their competition, remains unfulfilled.

An analysis of the Kazakh constitutional legislation, particularly the 1995 Constitution and the 1995 Law on Elections, assists us in proving the aforementioned notion. To start with, one should note that there exists a close relationship between the electoral systems, party systems and the quality and stability of government which is responsible for the enactment of laws and regulations.[16] Needless to say, the electoral process is perhaps the most important element of any democratic society because it provides a society with the possibility of not re-electing the power-holders should they fail to deliver what they had promised at previous elections. This component of political order is particularly significant for the evolving democracy in the former USSR, because it provides an avenue for the formation and incorporation of new political actors into the system of relationship between the state and society. In this sense, the electoral process in post-Soviet conditions could play two important roles – controlling the state and providing the background for the growth of political parties. Both objectives are essential for the newly emerged states, where the lack of a democratic tradition and many decades of highly authoritarian state oppression undermined any independent will of the people.

The recent constitutional reform undertaken in Kazakhstan by the executive indicates a clear retreat from this achievement of the period of *perestroika*.[17] This means that, because of particular interests pursued by the state, a democratic electoral process in Kazakhstan was viewed as a serious threat to the power-holders and, accordingly, was redesigned in order to 'freeze' the process of further democratization, in particular to prevent the emergence of 'spontaneous' (and thus difficult to control) civil society, as well as the entry of new political actors into the state structure.

As one of the main dimensions of democratic governance, electoral systems provide a major stimulus for the development of parties as well as bringing them to the centre of the political stage. In Kazakhstan, the political activism of people shaped into amorphous social movements, brought about by the Gorbachev reforms, has never been transformed into a stable process of the institutionalization of parties.[18] Again, the recent developments in the legislation regulating elections, undertaken as a part of the 1995 constitutional reforms, allows one to see that the electoral process was redesigned with a clear purpose of impeding the process of emergence of parties.[19] Accordingly, it is too early to say that a civil society has been formed here. The majority of the parties were established with the informal approval of the state.[20] President Nazarbayev himself joined none of these parties, although he came close to doing so on at least three occasions.[21] One explanation is that, according to the president's logic, the the fact that he is not identified with a particular party precludes the emergence of a strong opposing party or bloc of such parties, or the emergence of a serious impetus towards the process of party building. Thus, being without the left and right, he can enjoy flexibility in associating with or distancing himself from one or another party depending on the situation. This may leave the president with the bureaucracy as his only power base. This is no accident, inasmuch as the bureaucracy is the most well-organized social organization and is easy to control. At the same time, it can be viewed as being neutral.

The opposing parties in Kazakhstan are usually established and led by former members of the ruling elite, who now find themselves outside the decision-making process. Therefore, these parties are in fact not entities to link the state and society, but rather they are newly emerged mechanisms for inner-elite communication. Interestingly, the ruling elite has dealt with them not in the way of negotiations and bargains, as would be suggested by the literature on transition, but through assimilating the activists of such opposing groups into the power structures. Such a policy facilitates the establishment of an environment in which the orientation of parties is geared towards state power rather than towards society. In addition, the purpose of this policy is to incorporate as many contestants as possible into the state structure in order to bring them into a more controllable environment and, by so doing, avoid the institutionalizing influences on the citizenry. This guarantees the longevity of the present regime inasmuch as formerly opposing individuals, after having been incorporated into the system of power tend to get involved in the inner-elite competition and thus refrain from further criticism for reasons of self-preservation.

7.4 The internal organization of the state

It was shown earlier that the constitutional restraint of power is the prime prerequisite for achieving the optimal model of regulation. In an empirical survey Hellmann concludes that the concentration of executive power actually impedes economic reform. He argues that stable constitutions that place constraints on the executive power appear to have a positive effect on the process of economic reform, even at this early stage of the post-Communist transitions.[22] Accordingly, an examination of how this requirement is fulfilled in the case of Kazakhstan, paying particular attention to the executive, is needed. We need to examine the clause which establishes a cornerstone in restraining usurpation of power – Item 4 of Article 3. It proclaims: 'The state power in the Republic of Kazakhstan is unified and executed on the basis of the Constitution and laws in accordance with the principle of separation of powers into legislative, executive and judicial and a system of checks and balances that governs their interaction.' Let us examine the elaboration of this clause in the following provisions of the Constitution.

Because of the Romano-Germanic origins of the legal system in Kazakhstan, the analysis of the role of the legislator in the formation of the system of regulatory governance and thus in the overall process of legal regulation of FDI occupies a central place. Legislators are largely responsible for enacting regulatory legislation, and the form of this legislation often defines the responsibilities and constrains the behaviour of the regulatory agencies and the firms. For instance, if the goals of the regulatory agencies and the methods that may be used to implement those goals are spelled out in detail in the legislation, this will reduce the amount of discretion that is open to regulatory agencies in their subsequent administration of the legislative mandate.[23]

Recent legislation in Kazakhstan demonstrates a substantial shift in the inter-branch balance of power. Clearly, the principle of the separation of powers, but more importantly the system of checks and balances, has been severely undermined. In short, the essence of the last constitutional reforms can be defined as the limitation of institutional control over the executive, which is usually performed in conditions of a democratic society by the Parliament and the judiciary.

In a similar manner to the Russian legislature, the Kazakh Parliament became a rather influential actor in the political life of Kazakhstan immediately after independence.[24] In December 1993, two months after the anti-constitutional dissolution of the Russian Parliament by President Yeltsin, the Kazakh Parliament was 'self-dissolved' and thus peacefully ceased to exist. Having seen the attack on the Russian Parliament in early October 1993 and the West's passive reaction to this act, which in turn presented the Russian legislature as an anti-reform institution, the Kazakh MPs gave up their authority without any serious resistance. The truth of the matter is, however, that although formally this dissolution was initiated by the group of pro-presidential MPs, in fact it happened under the direct orchestration of the executive branch.[25] The assertive criticism on the side of the legislature of the financial abuses by the executive and, correspondingly, the growing reputation and influence of the Speaker of the Parliament undoubtedly expedited the decision to initiate 'self-dissolution'.

The dismissal of the second post-independence Parliament in March 1995 followed after the Constitutional Court ruled that the 1994 parliamentary elections were invalid. This was an unexpected event for the president, who was forced to cancel his visit to Copenhagen as a result of the ruling.[26] The OSCE and the United States welcomed the decision of the Constitutional Court and viewed it as a victory for the rule of law. However, the next move of the president, which emerged spontaneously and the actions accordingly undertaken by the executive after this decision of the Court, were rather unexpected. They resulted in two consequent referendums – of 30 April and 30 August 1995. The first referendum entailed a prolongation of the presidential mandate and correspondingly the cancellation of the 1996 elections.[27] The second cancelled the 1993 Constitution in the way of enactment of a new Constitution. The new Constitution substantially redesigned the whole structure of the state, limiting the authority of Parliament, broadening the authority of the executive branch, and subordinating all three branches of power to the president. As a result, because the president acquired the right to enact the decrees with the effect of laws, two legislative centres emerged. This, consequently, further undermined the role and overall significance of Parliament in society and resulted in an unpredictable legislative environment as well as a lack of transparency in the law-making processes.

Thus, in 1995 the Parliament became a representative branch of power with curtailed legislative and controlling functions. Structurally, according to the 1995 Constitution, Parliament was split into two chambers – the Senate and the Mazhilis. The number of members of the lower chamber – the Mazhilis, which is elected directly by the populace – was reduced to 67.[28] The upper chamber – the Senate – includes two members from each region of the republic who are elected at the joint session of the local representative bodies of the region.[29] For an individual to become a candidate to the Senate, it is necessary to get the support and approval from each local district council. For example, if a region consists of twenty districts, a candidate must receive approval from all twenty. These local councils can recall an earlier issued approval of a particular candidate. Given the fact that the local representative bodies are de facto subordinated to the regional executive – the head of the Regional Administration, who, in turn, is appointed by the president – one can imagine the likely outcome of such elections. Furthermore, as well as the Senate, composed of two members from every region of the republic and the capital city, the president appoints seven additional senators by his own decree. Each of these senators has to provide a written statement of loyalty to the president. The president has the right to discharge any of them at any time. Thus, overall, the Senate is designed to be a pro-presidential entity. It is not by accident that all procedures associated with issues vital for the president are vested in the upper chamber of the Parliament, which performs the function of a final screening forum.

In addition to the above structural changes, the legislative functions of the Parliament have been dramatically reduced as well. Along with the constitutional right to issue decrees with the effect of law, the president received the right to request the Parliament to grant him legislative authority for up to one year. This request is considered satisfied if it is supported by 31 members of the Senate and 45 members of the lower chamber.[30] In addition, the president is entitled to declare the consideration of the draft law submitted to the Parliament as 'urgent'. Item 2 of Article 61 of the Constitution states:

> The President of the Republic of Kazakhstan shall have the right to determine priority consideration of draft laws as well as to declare consideration of a draft of a law urgent, signifying that the Parliament must consider this draft within a month from the day of its submission. If the Parliament does not meet this requirement,

> the President of the republic shall have the right to issue a decree having the force of law which shall be in effect until Parliament adopts a new law as established by the Constitution.

This clause explicitly indicates that the Parliament is indirectly forced by the president to consider urgently any draft law because this law can be enacted by the president himself.

Under the new Constitution, the Cabinet of Ministers, which is part of the executive branch, is also given the right to impose pressure on the Parliament. In particular, Item 7 of Article 61 states:

> In the case when a draft of law submitted by the Government is not adopted, the Prime Minister shall have the right to raise an issue of non-confidence in the Government at a joint session of the Chambers. Voting on this issue shall be held not earlier than within forty-eight hours from the moment of calling for a vote of confidence. If the call for a vote of non-confidence does not receive the necessary number of votes established by this Constitution, a draft of law shall be deemed adopted without voting. However, the Government may not use this right more than twice a year.

If the Parliament does not express its confidence, then the president shall decide whether the Parliament or the Cabinet will be dissolved.

Although the lower chamber – the Mazhilis – is entitled to initiate the process of impeachment of the president, the procedures are designed in a rather complex way for the MPs. Item 2 of Article 47 says:

> [...] The decision to bring an accusation and conduct its investigation may be adopted by the majority of the deputies of the Mazhilis at the initiative of no less than one-third of the total number of its deputies. Investigation of the accusation shall be organized by the Senate and by the majority of votes of the total number of the deputies of the Senate. Its results are transferred for consideration at a joint session of the Parliament's Chambers. The final decision of this issue shall be adopted by the majority of no less than three-fourths of the total number of the deputies of each chamber, provided the Supreme Court concludes the validity of the accusation and conclusion by the Constitutional Council that the established constitutional procedures were observed. Failure to arrive at a final decision within two months from the moment of the accusation shall result in the recognition that the accusation against the

> President of the Republic is rejected. Rejection of the accusation of the President of the Republic in perpetration of high treason at any stage shall result in premature termination of the powers of the deputies of the Mazhilis who initiated the consideration of this issue.

The Constitution establishes other cases when Parliament can be dissolved. In particular, Article 63 states:

> The President of the Republic of Kazakhstan may dissolve Parliament in cases: expressing by Parliament of a vote of non-confidence in the Government, twice refusal of Parliament to give consent to the appointment of the Prime-Minister, political crisis resulting from the insurmountable contradictions between the chambers of Parliament or Parliament and other branches of state power.

Interestingly, the 1995 Constitution does not provide a definition of the term 'insurmountable contradictions'. In other words, in practice this will again be decided by the president.

Furthermore, Parliament is practically excluded from the process of amendment of the Constitution. Item 3 of Article 63 states: 'Amendments and additions to the Constitution shall be introduced by the majority of no less than three-fourths of votes from the total number of the deputies of each chamber.' However, Item 1 of Article 53 nullifies this right of Parliament by saying: '[Parliament at a joint session of the chambers shall] introduce amendments and make additions to the Constitution *at the proposal of the President* of the Republic of Kazakhstan' (emphasis added). Thus, the Parliament itself cannot initiate any amendment or addition to the Constitution unless the president allows it to do so ('at the proposal of the President').

It is clear from the above analysis that the executive branch has monopolized the legislative functions – the Constitution can be amended by referendum; however, only the president decides whether an issue should be submitted to referendum. The president may refuse a proposal made by the Parliament to submit an issue to referendum without giving a reason for his decision. Furthermore, the people themselves are deprived of the right to referendum or to initiate an amendment of the Constitution.[31] The latter reveals another important feature of the current stage of transition, namely that in constitutional terms the elections are considered to be the process of delegating the people's power to the state. According to this notion, between the elections people are deprived of the right to express their will. The constitutional clause, according to which citizens are not given the right of legislative initiative, reinforces the above notion.[32]

Another major function of Parliament in a democratic society is what is usually referred to as its controlling function. Legislators influence the conduct of the executive agency through the allocation of budgets to the agency and by monitoring its performance. This authority of the legislature plays an important role in the system of checks and balances between the branches of power. A comparative analysis of the two post-independence constitutions shows that in Kazakhstan the Parliament was deprived of this function. Basically, there are two forms of control that are usually undertaken by a parliament. The first is founding control, which is exercised when the legislature approves the nominees of the president or approves the establishment of the new executive bodies. The present Constitution curtails this form of control. In particular, in contrast to previous parliaments, the present Kazakh legislature does not have the right to form or to influence the process of formation of the Cabinet of Ministers. Furthermore, as analysis of the constitutional clauses shows, the latter is not accountable to the legislature. Item 6 of Article 53 of the Constitution states that:

> [Parliament at a joint session of the chambers shall] hear the report of the Prime-Minister on the Government's programme and approve or reject the programme. A second rejection of the programme can be made by the majority of two-thirds of votes from the total number of deputies of each chamber and means a vote of non-confidence in the Government. The absence of such majority implies the approval of the government's programme.

Thus, if the Parliament does not approve the programme of the government, this will be considered as an expression of 'no confidence' in the government. Accordingly, the fate of the Parliament becomes again vulnerable to the president's will, who, according to Article 63 of the Constitution, decides which organ, either the Parliament or the Cabinet of Ministers, shall be dissolved. One-third of the members of Parliament can request a report by an individual member of the Cabinet – however, this procedure is not precisely stipulated by the Constitution. The committees of Parliament are not entitled to call for those individual members of the Cabinet whose responsibilities correspond with the specialization of a committee.[33]

The second form of control exercised by a parliament, so-called 'current control', is inseparably linked to the law-making function of the legislature and is reflected chiefly in control over the implementation of enacted laws and decisions. The two previous Kazakh legislatures exercised the controlling functions actively. Unlike its predecessors, the present Parliament is not given such a right; neither has it a controlling chamber, which was a strong institution of the legislature in exercising controls over the implementation of laws by and the budgetary expenditures of the executive. As the practice of the first post-independence Parliament shows, the activities of such an entity can be dangerous to the executive. Furthermore, the 1995 Constitution deprived the Kazakh Parliament of the right to influence the economic decision-making process. In particular, Item 6 of Article 61 states: 'Draft laws introducing reduction of state revenues or increase in state expenditures may be submitted only after the Government of the Republic provides its approval.' Taking into account that in modern conditions any major economic undertaking is associated with the alteration of state expenditures and revenues, one may conclude that the real purpose of this clause is to prevent the involvement of the legislature in the process of economic decision-making, especially those decisions relating to the allocation of resources.

The 1995 constitutional reforms resulted in the elimination of the Constitutional Court and its substitution by the Constitutional Council. Interestingly, unlike the previous Constitution, and unlike the Constitutions of Russia and other CIS republics, the present Constitution does not define this Council as the supreme body of the state for protection of the Constitution. An explanation of this rather surprising innovation is in Article 40 which stipulates that: 'The President of the Republic shall be the symbol and guarantor of the unity of the people and the state power, inviolability of the Constitution, rights and freedoms of an individual and citizen.' Seemingly, this clause also explains why the president alone is entitled to decide whether the Constitution should be amended or a referendum be held.

Thus, for the present the executive shielded themselves from the uncertainties of an electoral process as well as from the controls of two main social institutions – Parliament and the judiciary. Equally important to emphasize is the fact that people were excluded from the active political process. The above analysis of the formal institutional framework may lead to the conclusion that the law-making process is presently characterized by the dominance of the executive branch over the legislature and judiciary. The centralized state, by its nature, still seeks to influence market activity through heavy regulatory controls designed to shape the direction and scope of private business. The situation is aggravated by the lack of bureaucrats who understand the techniques and mechanisms of the market economy. Lack of academic institutions and of relevant literature which could upgrade the professional outlook of civil servants further aggravates the situation. Several years ago the National Academy of Sciences was incorporated in the Ministry for Science and Technologies and thus became a part of the executive branch of power, an act that will stifle any academic discourse or pluralism of thought. Uncertainty in the decision-making process can be also explained by a gradual shift in recruitment policy toward bureaucrats – in particular, the involvement of those individuals who are close to the president by virtue of kinship or personal loyalty.

This section undertook an analysis of the inter-branch organization of the state. This clearly indicates a shift of formal and actual powers to the executive. Accordingly, an appraisal of the executive, a key rule-maker, is required for a complete understanding of the nature of the regulator. The following section deals with this issue.

7.5 The executive

In his empirical survey Hellman suggests that the concentration of executive power impedes economic reforms in conditions of transition.[34] Our study suggested in turn that the existing system of institutions generates a type of state regulation (and behaviour) which is not directed towards the achievement of long-term economic goals. Indeed, the main concern of the executive is to receive much-needed cash, which, in the conditions of an under-performing domestic economy, can be obtained only with FDI. FDI then becomes the source for fuelling the withering legitimacy of the inefficient power-holders.[35] This also explains why the executive has made little effort to make a long-term commitment in the sphere of economic policy. But what produces this kind of behaviour in the executive branch? This is the subject of the next part of our analysis.

The 1995 Constitution has not set any constraints on the government. On the contrary, it has curtailed the controls for the interactions of social institutions over the state and redistributed the power unequally between the three branches.[36] As a result, a clear shift of power towards the executive has occurred. However, at the same time, a further analysis of the constitutional clauses indicates that this shift does not only mean a concentration of the executive power. Certain clauses also display changes in the nature of the executive itself. In particular, Article 40 stipulates:

> The President of the Republic of Kazakhstan shall be the head of state, its highest executive officer determining the main directions of the domestic and foreign policy of the state and representing Kazakhstan within the country and in international relations.
>
> The President of the Republic shall ensure by his arbitration concerted functioning of all branches of state power and responsibility for the institutions of power before the people.

Article 67 states that 'the Government (i.e. the Cabinet of Ministers) shall implement the executive power of the Republic of Kazakhstan, head the system of executive bodies and exercise supervision of their activity'. This article, although clearly stating that the Cabinet of Ministers heads the system of the executive bodies, at the same time stipulates that the Cabinet does not actually formulate the policy of the executive – it only *implements* it.[37] Further, the present Constitution makes the Cabinet's orientation completely president-centred. In particular, the legislator does not influence the process of formation of the Cabinet and the latter is not accountable before the Parliament. Only Article 53 includes a provision which allows the MPs to listen to the annual report of the Cabinet. Its disapproval, however, means a vote of 'no-confidence' in the Cabinet. Consequently, the fate of MPs will become dependent on the president, who may decide to dissolve the recalcitrant Parliament. The likelihood of such a situation is high because the president stands behind the Cabinet and its programme.[38]

The above allows us to assume that the crucial feature of the 1995 Constitution can be defined more precisely as the concentration of power in the person of the president. The underlying *leitmotif* of the new Constitution is the ensuring of total loyalty to the personality of the president.[39] The latter notion is displayed in several constitutional clauses. For instance, the president is, to all intents and purposes, immune from impeachment. Indeed, the existing procedures cannot lead to impeachment in practice. First, the president can be removed from his office only in the case of the commitment of state treason.[40] It should, however, be noted that this constitutional provision, included in Article 47 of the Constitution, contradicts a clause in Article 14 which states that 'Everybody shall be equal before the law and the court'. In comparison, in Kyrgyzstan, the president can be impeached for state treason and *any other* crime. Furthermore, Article 47 stipulates that:

> The decision to bring an accusation and conduct its investigation may be adopted by the majority of the deputies of the Majlis at the initiative of no less than one-third of the total number of its deputies. Investigation of the accusation shall be organized by the Senate and by the majority of votes of the total number of the deputies of the Senate. Its results are transferred for consideration at a joint session of the Chambers of the Parliament. The final decision of this issue shall be adopted at a joint session of the Chambers of the Parliament by the majority of no less than three-fourths of the total number of the deputies of each Chamber, provided the Supreme Court concludes the validity of the accusation and conclusion by the Constitutional Council that the established constitutional procedures were observed. The failure to arrive at a final decision within two months from the moment of the accusation shall result in the recognition that the accusation against the President of the Republic is rejected. Rejection of the accusation of the President of the republic in perpetration of high treason at any stage shall result in premature termination of the powers of the deputies of the Majlis who initiated the consideration of this issue.

The provision of this article which stipulates that failure to arrive at a final decision within two months, in a hypothetical case of impeachment, will allow the artificial creation of such a situation where the decision will not be reached – for example, the convenient 'illness' of a certain number of members of the pro-presidential upper chamber – the Senate – might prevent the arrival at a final decision.

Interestingly, Kazakhstan is among a small number of countries where the protection of the dignity and honour of the president is given a status in the constitutional clause.[41] In practice, this clause is used to prosecute criticism of the president and was employed during the 1998–1999 presidential election campaign.[42] Furthermore, Article 46 includes a provision which cannot be found in the constitution of any other post-Soviet state:

2. Provision, service, and guard of the President of the Republic and his family shall be carried out at the state's expense.

3. The provisions of this article shall extend to ex-Presidents of the Republic.

Finally, personal loyalty to the president is secured at the regional level. The local governments are bound to be pro-presidential for two reasons incorporated in the 1995 Constitution. According to Article 4 (i) the heads of the regional administrations are appointed by the president, who also has the right to discharge the head of the local administrations of any lower level at any time; (ii) the authority of the heads of local administrations expires after the inauguration of the newly elected president.[43]

The above discussion points to the fact that the entire system of the separation of powers and of the checks and balances is undermined by constitutional provisions. The Constitution is designed in such a way as to prevent the strengthening of the Cabinet, Parliament or the judiciary. Dependence upon the personality of the president, clearly observed in the text of the present Constitution, results in inner-state and inner-executive uncertainty which in turn prevents the emergence of a strong bureaucratic corps with a long-term career perspective. In turn, uncertainty within the bureaucracy explains the desire by civil servants at all levels to take advantage of their unpredictable short-term tenure.

The above analysis of the existing constitutional framework explains why the agenda of the state as an entity is not economic development, but rather survival in an uncertain political environment. Correspondingly, governing takes place on a basis of mercenary incentives. With the autocratic leader personally controlling the civil service, personal loyalty and fear are the mainstays of the government, wrapped in a patina of familiar political symbols and traditionally respected practices. The patron–client relations is developed, through which the president recruits local and regional clients and perpetuates his rule by giving them privileged access to resources. It is also through such clientelist relations that personal control over the armed forces and the bureaucracy is ensured. Loyalty to the person of the president, to his clan and tribe, has become the main criterion for the promotion of civil servants. At the same time, considerable efforts are made to ensure that no one person or group of individuals gathers enough power and influence to be able to challenge the leader. Intra-elite discord and factionalism are deliberately sown in order to minimize the possibility of an assault on power by disaffected groups. Offices and institutions are created primarily to counter-balance the weight of others.

7.6 The 1999 presidential elections – shift towards an optimal model?

In the case of the South East Asian industrializing nations, the turn to export-led growth in the mid-1980s occurred in the wake of external shocks and a domestic economic crisis.[44] Fiscal and balance of payments deficits persuaded the political rulers to strengthen the hand of economic technocrats, who, in turn, pushed through market-oriented reforms. However, the underlying weakness of the state structures and the clientelist political institutions were left unchanged. Nevertheless, the established type of relationships backed by the autonomous state preserved the coherence of economic policy. It is equally important to note that this dynamic was not surprising because a distinguishing feature of their economic governance was not the creation of well-organized private interests, but rather the presence of a cohesive central political authority. Earlier discussion has already shown that both features are missing in the case of Kazakhstan.

The 1997 Asian and Russian crises entailed a significant drop in oil prices. Given that crude oil is the major export commodity for Kazakhstan, this undoubtedly reduced the level of cash inflows, leading to further cuts in social programmes and a further impoverishment of the population. Economic hardship in such conditions could be easily used by opposing the president's regime forces to provoke a major action of discontent. In such a situation, two possible solutions could be pursued by President Nazarbayev. First, he could undertake a major political reform which would provide the grounds for a gradual shift from a clientelist governance towards a coherent policy. Second, he could pre-empt political opponents in their effort to mobilize the masses against the present regime. The 1999 presidential elections illustrate which which course of action was actually taken.

In 1995 Nazarbayev's decision to prolong his mandate without holding elections and in the absence of the legislature, was clearly in violation of the existing Constitution. In early 1998, these actions were used by the opposition as the basis of a challenge to the legitimacy of Nazarbayev's mandate. In turn, this created tensions and finally forced Nazarbayev to make a decision to hold premature elections in January 1999. By so doing, the president pursued two goals: (i) to restore his formal legitimacy and (ii) to mobilize popular support from the populace in order to offset the strength of emerging political forces who used the growing dissatisfaction of the population as their major argument in criticizing Nazarbayev's policy, in their consolidation of their own powers, and in their strengthening of the social basis.

In early October 1998, President Nazarbayev initiated constitutional reforms. In his statement, he admitted that 'some persons were inducing me to tighten up the bolts', thus shifting the blame for the increased tensions and the faltering economic performance.[45] He further outlined the main directions for the democratization of Kazakh society. Again, the head of state used the emergency – 'danger from outside, namely the world economic crisis' – as the reason for initiating a few major amendments to the Constitution. The actual reason for holding premature elections, however, was not that suggested by the president. Nazarbayev had exaggerated the threat of the consequences of the Asian crisis for a country with no secondary market of securities, and cited this as a reason for calling the snap election. The actual reasons were a lack of inner-elite cohesion, on the one hand, and, on the other hand, increasing criticism of the economic inefficiency of the presidential regime, which presently resembles the Indonesian model under Suharto. To reinforce his position, Nazarbayev initiated major constitutional changes which, in particular, extended the presidential term up to seven years, and ended a rule that 50 per cent of voters must turn up in order for an election to be valid. This latter change neutralized the threat of a 'stay-at-home' protest vote. It was announced that the premature presidential elections would be held on 10 January 1999. It is clear from what the pre-election arrangements implied that the second option, of the further perpetuation of the present regime, had been chosen.

For the first time since the disintegration of the USSR, the presidential elections in one of its successor states were pre-emptively opposed by the OSCE and the US Administration as being undemocratic and unfair. The OSCE urged the Kazakh government to postpone the 10 January 1999 presidential election, saying that the nation's international reputation was at stake. The OSCE warned that it would not fully recognize the results of the poll, which in October 1999

President Nazarbayev agreed to bring forward from 2000. Nazarbayev's leading opponent, the former Prime Minister Kazhegeldin, was banned from taking part after an administrative irregularity – he had attended a meeting which was not formally registered by the authorities. Opposition candidates said that the snap election had given them little time to mount a challenge to Nazarbayev. Nevertheless, the elections did go ahead on 10 January 1999; Nazarbayev gained 80 per cent of the votes and accordingly secured for himself another seven years in office.[46] The presidential elections highlight a number of factors which have an implication for foreign investment.

First, Nazarbayev's attempts to bribe the US administration in December 1998 in order to soften its position towards the forthcoming elections by offering the Kazakh government's stakes in the oil enterprises indicated his fears of damaging relations with Washington. But was it a genuine desire of the top decision-maker to maintain good relations with the West in order to secure the movement of the entire Kazakhstan's system towards a market-type one? If the answer is 'yes', this would mean that the elections should also have a positive impact on the future regulatory framework for FDI. The answer is likely to be 'no', however. The clientelist state personified in the president seeks the support of the West not in order to maintain the country's positive investment image or because it is willing to rationalize its economic system. Rather, this support is sought for the purpose of prolonging Nazarbayev's personal rule. The international credentials of the latter became a strong tool to suppress domestic discontent and opposition. In fact, international recognition has been used to prop up his domestic legitimacy.[47]

Second, the OSCE's final report on the elections was expected by 10 February 1999. The president held the inauguration on 20 January 1999, just ten days after the elections, and held another significant event – the session of the Assembly of the Nations of Kazakhstan – on 22 January 1999. Such haste was not accidental. The president's intention was to demonstrate to the West his democratic commitment even as the final verdict of the OSCE was being prepared. This, however, was not a genuine desire on the part of the president. If this really had been his intention, it would have been easier to satisfy the request of the US Administration and the OSCE to postpone elections while ensuring that the electoral legislation was made democratic. The fact that the president reappointed the previous prime minister as well as the whole previous Cabinet of Ministers with only minor reshuffles is an indication that he was not going to relax his grip on power. In the context of the present analysis, Nazarbayev's attitudes mean that no substantial positive changes in the treatment of FDI and no shift in the existing model of legal regulation of FDI should be expected in the foreseeable future.

Third, the critical position of the West towards unfair elections in Kazakhstan indicate that this was not a triumph for democracy. Rather, the elections and associated events have re-emphasized the trend of personification of state power in Kazakhstan which was formalized in the 1995 Constitution, the most authoritarian in tone of those adopted by FSU states.[48] Nazarbayev's decision to hold elections despite the urgings of OSCE to postpone them is a clear confirmation of his adherence to the previous style of governance. More importantly, it indicates that he himself will find it difficult to break from the corrupt top bureaucrats who surround him. The latter could force him to sacrifice his last remaining asset – his international reputation – for the sake of preserving the regime serving its interests. This shows that the clientelist state is perpetuated not only by the top patron, but also by the lower clients. Furthermore, this means that one should not expect the restoration of a missing link between state and society. The executive has again given out the message that it is not willing to allow businesses to self-organize into an autonomous actor in order to foster collaborative relationships for the purpose of ensuring economic growth. A first post-election statement by the reappointed prime minister, who emphasized that the government's priority would be the pursuit of an import-substitution strategy, indicates that the executive will further promote patron – client relationships with domestic businesses.[49] This suggests that the 1999 elections can be viewed as yet another missed opportunity for radical sociopolitical reform and thus for establishing the optimal model for the regulation of FDI.

7.7 Summary

The 1999 elections in Kazakhstan have not given a strong enough impetus to replace the existing regime. In fact, they revealed a continuing deeper systemic crisis, the essence of which is further regression of the process of transition towards an authoritarian type of governance. The 1999 presidential elections confirmed the earlier findings of this study. Hence, in spite of the current rhetoric of the president, one should not expect that the state will be able to transform itself into a facilitator of a free market and break with the authoritarian style of governance, both economic and political. Neither is it likely that the state will allow the business class to emerge into an autonomous social actor. Accordingly, only profound reform of political institutions, namely the reform of the present Constitution with a clear limitation of the powers of the president and including implementation of the principle of the separation of powers, can create a true ground for transition to the optimal model.

8
Conclusion

This study was undertaken to provide an analytical overview of the legal regulation of FDI in conditions of transition. However, the focus was not solely on the legal superstructure; an effort was also made to go beyond a definition of the static regulatory framework for FDI. The aim was to start the investigation at an earlier analytical point and to adopt a multidisciplinary methodological approach through which the emerging legislation regulating FDI could be explained. This concluding chapter places what has been said in context, by indicating how the study may contribute to the development of the theory of the legal regulation of FDI in transitional countries.

Given the economic origin of FDI, our starting point was that the legal rules which govern FDI can be described and analysed in economic terms. The law and economics school has given us a number of tools with which to approach the research issue. Pursuing such an approach yielded important insights into the relationship between a host state and foreign investors, as well as other relevant issues to the legal regulation of FDI issues that come into play in conditions of transition. The preceding chapters have demonstrated these points. In general, the law and economics approach allowed us to build our analysis on the basis of the notion of the economic efficiency of the emerging legislation, including the normative acts indirectly relevant to FDI.

The law and economics school allowed us to consider the emerging regulatory framework for FDI in the context of a hypothetical bargaining model. The key point is that working through the FDI-related problems by envisaging what two parties – a foreign investor and a host government – would have contracted for under ideal conditions proved to be a useful intellectual exercise. In particular, this allowed us to include in our analysis the notion of an optimal and less optimal equilibrium in the nexus 'host state–foreign investor'. In the legal dimension, this notion was translated into two modes of legal regulation that were, in turn, analysed in terms of possible economic outcomes for both a multinational corporation and a host state.

Having provided definitions for the optimal and the less optimal equilibriums, we made an attempt to find out why disequilibrium emerges in relationships between a host government and a foreign investor. In order to do this, we employed another important notion, which affects the efficiency effectiveness and functionality of the FDI-related legislation. This is the perceptions of time and certainty by a host state, on the one hand, and a foreign investor on the other. These perceptions are crucial elements in the analysis of the emerging regulatory framework for FDI. The longer the time-span in the plans of a host nation's government, and the longer its developmental commitments, then the more far-reaching their effect will be on the expectations of a foreign investor, and the better will be the preconditions for the emergence of the optimal model of legal regulation. An approach incorporating a host nation government's strategy towards FDI allowed the linkage of those laws specifically designed for FDI to a host nation's political law. Incorporation of the latter into the analysis of the legal regulation of FDI also emphasized the necessity for and significance of adopting a multidisciplinary approach to FDI in conditions of transition.

Further, envisaging how a foreign investor and a host state would structure their affairs if they were acting entirely rationally produced some insights into the interaction between the actual FDI relationship and the legal framework. Having envisaged an idealized description of transactors in analysing conduct in terms of bargains, we could then introduce the notion of limitations and distortions into this bargaining process. In particular, we approached the transition, the main underlying process in post-Soviet countries, as a factor affecting the hypothetical bargaining between a foreign investor and a host government. This in turn enabled us to show that the Kazakh host government has chosen a less optimal model for the legal regulation of FDI. In order to understand why it has done so, we 'unpacked' the state, which had formerly, in analytical terms remained a 'black box'. In so doing, we approached the state at the macro, inter-branch level as well as conducting a micro-level analysis of the executive. Further, in undertaking the latter analysis, we utilized the notion of economic efficiency. This was considered as the benchmark to evaluate whether the state and its officials are dealing with FDI-related issues, particularly in the law-making process, in a manner consistent with efficiency considerations.

Of equal importance was the fact that the law and economics approach helped us to understand why certain principles in other realms of law, seemingly irrelevant to FDI – particularly in political legislation – do, in fact, matter in the analysis of the legal regulation of FDI in transitional societies. For instance, the relevant discussion has shown how the constitutional principle of separation of powers predetermines the choice and workings of a certain model of the legal regulation of FDI. Equally, it has demonstrated why this constitutional principle should be one of the governing principles in the formation of an optimal model of the legal regulation of FDI.

The methodological approach employed in this study with particular regard to emerging laws on FDI observed through the prism of the regulatory models also provided a fertile ground for assessment of the legislation within a tridimensional system of coordinates: legal, economic and political. This allowed us to assess the correlation between the economic and political dimensions of a transitional state and especially to incorporate into the analysis the driving forces within this tridimensional system. This exercise was helpful in explaining the reasons for choosing a particular model of legal regulation. An understanding of the works of such a tridimensional system could also provide a future researcher with helpful tools for a long-term forecast and an assessment of the further evolution of the legal regulatory framework for FDI in transitional societies, as we have done with respect to the case of Kazakhstan.

In this study, the underlying focus was on the property rights assignment, but the frame of reference in our work was fundamentally different to that adopted in the previous literature on FDI. The standard formulation treats property rights associated with FDI as being 'granted' – presumably by the state (or, more specifically, by the legislator) – and the distribution of the property rights as exogenous with respect to the behaviour of affected economic agents – the state and, principally, the foreign investor. Accordingly, the principal emphasis in such an approach is on the efficiency of bargaining outcomes. Implicit in this conceptualization is the presumption that economic agents will remain passive with respect to the property rights assignment. By contrast, this study has demonstrated that in conditions of post-Soviet transition, the state, as a party in the bilateral relationship with a foreign investor, has a greater incentive to rent-seek over the rights distribution than to bargain after the rights assignment. The conclusion is that rent-seeking behaviour in a 'missing-market' context, such as the Kazakh one, would appear to be particularly likely because of the absence of checks and balances among the different branches of the state and also of powerful civil society institutions. This, in turn, leads to a lack of clarity in the definition of property rights, and raises the possibility that the costs of influencing the rights definition are relatively low. In fact, more specifically, as our analysis of the recent legislative developments in Kazakhstan has shown, the state has undertaken steps to rearrange the existing institutional environment with the express purpose of lowering the costs associated with the definition and distribution of property rights.

Recent surveys allow one to see the present pivotal problem of the Kazakh investment climate, which is the paralysis of power: the incompetence of its bureaucracy, corruption at all levels, and the short-sightedness of civil servants. We have taken a deeper look by attempting to answer the questions as to why the less optimal model of legal regulation has been chosen and why the existing model cannot be replaced by an optimal one.

In particular, our study has emphasized the importance of the interrelations between institutional arrangements and economic behaviour, since account was taken of the fact that more than one pattern of property rights can exist and that profit maximization is not assured. Accordingly, the role of individual decision-makers within the regulating organization – that is, the state (or the executive) – was stressed. The state per se was no longer the monolithic central focus; rather, individuals were assumed to be pursuing their own interests and to be maximizing utility subject to the limits established by the existing organizational structure. Thus, in each instance, as was suggested, it has been necessary to define the particular utility function that reflects the decision-makers' preferences, and to determine the actual set of options that are attainable by the decision-maker.

We then considered the continued importance of the state as an agent of economic governance in the case of Kazakhstan. The state-centred approach was not incidental because, since the dissolution of the USSR, the state, the strongest of the surviving institutions, has gradually been restored to its dominant position which had started to diminish as a result of Gorbachev's reforms. We argued, on the basis of the analysis of the post-independence evolution of the Kazakh constitutions and the changes in the legislation governing FDI, that this process of the restoration of state domination has continued after independence. North has observed that organizations are a response to the institutional structure of societies and, at the same time, as they evolve, they may also alter that institutional structure.[1] Seemingly, the depth of embeddedness of the Soviet-type institutions was so profound that the new and independent institutions of the Gorbachev period could not survive after the demise of the Gorbachev administration itself, which had itself generated the liberalizing impetus. Accordingly, this explains the 'up–down' nature of institutional change in Kazakhstan in the post-independence period and the necessity for the adoption of a state-centred focus in the study of the legal regulation of FDI. It also implies that the key factor for the achievement of the optimal model of regulation depends on the cohesion of the central authority and its sustained effort to secure productive cooperation from the private sector, both domestic and foreign. Unrestrained state or business influence risks a deterioration into parochialism and clientelism in one form or another. In the case of Kazakhstan, however, because it lacks a market-economy history and a democratic tradition, the more difficult task for economic governance is not the creation of well-organized private interests, but the presence of a cohesive central political authority.

The study also suggested that, in the case of Kazakhstan, the evolution and present organization of the state reflects the lack of civil society institutions. As it has evolved since the collapse of the USSR, the Kazakh state has prevented such institutions from emerging.

Therefore, to date, the economy of Kazakhstan has not undergone any profound restructuring which could have promoted economic self-sustainability. The continuing inability of the Kazakh government to revive the country's economy has made Kazakhstan almost wholly reliant on foreign direct investment. Privatization has not produced a middle class, the principal agent of socioeconomic change and the guarantor of domestic stability needed for any long-term foreign investment. At the micro-level, post-Soviet privatization has not changed the system of corporate governance and, as a result, the internal engines of entrepreneurship and western-type investment attitudes have never been established. Equally, the absence of a domestic middle class explains the lack of any feasible 'spill-over' effects of FDI on the Kazakh economy. It also explains why sophisticated foreign investments, excluding those in the raw material sectors, still cannot be rooted in Kazakh soil. Earlier decisions by Siemens-Nixdorf, Daimler-Benz, Sagem, and other similar companies, to withdraw from the Kazakh market are the clearest proof of this claim.[2] The absence of domestic entities able to accept the transferring of knowledge-based assets by MNCs, in turn, indicates that the country is unlikely to upgrade its technological standing within the MNCs' networks and indigenize the technologies that could be brought into the country by the MNCs.

In addition, it has been shown that the content of the legislation on FDI has gradually undergone substantial transformations within the short time-span of the post-independence period between 1991 and 1997. Early post-independence legislation resembled and corresponded with the free entry model of regulation of FDI. Later, the evolution of the entire system went in the opposite direction. This process resulted in the enactment of the 1997 Law on State Support of Direct Investment, which can be viewed as a culmination of the formation of an inward-looking policy towards FDI and, accordingly, a final confirmation of the adoption of the less optimal model of legal regulation.

A linear cause of the legal developments in Kazakhstan is not a sudden chain of evolving events, nor is it a response of the rule-maker to changing global conditions, nor is it the adaptation of the domestic policy to coax the MNCs. Rather, these are manifestations of the deeper, state-centred transformations which have not evolved spontaneously, but originated at an earlier stage, even before independence. The remarkable feature of the post-Soviet transition is that the reforms originated from above, and thus lacked a popular base of support. Accordingly, the formation of property rights emerged not as the result of socioeconomic transformations nor as an outcome of the clashes between different interest groups in Kazakh society which could defend them in case of infringement. Instead, the new property rights, manifested through the legislation, were tailored and then granted by the state. At the same time, because no new class or ownership 'interest' emerged to mobilize people in order to make use of and, if necessary, to defend these granted property rights, the gap between the actual and the written rules increased.[3]

It is clear that the failed privatization process, which has not resulted in a restructured economy and has thus far not created the internal sources for the generation of investments, has made foreign investment the only source of much-needed finances for keeping the country's economy afloat. Foreign investment is being increasingly used to support the declining legitimacy of an economically ineffective and corrupt elite. Therefore, although another round of privatization was announced by the president for 1999 as part of his post-election programme, the prospects are that the acquired property will be vulnerable to domestic political instability because, in the presence of corrupt bureaucracy, any privatization is viewed as unfair by the impoverished population. In short, the past elections have not produced an impetus strong enough to replace the rent-seeking model by a developmental one. This accordingly will affect the actual execution of property rights, and the gap between the theoretical rules and how they operate in practice will inevitably increase.

We have also touched on the issue of the possible replacement of the less optimal model of regulation by a more optimal one. In particular, a significant event – the 1999 January presidential elections – was analysed in this context. A number of conclusions relevant to the regulation of FDI can be made in connection with this. One can assume that, following the January 1999 elections, the crumbling international image of the president, sacrificed for the sake of the prolongation of his rule, puts pressure on him to focus on improving the economic performance. Furthermore, the president is now seemingly compelled to set the groundwork for the emergence of a domestic class of entrepreneurs. This, however, would be done with his personal political survival in view because he recognizes that further reliance exclusively on the bureaucracy, which has been weakened by internal clashes, would be dangerous. Besides, because of the new inner-state arrangements, established by the 1995 Constitution, the bureaucracy focuses on its relations to the president, rather than on serving the public. As a result, it is increasingly out of touch with reality, and is producing a growing number of inconsistent laws and regulations which have resulted in the lack of a coherent policy towards FDI.

A new round of privatization could facilitate the emergence of a new social basis for the support of the president. In theory, this would, in turn, allow the business class to consolidate their powers and to emerge as an institutionalized political actor. The emergence of an organization of businessmen would prepare favourable grounds for a shift from rent-seeking relationships with the state towards ones which are collaborative and growth-oriented. At present, business people prefer to deal with the state on an individual basis, via their patrons in the power structures. The rent-seeking system of relationships better serves their business interests. Furthermore, the emergence of the latter would be vital because it is that missing element in the domestic system which can facilitate the 'spill-over' effect of FDI into the host economy. The obsolete state of their equipment and machinery would also open the prospect for foreign investors willing to cooperate with the domestic participants of the 1999 privatization who lack their own resources to revitalize backward Soviet enterprises. However, privatization is likely to fail again because there is no developed link between the state and society. The relatives of the president, who have monopolized the key sectors of the Kazakh economy, play a major role in eroding the grounds for the consolidation and the institutionalization of private interest.

The dissolution of the USSR and the consequent emergence of the 15 independent states presents a unique case for the study of the post-independence evolution of political, economic and legal systems. This study has made a modest effort to provide a framework for understanding one of the aspects of these profound changes by analysing the emerging law on foreign direct investment. Undoubtedly, the posing of the issues and presenting them in a certain systematic form along the lines of this study was perhaps, at this stage, more important than providing a solution. It is hoped that this study has contributed to a better understanding of the legal aspects of post-Soviet transition and has constructed an initial framework for future scholarly inquiry.

Appendix: The Normative Acts of the USSR and the Republic of Kazakhstan

The Law of the USSR 'On the Fundamental Principles of the Legislation on Foreign Investment', *Vedomosti S'yezda Narodnyh Deputatov i Verhovnogo Soveta SSSR*, 1991, No. 29, st. 1008.

The Decree No. 49 of the Council of Ministers of the USSR 'On the Establishment in the Territory of the USSR and the Operation of Joint Enterprises with the Participation of Soviet Organizations and Firms of Capitalist and Developing Countries', *Sobranie Postanovlenii Pravitel'stva SSSR*, 1987, otd. 1, No. 9, st. 40.

The Law of the Republic of Kazakhstan 'On Basic Principles of the Foreign Economic Activity', *Vedomosti Verhovnogo Soveta Kazahskoi SSR*, 1990, No. 1, st. 3.

The Law of the Republic of Kazakhstan 'On Lease', *Vedomosti Verhovnogo Soveta Kazahskoi SSR*, 1990, No. 10, st. 87.

The Law of the Republic of Kazakhstan 'On the Development of Competition and Limitation of Monopolistic Activity', *Vedomosti Verhovnogo Soveta Kazahskoi SSR*, 1990, No. 24, st. 83.

The Land Code of the Kazakh SSR, *Vedomosti Verhovnogo Soveta Kazahskoi SSR*, 1990, No. 47, st. 429.

The Law of the Republic of Kazakhstan 'On Special Economic Zones', *Vedomosti Verhovnogo Soveta Kazahskoi SSR*, 1990, No. 49, st. 455.

The Law of the Republic of Kazakhstan 'On Foreign Investment', *Vedomosti Verhovnogo Soveta Kazahskoi SSR*, 1990, No. 50, st. 474.

The Law of the Republic of Kazakhstan 'On Banks and Banking', *Vedomosti Verhovnogo Soveta Kazahskoi SSR*, 1990, No. 50, st. 475.

The Law of the Republic of Kazakhstan 'On Freedom of Economic Activity and the Development of Entrepreneurship', *Vedomosti Verhovnogo Soveta Kazahskoi* SSR, 1990, No. 51, st. 483.

The Law of the Republic of Kazakhstan 'On Enterprises in the Republic of Kazakhstan', *Vedomosti Verhovnogo Soveta Kazahskoi SSR*, 1991, No. 8, st. 96.

The Law of the Republic of Kazakhstan 'On Circulation of Securities and Stock Exchange', *Vedomosti Verhovnogo Soveta Kazahskoi SSR*, 1991, No. 24, st. 287.

The Law of the Republic of Kazakhsan 'On Currency Regulation', *Vedomosti Verhovnogo Soveta Kazahskoi SSR*, 1991, No. 25, st. 310.

The Law of the Republic of Kazakhstan 'On Citizenship', *Vedomosti Verhovnogo Soveta Respubliki Kazahstan*, 1991, No. 52, st. 636.

The Law of the Republic of Kazakhstan 'On Concessions', *Vedomosti Verhovnogo Soveta Kazahskoi SSR*, 1992, No. 52, st. 640.

The Law of the Republic of Kazakhstan 'On Foreign Investment', *Vedomosti Verhovnogo Soveta Respubliki Kazahstan*, 1994, Nos 9–10, st. 69.

The Civil Code of the Republic of Kazakhstan. *Vedomosti Verhovnogo Soveta Respubliki Kazahstan*, 1994, Nos 23–4.
The Law of the Republic of Kazakhstan 'On the Legal Status of Foreign Citizens', *Vedomosti Verhovnogo Soveta Respubliki Kazahstan*, 1995, Nos 9–10, st. 68.
The Constitution of the Republic of Kazakhstan (1995) Almaty: Zheti Zhargy.
The Law of the Republic of Kazakhstan 'On State Support of Direct Investment', *Vedomosti Parlamenta Respubliki Kazahstan*, 1997, No. 4, st. 36.
The Law of the Republic of Kazakhstan 'On Normative Acts', *Kazahstanskaya Pravda*, 28 March 1998.
The Edict of the President of the Republic of Kazakhstan having the force of law 'On Economic Partnerships'. *Vedomosti Verhovnogo Soveta Respubliki Kazahstan*, 1995, No. 15, st. 109.
The Edict of the President of the Republic of Kazakhstan having the force of law 'On Banks and Banking', *Vedomosti Verhovnogo Soveta Respubliki Kazahstan*, 1995, Nos 15–16, st. 106.
The Edict of the President of the Republic of Kazakhstan having the force of law 'On Licencing', *Vedomosti Verhovnogo Soveta Respubliki Kazahstan*, 1995, No. 3, st. 37.
The Edict of the President of the Republic of Kazakhstan having the force of law 'On Land', *Vedomosti Verhovnogo Soveta Respubliki Kazahstan*, 1995, No. 24, st. 159.
The Edict of the President of the Republic of Kazakhstan having the force of law 'On Petroleum', *Vedomosti Verhovnogo Soveta Respubliki Kazahstan*, 1995, No. 11, st. 76.
The Decree of Parliament of the Republic of Kazakhstan 'On Order of Implementation of the Law on Foreign Investment', *Vedomosti Verhovnogo Soveta Respubliki Kazahstan*, 1994, Nos 23–4.
The Decree of the Cabinet of Ministers of the Republic of Kazakhstan 'On Licencing of the Subsoil-Use', *Sbornik Aktov Prezidenta Respubliki Kazahstan i Pravitel'stva Respubliki Kazahstan*, 1996, No. 34, st. 321.
The Letter of the Tax Inspectorate of 2 February 1996 No. 12–10–3–12/674 'On Taxation of Enterprises with Foreign Investment', *Informatsionnyi Bulleten' Ministerstva Finansov Respubliki Kazahstan*, 1997, No. 17, 218.
The Letter of the Tax Inspectorate of 24 April 1996 No. 12–10–3–12/2174 'On Taxation of Enterprises with Foreign Investment', *Finansy Kazahstana*, 1996, No. 9, 64.

Notes

1 Introduction

1. See, e.g., T.W. Waelde and J.L. Gunderson, 'Legislative Reform in Transition Economies: Western Transplants – Short-Cut to Social Market Economy Status?' (1994) 43 *The International and Comparative Law Quarterly* 347; D.F. Black, 'So You Want to Invest in Russia? A Legislative Analysis of the Foreign Investment Climate in Russia' (1996) 5 *Minnesota Journal of Global Trade* 123; B.L. Zimbler, 'Russian Foreign Investment Laws and Natural Resources' (1993) 14 *Whittier Law Review* 477; C. Osakwe, 'Navigating the Minefields of Russian Joint Venture Law and Tax Regulations: a Procedural Compass' (1993) 22 *Vanderbuilt Journal of Transnational Law* 1; W.G. Frenkel and M.Y. Sukhman, 'New Foreign Investment Regimes of Russia and Other Republics of the Foremer USSR: a Legislative Analysis and Historical Perspective' (1993) 16 *Boston College International and Comparative Law Review* 321; G.D. Jackson, 'Doing Business in Russia: Practical Guide for American Investors' (1994) 3 *Journal of International Law and Practice* 111; P. Cameron, 'Creating a Legal Framework for Investment in the Commonwealth of Independent States Energy Sector: Lessons from the Energy Charter Experiment' (1994) 1 *Tulsa Journal of Comparative and International Law* 233.
2. The present legal superstructure in the countries of the former USSR – that is, the texts of statutes – has adopted a western-type legal language. However, the dysfunctionality of these laws in reality makes one conclude that mere western-type language and style of laws is not a sufficient basis for the application of methodological tools utilized by western legal students.
3. These misconceptions have also affected the policy of international institutions involved in post-Soviet transition. The International Monetary Fund's (IMF) 1991 report stated that 'attracting substantial flows of foreign investment could be crucial in the transition to a market economy'. See *IMF 1991 Report* (1991) 75. The United Nations Economic Commission for Europe asserted more pointedly that 'foreign direct investment is expected to play a major role in the transformation of the eastern economies'. See *United Nations/ECE* (1992) 96. A report issued in 1992 by the United Nations Centre on Transnational Corporations labeled investment, made by transnational corporations, as 'engines of development'. See *World Investment Report 1992: Transnational Corporations as Engines of Growth* (1992).
4. See C.D. Wallace, *Legal Control of the Multinational Enterprise* (1982) 6. She accurately points out that: 'In developed states, where a reasonably stable political structure has existed long enough to give governmental policy and legal solutions sufficient continuity to be of interest in our study, the development of legal means of dealing with the multinational are more easily traceable and more juridically significant than in the developing world

where, due to historical forces, such a continuity is often lacking ... *The investment problem* of the less developed nations and those of the advanced industrialized states *differ substantially in kind* – those of developing nations tending to fall more in the politico-socio-economic sphere, and those of the developed states arising generally in the legal arena'.

5. W.W. Powell and P.G. DiMaggio (eds), *The New Institutionalism and Organizational Analysis* (1991). M.C. Suchman and L.B. Edelman, 'Legal Rational Myths: the New Institutionalism and the Law and Society Tradition' (1996) 21 (4) *Law and Social Inquiry* 903.
6. J.G. March and J.P. Olsen, 'The New Institutionalism: Organizational Factors in Political Life' (1984) 78 (3) *American Political Science Review* 734, 735. These authors provide a useful sketch of the main theories of politics since the 1950s. They define 'neo-institutionalism' as follows: 'neo-institutionalism insists on a more autonomous role for political institutions. The state is not only affected by society but also affects it. Political democracy depends not only on economic and social conditions but also on the design of political institutions. The bureaucratic agency, the legislative committee, and the appellate court are arenas for contending social forces, but they are also collections of standard operating procedures and structures that define and defend interests. They are political actors in their own right ... Political outcomes are a function of three primary forces: the distribution of preferences (interests) among political actors, the distribution of resources (powers), and the constraints imposed by the rules of the game (constitutions).' (p. 738) As March and Olsen note, new institutionalism is not completely different from the 'old' institutionalism. Rather, it can be viewed as 'blending elements of an old institutionalism into the non-institutionalist styles of recent theories of politics' (J.G. March and J.P. Olsen, *Rediscovering Institutions: the Organizational Basis of Politics* (1989) 2).
7. It is not by accident that the Tsarist administration exiled more than 100 000 Poles here at the beginning of the twentieth century. Likewise, the Stalin administration exiled Germans, Caucasians and other disloyal ethnic groups during the Second World War. Both decision-makers realized that the native population of Kazakhstan would be able to co-habit even with ethnic groups treated as potential enemies.
8. During the past years a few monographs have been published with particular focus on foreign direct investment – C.D. Wallace, *Legal Control of the Multinational Enterprise* (1982); M. Sornarajah, *International Law on Foreign Investment* (1995); P. Muchlinski, *Multinational Enterprise and Law* (1996); I. Rapakko, *Unlimited Shareholder Liability in Multinational Enterprise* (1997). The focus of all of these books is primarily on various international aspects of foreign direct investment or legal aspects, both external and internal, of multinational companies undertaking FDI. A few studies have also been undertaken with emphasis on the domestic level of legal regulation. In particular, a publication by E. El-Sheikh, *The Legal Regime of Foreign Private Investment in the Sudan and Saudi Arabia: a Case Study of Developing Countries* (1984), has a rather descriptive country-specific character which is mainly focused on the formalistic superstructure which reflects the static portrayal of laws regulating foreign investment. It is not by accident that the author arrives at a conclusion, which could change the pattern of his whole study

should it be used as a starting point: 'What is significant for foreign investors is not the quantum and quality of incentives, but their effective enjoyment and guarantee of their performance. There should be an effective legal machinery for the protection of the acquired rights of foreign investors to enjoy these incentives without any disturbance.' Another study by Juha Kuusi, which grew out of his DPhil thesis submitted to the Law Faculty of Oxford University, *The Host State and the Transnational Corporation* (1979), though it points to the term 'host-nation' in its title, nevertheless, again builds its arguments within the realm of international law. In the preface to his book, he explicitly points out: 'If this book contributes, in however small a degree, to a better understanding of the role that international legal doctrines have played in the past and what alternative roles they could play in the future in the development of world economy, it has fulfilled its purpose'. In other words, Kuusi's focus, though implying the host nation's level of legal regulation, is in fact on the responses of international law to changes in world's political and economic arenas emanating from the change in status and behaviour of individual or group states.

9. R. Bilder and I. Murphy, 'Book Review of *The International Law on Foreign Investment* By M. Sornarajah. Cambridge, New York: Cambridge University Press, 1994.' In 89 *American Journal of International Law* (1995) 666, 668.
10. The scope of this book, therefore, does not include bilateral investment treaties as they are studied within the field of international public law.
11. In this study, the effectiveness of law is understood by using economic indicators such as (i) the overall volume of FDI which came into the country; (ii) the sectoral and geographical distribution of these inflows; (iii) the duration of the investment project; (iv) the volume of re-investment. It is assumed that even in the study of a non-economic character, a perception of FDI only in terms of overall volume of FDI can be misleading.

1 Methodological Approach

1. T.W. Waelde, 'The 1994 Energy Charter Treaty' (1995) 29 (5) *Journal of World Trade* 5, 11.
2. Although the FDI relationship may theoretically occur between either a foreign investor and the state or a foreign investor and a host country's private companies, the focus of this study is on the former. In contrast with industrialized countries, due to the state-owned structure of the post-Soviet economy, the absence of domestic enterprises capable of entering into long-term investment relationships, as well as the remaining state monopoly of natural resources, which attracts the absolute majority of FDI in the former USSR (in the case of Kazakhstan, this FDI comprises nearly 80 per cent), the relationship occurs mainly within the nexus of a foreign investor and the state. Furthermore, due to the lack of democratic and market institutions during transition, the unrestrained state can unilaterally significantly affect the relationships between a foreign investor and a private entity, thus making this relationship dependent mainly on the state, not market forces. This, along with the above reasons, explains why the chosen nexus is so

important in the study of legal regulation of FDI in transitional states of the former USSR.

3. C.D. Wallace, *Legal Control of the Multinational Enterprise* (1982) 6.
4. R. Bilder and I. Murphy, 'Book Review. *The International Law on Foreign Investment.* By M. Sornarajah. Cambridge, New York: Cambridge University Press, 1994' (1995) 89 *American Journal of International Law* 666, 668.
5. T. Rapakko, *Unlimited Shareholder Liability in Multinationals* (1997) 7.
6. D.S. Lev, 'Book Review. *Russian Law: Trying to Make Law Matter. Legal Reform and Labour Law in the Soviet Union.* By Kathryn Hendley. University of Michigan Press: 1996' (1997) 44 *American Journal of Comparative Law* 531.
7. Similarly, Lankes and Venables found that 'host country transition progress, political stability and perceived risk influence FDI inflows as well as the predominant type of investment'. See H.-P. Lankes and A.J. Venables, 'Foreign Direct Investment in Economic Transition: the Changing Pattern of Investments' (1996) 4 (2) *Economics of Transition* 331.
8. S.H. Robock, 'Political Risk: Identification and Assessment' (1974) 6 (4) *Columbia Journal of World Business* 6, 6.
9. Ibid., 8.
10. Robock states that political risk in international business exists (i) when discontinuities occur in the business environment, (ii) when they are difficult to, anticipate, and (iii) when they result from political change. Most important is that to constitute a 'risk' these changes in the business environment must have the potential to significantly affect the profit or other goals of a particular enterprise. See S.H. Robock, 'Political Risk: Identification and Assessment', 'Assessing and Forecasting Political Risk' (*Abstract Paper for the Research Conference on the Multinational Corporation in the Global Political System, Philadelphia, 22–23 April 1971*), p. 7. Root notes that a company investing abroad faces a wide spectrum of political risks that are generated by the attitudes, policies, and overt behaviour of host governments and other local power centres such as rival political parties, labour unions and nationalistic groups. See F. Root, 'U.S. Business Abroad and the Political Risks' (1968) *MSU Business Topics* 73. Greene defines it as uncertainty stemming from unanticipated and unexpected acts of governments or other organizations which may cause loss to the business firm. See F. Green, 'The Management of Political Risk' (1974) *Bests Review.* Fatehi-Sedeh and Safizadeh suggest that political risk is defined as negative perception emanating from internal instability, intergovernmental relationship or unanticipated government actions, or government discontinuities all brought about by social, economic, or political imperatives existing in a country's internal or relevant external environment. See K. Fatehi-Sedeh and M. Safizadeh, 'The Association Between Political Instability and Flow of Foreign Direct Investment' (1989) 29 (4) *Management International Review* 4, 10.
11. C. William and R. Heins, *Risk Management and Insurance* (1964) 4–7.
12. I. Pfeffer, *Insurance and Economic Theory* (1956) 42.
13. A. Willet, *The Economic Theory of Risk and Insurance* (1951) 6.
14. See T. Rapakko, *Unlimited Shareholder Liability in Multinationals* (1997) chapter 3.4.1.
15. R.A. Posner, 'The Future of the Law and Economics Movement in Europe' (1997) 17 *International Review of Law and Economics* 3.

16. K.H. Parsons, 'John R. Commons Point of View' (1942) 18 *Journal of Land and Public Utility Economics* 245.
17. H. Kohler, *Intermediate Microeconomics* (1986) 474.
18. D.C. North, *Institutions, Institutional Change and Economic Performance* (1990) 6.
19. R.E. Scott, 'A Relational Theory of Default Rules for Commercial Contracts' (1990) 29 *Journal of Legal Studies* 598.
20. M.J. Rizzo, 'Uncertainty, Subjectivity, and the Economic Analysis of Law' in M.J. Rizzo (ed.), *Time, Uncertainty and Disequilibrium: Exploration of Austrian Times* (1979) 74.
21. See G.P. O'Driscoll and M.J. Rizzo, *The Economics of Time and Ignorance* (1985). They note that in economics there are three conceptions of time: static, dynamic and analytical. In the static conception, time is analogous to space. Economic agents can allocate fragments of time to different activities. The passage of time may be represented by 'movements' along a line. The future exists just like the points on a line that are given simultaneously. The dynamic conception perceives time as a flow of events, which implies novelty or a 'continuous flow of novel experiences'. This flow is not in time, as would be the case from a static perspective; rather it *is* or constitutes time. The concept of analytical time resembles that of historical time insofar as it is characterized by path dependence. It leaves no room for a 'continuous flow of novel experiences', however, as it merely distinguishes 'before' and 'after'.
22. See A. Leff, 'Economic Analysis of Law: Some Realism about Nominalism' (1975) 60 *Virginia Law Review* 451. He puts this point as follows: 'If a state of affairs is a product of n variables, and you have knowledge of or control over less than n variables, if you think you know what's going to happen when you "vary" your variables, you're a booby'. See ibid., 476.
23. A.A. Alchian, *Economic Forces at Work* (1977) 301.
24. Ibid., 310.
25. K.I. Vaughan, 'Does It Matter That Costs Are Subjective?' (1979) 46 *Southern Economic Journal* 702.
26. Fenwick illustrates this point: 'Many of the most crucial and noticeable problems and trends in the evolution of joint ventures [in China] during their first five years are the outcome of the at-times conflictual interplay between two key roles envisaged for joint ventures: that of component of national development strategy (a role envisaged, by Beijing) and that of profit-making entrée into the China market (a role envisaged by foreign investors).' See A. Fenwick, 'Equity Joint Ventures in the People's Republic of China: An Assessment of the First Five Years' (1985) 40 *Business Lawyer* 839.
27. Decision models are based on the models for the legal regulation of FDI which will be discussed in the subsequent chapter.
28. C. Lindblom, 'The Science of Muddling Through' (1959) 19 *Public Administration Review* 79, 83.
29. S. Breyer, 'Analyzing Regulatory Failure: Mismatches, Less Restrictive Alternatives and Reform' (1979) 92 *Harvard Law Review* 549, 550.
30. Ibid., 586.
31. R. Cooter and T. Ulen, *Law and Economics* (1988) 7.
32. Ibid., 11.

33. A Przeworski, *Democracy and the Market: Political and Economic Reforms in Eastern Europe and Latin America* (1991) ix.
34. R. Bova, 'The Political Dynamics of the Post-Communist Transition: a Comparative Perspective' (1991) 44 (1) *World Politics* 113, 117.
35. W.W. Powell and P.J. DiMaggio (eds), *The New Institutionalism and Organizational Analysis* (1991) 1.
36. Ibid., 3.
37. Ibid.
38. V.W. Ruttan and Y. Hayami, 'Toward a Theory of Induced Institutional Innovation' (1984) 20 *Journal of Development Studies* 203, 204 in D.W. Bromley, *Economic Interests and Institutions: the Conceptual Foundations of Public Policy* (1989) 18–19.
39. D.W. Bromley, *Economic Interests and Institutions: the Conceptual Foundations of Public Policy* (1989) 11.
40. J.M. Buchanan, 'The Domain of Constitutional Economics' (1990) 1 *Constitutional Political Economy* 1, 4.
41. W.J. Samuels, 'Interrelations Between Legal and Economic Processes' (1971) 14 *Journal of Law and Economics* 435, 444.
42. See M.C. Suchman and L.E. Edelman, 'Legal Rational Myths: the New Institutionalism and the Law and Society Tradition' (1996) 21 (4) *Law and Social Inquiry* 903–43; P.A. Hall and R.C.R. Taylor, 'Political Science and the Three Institutionalisms' (1996) XLIV *Political Studies* 936; J.G. March and J.P. Olsen, 'The New Institutionalism: Organizational Factors in Political Life' (1984) 78 (3) *American Political Science Review* 734.
43. J.G. March and J.P. Olsen, *Rediscovering Institutions: the Organizational Basis of Politics* (1989) 2.
44. J.G. March and J P. Olsen 'The New Institutionalism: Organizational Factors in Political Life' (1984) 78 (3) *American Political Science Review* 734, 738–39.
45. D.C. North, *The Contribution of the New Institutional Economics to an Understanding of the Transition Problem* (1997) 83.
46. W.W. Powell and P.J. DiMaggio, *The New Institutionalism and Organizational Analysis* (1991) 7.

2 Units of Analysis

1. In particular, the Heckscher–Ohlin theory remains ubiquitous in the relevant theory. According to this factor-proportions theory of comparative advantage, international commerce compensates for the uneven geographical distribution of productive resources. The fundamental insight of the Heckscher–Ohlin model is that traded commodities are really bundles of factors (land, labour and capital). The international exchange of commodities is therefore indirect factor arbitrage, transferring the services of otherwise immobile factors of production from locations where these factors are abundant to locations where they are scarce. Under some circumstances, this indirect arbitrage can completely eliminate factor-price differences. The most important implication of the Heckscher–Ohlin theory is that the option to sell factor services externally (through the exchange of commodi-

ties) transforms a local market for factor services into a global market. As a result, the derived demand for inputs becomes much more elastic, and also more similar across countries. For discussion, see E.E. Leamer, *The Heckscher–Ohlin Model in Theory and Practice* (1995); E.E. Heckscher and B. Ohlin, *Heckscher–Ohlin Trade Theory* (1991); D.R. Davis, D.E. Weinstein, S.C. Bradford and K. Shimpo, *The Heckscher–Ohlin–Vanek Model of Trade: Why Does it Fail? When Does It Work?* (1996).

2. I.S. Johnston, 'Law, Economics, and Post-Realist Explanation' (1990) 24 (5) *Law & Society Review* 1217, 1221.
3. S. Hymer, *The International Operations of National Firms* (1976).
4. R. Vernon, 'International Trade and International Investment in the Product Cycle' (1966) 83 (1) *Quarterly Journal of Economics* 190–207; R. Vernon, *Sovereignty at Bay* (1971); J.H. Dunning (ed.), *The Location of Economic Activity in Economic Analysis and Multinational Enterprise* (1971).
5. P.J. Buckley and M. Casson, *The Future of Multinational Enterprise*, 2nd edn (1976) 2.
6. Ibid., 59. They point out that by comparison before the Second World War, multinationality was a by-product of the internalization of intermediate product markets in multi-stage production processes, particularly in primary industries as food, minerals, oil, and so on.
7. This includes infrastructure, legal regime for protection of knowledge-based assets, the educational level of local personnel and its managerial experience.
8. Ibid., 61.
9. T.L. Brewer, 'Government Policies, Market Imperfections and Foreign Direct Investment' (1993) 24 *Journal of International Business Studies* 101, 105.
10. See J. Dunning, *Multinational Enterprise and the Global Economy* (1992).
11. Ibid., 68.
12. See J. Dunning, *Globalization: the Challenge for National Regimes* (1993).
13. Ibid., 2.
14. Ibid., 3.
15. As a proportion of world gross national product (GNP), such transactions have more than doubled. See *UNCTAD World Investment Report* (1998).
16. Ibid., xvii–xxxi.
17. Dunning, *Globalization*, 6.
18. Similarly, Ricupero says: 'to attract such competitiveness-enhancing FDI, it is no longer sufficient for host countries to possess a single locational determinant. When it comes to the economic determinants, firms that undertake cometiteveness-enhancing FDI seek not only cost reduction and bigger market shares, but also access to technology and innovative capacity. These resources, as distinct from natural resources, are people-made, they are "created assets". Possessing such assets is critical for firms' competiteveness in a globalizing economy'. See *UNCTAD World Investment Report* (1998) xxx.
19. Ibid., 8.
20. S. Haggard, 'The Newly Industrializing Countries in the International System' (1986) 38 (2) *World Politics* 343.
21. P. Evans, 'State, Capital, and the Transformation of Dependence: the Brazilian Computer Case' (1986) 14 (7) *World Development* 791, 804.
22. See R. Cox, *Production, Power, and World Order: Social Forces in the Making of History* (1987).

23. M. Bernard and J. Ravenhill, 'Beyond Product Cycles and Flying Geese: Regionalization, Hierarchy, and the Industrialization of East Asia' (1995) 47 *World Politics* 171; K. Ohmae, *The End of the Nation State: the Rise of Regional Economies* (1995); P.G. Cerny, 'Globalization and the Changing Logic of Collective Action' (1995) 49 (4) *International Organization* 595.
24. See S. Huntington, *The Third Wave: Democratization in the Late Twentieth Century* (1991) 21.
25. Ibid., 114.
26. T.L. Karl and P.C. Schmitter, 'Modes of Transition in Latin America, Southern and Eastern Europe' (1991) 128 *International Social Science Journal* 269, 280.
27. D.A. Rustow, 'Transition to Democracy: Toward a Dynamic Model' (1970) 2 (3) *Comparative Politics* 337
28. Ibid., 345.
29. H. Welsh, 'Political Transition Processes in Central and Eastern Europe' (1994) 26 (4) *Comparative Politics* 379.
30. N. Genov, 'The Transition to Democracy in Eastern Europe: Trends and Paradoxes of Social Rationalization' (1991) 128 *International Social Science Journal* 331, 336.
31. See M.G. Burton and J. Higley, 'Elite Settlements' (1987) 52 *American Sociological Review* 295.
32. J. Linz, 'Authoritarianism' in J Krieger (ed.), *The Oxford Companion to Politics of the World* (1993) 63.
33. G.L. Munck, 'Democratic Transitions in Comparative Perspective' (1994) 26 (3) *Comparative Politics* 355, 361.
34. See G. O'Donnell and P. Schmitter, *Transitions from Authoritarian Rule: Tentative Conclusions about Uncertain Democracies* (1986) chapter 5.
35. Munck, 'Democratic Transitions', 362.
36. A. Przeworski, *Democracy and the Market: Political and Economic Reforms in Eastern Europe and Latin America* (1991) 51.
37. Munck, 'Democratic Transitions', 362.
38. S. Mainwaring, G. O'Donnell and J.S. Valenzuela (eds), *Issues in Democratic Consolidation: the New South American Democracies in Comparative Perspective* (1992) 60–62.
39. Huntington, *The Third Wave*, 120.
40. O'Donnell and Schmitter, *Transitions from Authoritarian Rule*, 31–37.
41. Przeworski, *Democracy and the Marke*, 94–99.
42. Huntington, *The Third Wave*, 276.
43. Munck, 'Democratic Transitions', 364.
44. Huntington, *The Third Wave*, 270–3.
45. Przeworski, *Democracy and the Market*, 183.
46. Ibid., 187.
47. The term 'civil society' has more than one definition. For example, Roniger says: 'the concept of civil society alludes to the existence of organized public life and free associations beyond the tutelage of the state, yet oriented toward the public sphere and toward influencing public policy'. See L. Roniger, 'Civil Society, Patronage, and Democracy' in J.C. Alexander (ed.), *Real Civil Societies: Dilemmas of Institutionalization* (1998) 66–84. Norton states: '. . . by civil society we mean the emergence of institutions

autonomous from the state which facilitate orderly economic, social and political activity . . .'. See A.R. Norton, *Civil Society in the Middle East* (1995–96), x. Shils, in turn, emphasizes that civil society is 'a society where law prevails, binding the state and citizen equally, protecting the latter from the arbitrary and unjust use of power by the former'. See E.A. Shils, 'The Virtue of Civil Society' (1992) 26 (1) *Government and Opposition* 3, 16.

48. E. Hayek, *The Road to Serfdom* (1944); M. Friedman, *Capitalism and Freedom* (1962).
49. C. Lindblom, *Politics and Markets: The World's Political-Economic Systems* (1977) 161–9.
50. C.B. MacPherson, *The Political Theory of Possessive Individualism* (1962) 3.
51. See S. Huntington and I. Nelson, *No Easy Choice* (1976).
52. T.W. Waelde and J.L. Gunderson, 'Legislative Reform in Transition Economies: Western Transplants – Short-Cut to Social Market Economy Status?' (1994) 43 *The International and Comparative Law Quarterly* 347, 376.
53. K.A. Shepsle, 'Institutional Equilibrium and Equilibrium Institutions' in H Weisburg (ed.), *Political Science: the Science of Politics* 51–82 (1986) 74.
54. See M. Pastor and E. Hilt, 'Private Investment and Democracy in Latin America' 21 *World Development* 489.
55. See M. Olson, 'Dictatorship, Democracy, and Development' (1993) 87 *American Political Science Review* 567.
56. Ibid.
57. A. Goldsmith, 'Democracy, Property Rights and Economic Growth' (1995) 32 (2) *The Journal of Development Studies* 157.
58. Ibid., 168.
59. J. Umbeck, 'Might Makes Right – Theory of the Formation and Initial Distribution of Property Rights' (1986) 19 (I) *Economic Inquiry* 38, 39.
60. R. Putnam, 'Diplomacy and Domestic Politics: the Logic of Two-Level Games' (1988) 42 *Organization* 427.
61. See B.R. Cheffins, *Company Law: Theory, Structure and Operation* (1997) 19–21.
62. Ibid., 21.
63. See G. Tsebelis, *Nested Games: Rational Choice in Comparative Politics* (1990).
64. Ibid 32–3.
65. See R.L. Calvert, 'The Rational Choice Theory of Institutions: Implications for Design' in D.L. Weimer (ed.), *Institutional Design* (1995).
66. B. Geddes, 'Building "State" Autonomy in Brazil, 1930–1964' (1990) 22 (2) *Comparative Politics* 217.
67. C. Lindblom, *Politics and Markets: the World's Political-Economic Systems* (1977).
68. R.F. Doner and G. Hawes, 'Southeast and Northeast Asia' in M Dorraj (ed.), *The Changing Political Economy of the Third World* (1995); D. Okimoto, *Between MITI and the Market* (1989).
69. D.C. North, 'Privatization, Incentives, and Economic Performance' in H. Giersch and H. Siebert (eds), *Privatization: Symposium in Honour of Herbert Giersch* (1992) 4.
70. The term 'rent-seeking' is a broad concept with many terminological and paradigmatic differences. Nevertheless, for the purpose of this study, a definition provided by Buchanan can be employed. He defines 'rent-seeking'

as behaviour in institutional settings where individual efforts to maximize value generate social waste rather than social surplus. See J.M. Buchannan, 'Rent-seeking and Profit-seeking' in R.D. Tollison and G. Tullock (eds), *Toward a Theory of the Rent-Seeking Society* (1980). See also C.K. Rowley, R.D. Tollison and C. Tullock, *The Political Economy of Rent-Seeking* (1988); K.M. Murphy, A. Suleiker and R. Vishny, *Why is Rent-Seeking so Costly to Growth?* (1993); *Foreign Aid and Rent-Seeking* (1998).

71. Doner and Hawes, 'Southeast and Northeast Asia' 156.
72. See O. Williamson, *The Economic Institutions of Capitalism* (1985); D.C. North, *Institutions, Institutional Change and Economic Performance* (1990).
73. K. Thelen and S. Steinmo, 'Historical Institutionalism in Comparative Politics' in S. Steinmo, K. Thelen and E. Longstreth (eds), *Structuring Politics: Historical Institutionalism in Comparative Analysis* (1992) 1–32, 13.
74. For instance, Demze and Posner believe that a pre-market economy left to develop its own manner would gradually generate market institutions and these would be optimal.
75. B. Levy and P. Spiller, 'The Institutional Foundations of Regulatory Committment: a Comparative Analysis of Telecommunications Regulation' (1994) 10 (2) *Journal of Law, Economics & Organization* 201, 205.
76. O.E. Williamson, 'The Evolving Science of Organization' (1993) 149 *Journal of Institutional and Theoretical Economics* 35, 53, emphasis added.
77. Levy and Spiller, 'Institutional Foundations', 205.
78. See D.C. North, *Institutions, Institutional Change and Economic Performance* (1990).
79. For more discussion, see A.A. Baev, 'The Transformation of the Role of the State in Monitoring Large Firms in Russia: From the State's Supervision to the State's Fiduciary Duties' (1995) 8 (2) *The Transnational Lawyer* 247.
80. See B. Dallago, G. Ajani and B. Grancelli (eds), *Privatization and Entrepreneurship in Post-Socialist Countries* (1992); T. Popova, 'Privatizatsiya: Tempy, Mashtaby, Prioritety' (1992) 2 *Ekonomist* 65; M. Odle, 'Foreign Investment as Part of the Privatization Process' (1993) (2) *Transnational Corporations* 7; V.V. Ramandham, *Privatization in Developing Countries* (1989).
81. C. Gray, *In Search of Owners: Lessons of Experience with Privatization and Corporate Governance in Transition Economies* (1996) 1.
82. See T. Buck, I. Filatotchev and M. Wright, 'Agents, Stakeholders and Corporate Governance in Russian Firms' (1998) 35 (1) *Journal of Management Studies* 81.
83. See D.C. North, 'Privatization, Incentives, and Economic Performance' in H. Giersch and H. Siebert (eds), *Privatization: Symposium in Honour of Herbert Giersch* (1992).

3 The Legal Framework for FDI: Origins, Principles and Structure

1. J. Gordley, 'Comparative Legal Research: its Function in the Development of Harmonized Law' (1995) 43 *American Journal of Comparative Law* 555.
2. B.R. Cheffins, *Company Law: Theory, Structure and Operation* (1997) 213.

3. C.S. Diver, 'Regulatory Precision' in K. Hawkins and J. Thomas, *Making Regulatory Policy* (1989) 199.
4. For more detailed analysis of the NEP period, see A.C. Sutton, *Western Technology and Soviet Economic Development 1917 to 1930* (1968); A.M. Ball, *Russia's Last Capitalists: the Nepmen, 1921–1929* (1987); A.G. Dongarov, *Inostrannyi Kapital v Rossii i v SSSR* (1990); O.I. Sekushin, *Ottorzhenie NEP i Kommandno-Administrativnaya Sistema* (1990); L.G. Lyandau, *Inostrannyi Kapital v Dorevolyutsionnoi Rossii i SSSR* (1925); B.A. Landau and I.N. Bernshtein, *Pravovye Usloviya Kontseionnoi Deyatel'nosti v SSSR* (1930); A.V. Karass, 'Kontsessii v Sovetskom Prave' 2 *Sovetskoye Pravo* (1925) 30; M. Reihel, 'Kontsessii v Sovetskom Zakonodatel'stve i Praktike' 4 *Sovetskoye Pravo* (1927) 3–27.
5. This decree was replaced by the law of 23 August 1923 which was further amended in 14 December 1927 and supplemented by special ordinances of 23 May 1926 and 17 April 1928. The 1923 law established a Chief Concessions Committee and the legal basis for the conduct of negotiations and the transfer of Russian property to foreign enterprises. See A.C. Sutton, *Western Technology and Soviet Economic Development 1917 to 1930* (1968) 7.
6. Sutton provides the following definition of concession: 'A pure concession is an economic enterprise in which a foreign company enters into a contract with the host country to organize, equip, and exploit a specific opportunity, under the legal doctrine of *usufruct*. In return for the burden of development, exploitation, and production, the foreign company receives a non-contractual surplus of profit, usually taxed by the host country.' See Sutton, *Western Technology and Soviet Economic Development*, 7.
7. See M.A. Sarsembayev (ed.), *Pravovoye Regulirovaniye Vneshneekonomicheskoi Deyatel'nosti'* (1995) 14–29; T.L. Fridman, *Inostrannvi Kapital v Dorevolyutsionnom Kazahstane* (1960).
8. G. Chulanov, *Promyshlennost' Dorevolyutsionnogo Kazahstana* (1960) 9.
9. For example, the Soviet government was prepared under the concession agreements to give copper and nickel mines of the Ural and Northern Kazakhstan to Leslie Urquhart, who was the only western investor in prewar Russia to return to invest in the plants which he built under the Tsarist administration. His 'Russkaya Gornopromyshlennaya Korporatsiya' was re-established under the name 'Lena Goldfields'. He was granted a concession for a period of sixty years. The contract signed in April 1923 was then approved by the Soviet government in August 1925. It stipulated that Urquhart was to invest no less than 22 million roubles in order to achieve a level of production of 7 tons of gold (or more), 16 tons of silver, approximately 10 000 tons of zinc, and 1 million tons of copper per year. In 1926 the company was capable of producing 10 tons of gold a year, which constituted 30 per cent of the USSR overall production, and employed more than 12 000 people. In December 1929, the concession agreement was terminated by the Soviet government. See K.H. Kennedy, *Mining Tsar: the Life and Times of Leslie Urquhart* (1986); V.V. Veeder, 'The Lena Goldfields Arbitration: the Historical Roots of Three Ideas' (1998) 47 *International and Comparative Law Quarterly* 747.
10. The Spasskii copper melting plant was the second largest in Tsarist Russia before the First World War.

11. Sarsembayey, *Pravovoye Regulirovariye*, 21–2.
12. O. Freund, 'Economic Organization, Commercial Regulations and Concessions in the Soviet Union' (1928) 22 *Illinois Law Review* 852, 878.
13. Concessions were briefly introduced in the Kazakh legislation on FDI in the late Soviet–early post-independence period. The Law on Concessions was passed in 1990. However, the main driving force behind this law was political, namely the assertive policy of the Kazakh government which sought to manifest and strengthen its independence from Moscow. The language of the law, which included only 22 articles, was rather vague and it did not have any meaningful impact on the Kazakh economy. Nevertheless, this law gave a strong signal, domestically and internationally, that the Kazakh government, although still subordinated to Moscow at that time, intended to take control over its natural resources and to become a legitimate negotiator with foreign investors. This was especially important in context of the negotiations conducted at that time between the USSR government and Chevron to explore the vast Tengiz and Korolevsoye oilfields discovered in Kazakhstan. In 1993, the 1990 Law on Concessions was rescinded. This occurred mainly because of the further sophistication, marketization and de-ideologization of the Kazakh legislation. This trend, conceived during the Gorbachev period of liberalization, was further reinforced by the collapse of the Soviet Union and the gained independence.
14. *Sobranie Postanovlenii Pravitel'stva SSSR*, 1987, otd. 1, No. 9, st. 40.
15. Ibid.
16. However, this decree did not (although it should have done so) include a precise procedure of registration of 100 per cent foreign-owned enterprises. Thus, it was rather an ambiguous document. Nevertheless, in terms of the general evolution of investment legislation, what is important is that the possibility of the establishment of a 100 per cent foreign-owned enterprise was formally recognized. Later, the Resolution of the Council of Ministers of the USSR provided a detailed procedure for the establishment of such enterprises.
17. *Vedomosti S'yezda Narodnyh Deputatov i Verhovnogo Soveta SSSR*, 1991, No. 29, st. 1008.
18. According to the legal practice existing at that time the republican legislatures were required to pass more detailed law on their territory, which could not contradict the federal legislation.
19. For useful discussion, see M.L. Braginskii, W.E. Butler and A.A. Rubanov, *Foreign Investment Legislation in the Republics of the Former Soviet Union* (1993).
20. For more detailed description of the federal legislation on foreign investment see C. Osakwe, Navigating the Minefields of Russian Joint-Venture and Tax Regulations: Procedural Compass' (1993) 25 *Vanderbilt Journal of Transnational Law* 799. D.F. Black, 'So You Want to Invest in Russia? A Legislative Analysis of the Foreign Investment Climate in Russia' (1996) 5 *Minnesota Journal of Global Trade* 123.
21. *Vedomosti Verhovnogo Soveta Kazahskoi SSR*, 1990, No. 50, st. 474.
22. *Vedomosti Verhovnogo Soveta Kazahskoi SSR*, 1990, No. 1, st. 3.
23. *Vedomosti Verhovnogo Soveta Kazahskoi SSR*, 1990, No. 49, st. 455.
24. *Vedomosti Verhovnogo Soveta Kazahskoi SSR*, 1992, No. 52, st. 640.

25. *Vedomosti Verhovnogo Soveta Kazahskoi SSR*, 1990, No. 51, st. 483.
26. *Vedomosti Verhovnogo Soveta Kazahskoi SSR*, 1991, No. 8, st. 96.
27. *Vedomosti Verhovnogo Soveta Kazahskoi SSR*, 1991, No. 24, st. 283.
28. *Vedomosti Verhovnogo Soveta Kazahskoi SSR*, 1990, No. 10, st. 87.
29. *Vedomosti Verhovnogo Soveta Kazahskoi SSR*, 1990, No. 47, st. 429.
30. *Vedomosti Verhovnogo Soveta Kazahskoi SSR*, 1991, No. 25, st. 310.
31. *Vedomosti Verhovnogo Soveta Kazahskoi SSR*, 1991, No. 24, st. 287.
32. *Vedomosti Verhovnogo Soveta Kazahskoi SSR*, 1990, No. 50, st. 475.
33. A. Brown, *The Gorbachev Factor* (1996) 22.
34. For example, the Law of the USSR 'On the Fundamentals of the Civil Legislation of the USSR' was enacted in early 1991. Nevertheless, its provisions were applied after the dissolution of the USSR up to the enactment of the Civil Codes in the former Soviet republics.
35. G. Ajani, 'By Chance and Prestige: Legal Transplants in Russia and Eastern Europe' (1995) 43 *American Journal of Comparative Law* 93, 95; C.M. Lawson 'The Family Affinities of Common-Law and Civil-Law Systems' (1982) 6 (1) *Hastings International & Comparative Law Review* 85; H.J. Berman, *Law and Revolution: the Formation of the Western Legal Tradition* (1983); W. Wigand, 'The Reception of American Law in Europe' (1991) 39 *American Journal of Comparative Law* 229, 236.
36. Ajani, 'By Chance and Prestige', 96.
37. N.A. Nazarbayev, *Kazakhstan-2030. Message of the President of the Country to the People of Kazakhstan* (1997) 212.
38. T.W. Waelde and J.L. Gunderson, 'Legislative Reform in Transition Economies: Western Transplants – Short-Cut to Social Market Economy Status?' (1994) 43 *The International and Comparative Law Quarterly* 347, 360.
39. Hungary introduced Decree No. 28 'On Economic Associations with Foreign Participation' in 1972. This decree was later amended by Decree No. 7 of 1977, Decree No. 35 of 1978, Decree No. 63 of 1982, and Order No. 35 of 1979 of the Hungarian Ministry of Finance. In Poland, in 1970, wholly foreign-owned enterprises were allowed in light industries: crafts, catering, domestic trade, hospitality. In 1982, the Polish Parliament passed the Law 'On Principles of Carrying on Economic Activity in Small Industry in the Territory of the People's Republic of Poland by Foreign Juridical and Natural Persons'. Later, in 1986, more liberal legislation was passed, in particular, the Law on Companies with Foreign Participation. However, participation of foreign capital in Eastern European socialist economies was limited and controlled by the state until the late 1980s. See C.L. Jadach, 'Ownership and Investment in Poland' (1985) 18 *Cornell International Law Journal* 63; K. Malfriet, 'The Hungarian Quest for a Valid Theory of "Socialist" Property: Still a Long Way to Go' (1987) 13 *Review of Socialist Law* 241; D. Gordon, 'The Polish Foreign Investment Law of 1990' (1990) 24 *International Lawyer* 335.
40. This statement is true for the oil and minerals sector of Kazakhstan's economy, from where the vast majority of foreign investment inflows has come during the first years of independence.
41. 1994 was probably one of the most active years for negotiations with major and independent oil companies. Furthermore, the consortium 'Kazakhstancaspishelf', which includes seven major oil companies, also

played an increasingly active lobbying role in expediting the drafting work. Another fact is that in December 1994 the Presentation of the Mineral Complex of Kazakhstan was scheduled to be held in Houston. This event, too, put a significant pressure on a drafting committee, for the newly appointed, two-month-old government wished to report a breakthrough in a legislative field to the international oil community to show that it was more responsive than the previous government to the criticisms of the business community and to demonstrate its commitment to the expansion of foreign participation in mineral exploration and production. CEELI ABA (Central and Eastern European Legal Initiative programme of the American Bar Association) and UNDP (United Nations Development Programme) provided substantial inputs to the drafting activities by sending highly qualified (in the Anglo-American way) scholars who convinced the drafting committee to choose the Anglo-American design for petroleum regulation.

42. See The Law of the Republic of Kazakhstan 'On Normative Acts', *Kazahstanskaya Pravda*, 28 March 1998.
43. It should be also noted that there is a special procedure to make amendments to the Civil Code, which is different from that provided for other laws.
44. M. Herbiet, 'The Constitutional Basis of the Economic Order During a Period of Transition From a Planned to a Market Economy' in *Rule of Law and Transition to a Market Economy* (1993) 19.
45. D.C. North, 'Privatization, Incentives, and Economic Performance' in H. Siebert (ed.), *Privatization* (1992).
46. The Constitution of 1977 acted indirectly but through the subconstitutional laws and regulations, that are passed by the Supreme Council, Council of Ministers and ministries.
47. See *Rossiiskaya Gazeta*, 8 December 1994.
48. B. Rudden, 'Civil Law, Civil Society, and the Russian Constitution' (1994) 110 *The Law Quarterly Review* 56, 61.
49. O.S. Ioffe, *Development of Civil Law Thinking in the USSR* (1989).
50. Referred to in the Kazakh legislation as 'juridical persons'.
51. In the Kazakh legislation, the organizational form of entity includes joint-stock company, limited liability company, full partnership, etc.
52. An implied formula of the previous Civil Code was that 'someone is allowed to do something which is explicitly specified in and allowed by law'.
53. *U.S. Uniform Commercial Code* paragraph 1–201 (19) (1990).
54. B. Rudden, 'Civil Law, Civil Society, and the Russian Constitution' (1994) 110 *The Law Quarterly Review* 56, 64.
55. Yet, from the legal point of view one may believe that that approach was incorrect, inasmuch as the ownership right is always one irrespective of who holds it, and the regime of property also has to be the same irrespective of who owns it.
56. Justice Brandeis in *Myers* v. *US* (1926) says: 'The doctrine of the separation of powers was adopted by the Convention of 1787, not to promote efficiency but to preclude the exercise of arbitrary power. The purpose was, not to avoid friction, but, by means of the inevitable friction incident to the distribution of the governmental powers among three departments, to save the

people from autocracy'. See *Meyers* v. *US* 272 US 52, 475 S Ct. 21 (1926) [a Supreme Court case]. For discussion, see L. Tribe, *American Constitutional Law*, 2nd edn (1988).

57. This philosophy, that the Constitution recognizes values based on protection of the citizenry from government action above values of efficiency, has been reiterated in American jurisprudence by the US, Supreme Court. In *Stanley* v. *Illinois* (1972), the Court stated: 'The establishment of prompt efficacious procedures to achieve legitimate state ends is a proper state interest worthy of cognisence in constitutional ajudication. But the constitution recognizes higher values than speed and efficiency. Indeed, one might fairly say of the Bill of Rights in general, and the Due Process Clause in particular, that they were designed to protect the fragile values of a vulnerable citizenry from the overbearing concern for efficiency and efficacy that may characterize praiseworthy government officials no less, and perhaps more, than mediocre ones'. See *Stanley* v. *Illinois* 405 US 645, 92 S. Ct. 1208 (1972) [a Supreme Court case].
58. See, for example, W. Fischel, *Regulatory Takings: Law, Economics, and Politics* (1995).

4 Types and Choice of the Model of Legal Regulation of FDI

1. C.W. Gray and W.J. Jarosz, 'Law and the Regulation of Foreign Direct Investment: the Experience from Central and Eastern Europe' 33 (1) *Columbia Journal of Transnational Law* 3, 18.
2. T.W. Waelde, 'Book Review. Kazakhstan: Investment Opportunities in the Energy Sector. By Paul Thomas. London: Financial Times Energy Publishing. 1995' (1995) 13 (4) *Journal of Energy and Natural Resources Law* 352.
3. W.G. Frenkel and M.Y. Sukhman, 'New Foreign Investment Regimes of Russia and Other Republics of the Former USSR: a Legislative Analysis and Historical Perspective' (1993) 16 *Boston College International and Comparative Law Review* 321, 422–3.
4. As of mid-1997, 18 draft bilateral treaties were in the process of negotiation. For discussion of Kazakhstan's bilateral investment treaties, see G.S. Sattarova, 'Mezhdunarodno-Pravovoye Regulirovanie Inostrannyh Investitsii (Na Primere Dvustoronnih Soglashenii Respubliki Kazahstan o Pooshrenii i Zashite Investitsii' in *Aktual'nye Voprosy Kommercheskogo Zakonodatel'stva Respubliki Kazahstan i Praktika Ego primeneniya* (1996), 135–50.
5. Sornarajah points out: 'The satisfaction of nationalistic lobbies resenting the increasing control of the economy by foreign states, the perception that some types of investment are deleterious to the interests of the state, the fear that national companies may not be able to withstand competition from an incoming foreign company which may have superior technology and other resources are reasons for developed states seeking to control the influx of foreign investment'. See M. Sornarajah, *International Law on Foreign Investment* (1996) 88.
6. Ibid., 87.

7. See G. Rodan, *The Political Economy of Singapore's Industrialization* (1989).
8. Blomstrom and Persson provide the following definition for the 'spill-over effect': 'Foreign investment can give rise to indirect gains for the host economy through the realization of external economies. Generally these benefits are referred to as "spillover" effects. This indicates the importance of the way in which the influence is transmitted'. See M. Blomstrom and H. Persson, 'Foreign Investment and Spillover Efficiency in an Underdeveloped Economy: Evidence from Mexican Manufacturing Industry' (1983) 11 (6) *World Development* 493.
9. Bond and Samuelson note: 'Once a firm builds a plant in a foreign country, the plant becomes a potential hostage to the host country government.' See E.W. Bond and L. Samuelson, 'Bargaining with Commitment, Choice of Techniques, and Direct Foreign Investment' (1989) 26 *Journal of International Economics* 77.
10. The bilateral treaties for the promotion and protection of investments (BITs) considered to be a most effective tool of international public law protection of FDI, began to appear on the scene in the late 1950s, first as an instrument of West German development policy and soon to be copied by other European countries. During the first 25 years, until the mid-1980s, the number of BITs increased gradually to about 250; then the annual growth rate became rapid with the result that by mid-1995 the number of treaties had risen to some 820. During the 1970s, most developing countries were opposed to investment protection by treaty. Latin American states stuck to the Calvo doctrine which was considered to prohibit international regulation of investment and international arbitration of investment disputes as laid down in BITs. Most other developing countries drew similar conclusions from the Charter of Economic Rights and Duties of States (CERDS) which had been adopted in 1974 by the General Assembly of the UN, with support from all the developing countries. Communist countries were also opposed on doctrinal grounds, with the sole exception of Romania, which started concluding BITs as early as 1976. All these objections dwindled away during the 1980s and there are now very few countries left which abstain. Most of the European Communist countries started concluding BITs several years before the regime came to an end. The break-up of the USSR has significantly contributed to the increase in the number of BITs. This shows the extent to which international investment protection and arbitration is now generally accepted and confirms that the extreme doctrines on permanent sovereignty, as interpreted in CERDS, have given way to more pragmatic views. Thus, the growth of BITs indeed reflects the near consensus gradually achieved among non-industrialized states that BITs are a useful tool in the competition for scarce investment capital. Equally, this rapid growth indicates the increasing desire for FDI in the non-industrialized world.

    Various types of clauses can be found in BITs, in particular, regarding treatment of investments by the host country, the investor's right to repatriate capital and profit, the rules applicable to expropriation, settlement of disputes, subrogation of an insurer to the rights of the investor, and a host of other subjects. In short, BITs constitute an important part of the host country's overall investment image in its relationship with prospective foreign investors. This is because by entering into BIT a host state voluntarily sets up a legal basis, namely one in the domain of international public law, which provides a foreign investor with an additional mechanism of protection for his investment. Furthermore, the fact that a host state is willing to enter into a BIT relationship clearly indicates an economic rationale behind a host state government's desire to enter into a BIT. This means that the actual source of effectiveness of any BIT is rooted here, that is, in the degree of willingness of a host state itself to seek FDI and for this purpose to adhere to international standards. This also means that such an adherence is dependent upon changes in domestic policy towards BITs. Furthermore, account should be taken of the fact that the whole notion of BIT emerged as a tool to offset the negative consequences of a potential conflict between a host state and a foreign investor. Thus, a BIT is a legal arrangement designed as a response to the expectations of a potential conflict. Accordingly, if viewed as a part of an international level of the two-level system of FDI regulation (domestic and international), BIT undoubtedly plays a significant, though at the same time auxiliary, role in treatment of FDI.

For the purpose of this study, which deals with the domestic and normal, rather than conflictual, aspects of FDI relationships it should be admitted that BITs undoubtedly play an important role in filling the gaps in the cases when a national level of legal regulation lacks sufficient mechanisms for protection or promotion of FDI. More importantly, they indirectly contribute to the consistency of national legislation in the sense that they impose certain pressures on the newly elected governments to comply with international commitments (say, to adhere to a certain model of regulation) made by the previous government. This, in turn, means that BITs may well play a facilitating, although again not a driving, role in implementation of certain model of legal regulation. For more detailed discussion on multilateral agreements and BITs, see R. Dolzer and M. Stevens, *Bilateral Investment Treaties* (1995) and for discussion on the Kazakh BITs, see G.S. Sattarova, 'Mezhdunarodno-Pravovoye Regulirovanie Investitsii (Na Primere Dvustoronnih Soglashenii Respubliki Kazahstan o Pooshrenii i Zashite Investitsii)' in *Aktual'nye Voprosy Kommercheskogo Zakonodatel'stva Respubliki Kazahstan i Praktika Ego Primeneniva* (1996) 135–50; T.L. Brewer and S. Yound, 'Towards a Multilateral Framework for Foreign Direct Investment: Issues and Scenarios' (1995) 4 (1) *Transnational Corporations* 69 J.W. Messing, 'Towards a Multilateral Agreement on Investment' (1997) 6 (1) *Transnational Corporations* 123; A.R. Parra, 'The Scope of New Investment Laws and International Instruments' (1995) 4 (3) *Transnational Corporations* 27; A. Stockmayer, 'Bilateral Investment Promotion Protection and Treaties: A Model for Community Promotion of Mining Investment' (1986) 4 (4) *Journal of Energy and Natural Resources Law* 247; M.R. Reading, 'The Bilateral Investment Treaties in ASEAN: a Comparative Analysis' (1992) 42 *Duke Law Journal* 679; G.D. Aldonas, 'Multilateral Investment Agreements' (1997) 31 *International Lawyer* 447; J.S. Siqueiros, 'Bilateral Treaties on the Reciprocal Protection of Foreign Investment (1994) 24 *California Western International Law Journal* 255.

11. See D. Gross and A. Steinherr, *Winds of Change: Economic Transition in Central and Eastern Europe* (1995); W. Easterly and S. Fischer, 'Growth Prospects for the ex-Soviet Republics: Lessons from Soviet Historical Experience' in A. Aganbegyan, O. Bogomolov and M. Kaser (eds), *Economics in a Changing World. Vol 1. System Transformation: Eastern and Western Assessments* (1994); M. Ellmann and V. Kantorovich, *The Destruction of the Soviet Economic System: An Insider's History* (1998).
12. See *TSSU (Goskomstat)* (1988) 298.
13. See *Materialy XXYII Siezda KPSS* (1987).
14. *Pravda*, 28 March 1986, 2.
15. A Pyatkin, 'Inostrannye Investitsii – Rezerv Economicheskogo Razvitiya' (1992) 4 *Rossiiskii Economicheskii Zhurnal* 10, 14.
16. See *OECD Transition Economics: Short Term Economic Indicators* 3/1994.
17. Professor Pyatkin says in his article: 'Because of backward technologies in the agro-industrial sphere of the economy millions of tonnes of meat never reach a consumer annually, near half of a milk protein is left unutilized, 30–40 per cent of vegetables and fruits are lost'. See Pyatkin, 'In ostrannye Investitsii', 15.
18. R. Pomfret, *The Economies of Central Asia* (1995) 168.
19. *FAO Production Yearbook 1988* (1989) 70–76.
20. Pomfret, *Economies of Central Asia*, 136.
21. See J. Humphrey and H. Schmitz, 'Trust and Inter-Firm Relations in Developing and Transition Economies' (1988) 34 (4) *The Journal of Development Studies* 32.
22. R. Jungnickel, *Foreign Direct Investment: Recent Trends in a Changing World* (1993) 4.
23. See *UNCTAD World Investment Report* (1998).
24. 'Kazakhstan Receives Over 1 Billion Dollars in Foreign Investment', *BBC Monitoring, Summary of World Broadcasts, Part I, Former USSR*, 21 April 1998.
25. R. Ballance, I. Ansar and H. Singer, *The International Economy and Industrial Development: the Impact of Trade and Investment on the Third World* (1991) 33.
26. Ibid., 33.
27. The founder of the Soviet state, Vladimir Lenin, realized the importance of private initiative in industrialization of the country. He therefore initiated the New Economic Policy (NEP) which encouraged private entrepreneurship and 'worker–peasant' alliance. However, after he fell ill in 1922, the dominant centre faction in the ruling Bolshevik Party cancelled the NEP course, mainly because of fears that the growing private sector could make an alliance with external forces and destroy the Soviet power.
28. As of January 1999, the total amount of FDI in Kazakhstan was equal to approximately US$6 billion, of which approximately 75 per cent was in extracting industries (see *Statisticheskoye Obozrenie Kazahstana*, No. 1, 1999). In particular, the Caspian Pipeline Consortium, which includes Chevron and Mobil of the United States, Lukoil and Rosneft of Russia, British Gas of Britain, Agip of Italy and the government of Oman as well as the Kazakh state company, Kazakhoil, signed a US$2 billion agreement to build the 1500-kilometre link between the huge Tengiz oilfield in Western Kazakhstan and the Russian port Novorossiisk on the Black Sea in 1997, but delays over the shareholding and transit rights have delayed the start of construction.

This was expected to begin in late 1999 (See 'Pipelines: Getting the Goods to Market', *International Herald Tribune*, 3 June 1998). Under the terms of a production-sharing agreement signed in 1998 with the Kazakh government, an international consortium consisting of Texaco, British Gas, Agip and Lukoil will have the rights to develop the Karachaganak reservoir of gas in the Aktyubinsk region, which comprises two-fifth of the country's total gas reserves of 2 trillion cubic metres (see 'Natural Gas: Maximum Potential', *International Herald Tribune*, 3 June 1998). A number of major enterprises were given under management contracts to foreign companies. In particular, Zhezkazgantsvetmet, a major copper producer, was transferred to the management of the South Korean company Samsung. Later, Samsung bought out 40 per cent of shares. An expected volume of investment by Samsung in Zhezkazgantsvetmet is an estimated US$350 million (see 'K Kontsu 1997 Goda AO "Zhezkazgantsvetmet" Planireut Nachat' Pasplachivat'sya po Svoim Dolgam', *Panorama*, No. 34, September 1997). Central Asia Petroleum Ltd, a unit of the Indonesian conglomerate Setdco, has bought a 60 per cent stake in Kazakhstan's largest oil company, Mangistaumunaigaz, for US$4.35 billion and paid a US$248 million bonus to the government (see 'Kazakhstan Sells 60 per cent of Largest Oil Firm', *International Herald Tribune*, 13 May 1997). The western and southern gas-distribution systems of Kazakhstan were transferred under the management of the Belgian utility group Tractebel which promised to invest US$600 million in total and to pay a bonus of US$130 million as well as royalties. According to the contract, the Kazakh government is to receive 40 per cent of the expected net profits; this rate to be reconsidered every five years (see 'Teper' Bel'giitsy Zaimutsya i Gazom', *Delovaya Nedelya* No. 23, June 1997). In April 1997, the Kazakh company managing the national electricity network was transferred to the Anglo-Swedish-Swiss company 'ABB Power Grid' for a period of 25 years. According to the contract, ABB Power Grid paid a bonus of US$20 million. The expected profit to be shared between the Kazakh government and 'ABB Power Grid' is at a ratio of 85/15 per cent respectively. ABB Power Grid guaranteed to invest between US$900 and US$1400 million in total (see 'Kazahstanskie Elektricheskie Seti Peredany v Kontsessiyu na 25 let Konsortsiumu 'ABB Power Grid', *Panorama*, No. 16, April 1997). According to Kazakh media reports, Japan Chrome Corporation, which acquired a 55.2 per cent stake in the state concern, Kazchrom, in August 1996, invested US$407 million in the chromium industry of Kazakhstan. Britain's White Swan has invested more than US$540 million in aluminum oxide production since 1995, mainly through Kazakhstanskii Aluminium, one of the country's eight largest companies, in which it has a shareholding of just under 56.6 per cent. In December 1997 the London-stock -exchange-registered company Bakyrchik and the Toronto-registered Indochina Goldfields became co-owners of the Bakyrchik gold reserves, one of the largest underdeveloped mines in the world. Santa Fe Pacific Gold, a subsidiary of Newmont Mining of the United States, raised its shareholding in the Sharaltyn gold exploration project in northeastern Kazakhstan from 50 per cent to 100 per cent. One of the biggest success stories so far is undoubtedly the Ispat-Karmet works, a former Soviet complex in Temirtau, near Karaganda, which has a capacity of 6 million tons of liquid steel. Ispat

International, part of the London-based LNM Group, has managed to raise output from 2 million tons in 1995 to 3.8 million tons in 1997, following its purchase of the facility in November 1995. By the year 2000, the figure is forecast to raise to 4.5 million tons, according to company officials (see 'Na Minuvshei Nedele Upravlyayushie Firmy Osushestvili Moshnyi Propagandistskii Proryv, Prizvannyi Dezavuirovat' Dovody Skeptikov", *Panorama*, No. 11, March 1996; 'The Mining Sector: Back to Profit', *International Herald Tribune*, 3 June 1998).

29. C.L. Dahlman, *Impact of Technological Change on Industrial Prospects for the LDCs* (1989).
30. See, for example, P.J. O'Sullivan, 'An Assessment of Ireland's Export-Led Growth Strategy via Foreign Direct Investment, 1960–1980' (1993) 129 *Weltwirtschaftliches Archiv* 139; L.R. De Mello, 'Foreign Direct Investment in Developing Countries and Growth: a Selective Survey' (1997) 34 (1) *The Journal of Development Studies* 1.
31. As the practice of other late industrializations has shown, the labour-intensive subcontracting role available to the domestic manufacturers within the previous MNCs' simple integration strategies had proved to be a developmental ladder rather than a dead end. Gereffi noted in this regard, however, that the East Asian states, in moving beyond their roles as assembly subcontractors, relied on the development of indigenous supplier bases and technological capabilities. He says: 'In contrast to those who would argue that [export oriented industrialization] by itself can lead to sustained economic growth, the experiences of the East Asian newly industrializing countries actually shows that a diverse array of backward linkages is essential in moving toward a more complex component supply, OEM and OBM export roles. These countries have been successful in upgrading their export industries in large measure because of their highly efficient networks of suppliers for international goods ... In addition, these countries have developed a full range of local design, financial, transportation, and communication services that give them major advantages over other third world production sites'. See G. Gereffi, Global Production Systems and Third World Development' in B. Stallings (ed.), *Global Change, Regional Response* (1995) 100, 133.
32. See J.M. Stopford, 'The Growing Interdependence Between Transnational Corporations and Governments' (1994) 3 (1) *Transnational Corporations* 53; J.H. Dunning, 'The Global Economy, Domestic Governance, Strategies and Transnational Corporations: Interactions and Policy Implications' (1992) 1 (3) *Transnational Corporations* 7; P.W. Beamish, 'Joint Ventures in Less Developed Countries: Partner Selection and Performance' (1994) 2 *Management International Review* 60.
33. See P. Hirst and G. Thompson, *Globalization in Question: the International Economy and the Possibilities of Governance* (1996); R. Boyer and D. Drache (eds), *States Against Markets. the Limits of Globalization* (1996).

5 The Kazakh Model for the Legal Regulation of FDI

1. *Vedomosti Parlamenta Respubliki Kazahstan*, 1997, No. 4, st. 36.
2. This chapter deals with the legislation effective as at 1 April 1998.

3. *Vedomosti Verhovnogo Soveta Respubliki Kazahstan*, 1995, Nos. 9–10, st. 69.
4. *Constitution of the Republic of Kazakhstan* (1995).
5. *Vedomosti Verhovnogo Soveta Respubliki Kazahstan*, 1991, No. 52, st. 636.
6. *Vedomosti Verhovnogo Soveta Respubliki Kazahstan*, 1995, Nos. 9–10, st. 68.
7. *Vedomosti Verhovnogo Soveta Respubliki Kazahstan*, 1994, Nos. 23–4.
8. *Vedomosti Verhovnogo Soveta Respubliki Kazahstan*, 1995, No. 15, st. 109.
9. *Vedomosti Verhovnogo Soveta Respubliki Kazahstan*, 1995, Nos. 15–16, st. 106.
10. *Vedomosti Verhovnogo Soveta Respubliki Kazahstan*, 1995, No. 3, st. 37.
11. *Vedomosti Verhovnogo Soveta Respubliki Kazahstan*, 1995, No. 24, st. 159.
12. *Sbornik Aktov Prezidenta Respubliki Kazahstan i Pravitel'stva Respubliki Kazahstan*, 1993, No. 30, st. 3.
13. *Vedomosti Verhovnogo Soveta Respublii Kazahstan*, 1995, No. 11, st. 76.
14. *Informatsionnyi Bullenten' Ministerstva Finansov Respubliki Kazahstan*, 1995, No. 3.
15. *Vedomosti Verhovnogo Soveta Respubliki Kazahstan*, 1994, Nos 23–4.
16. *Informatsionnyi Bullenten' Ministerstva Finansov Respubliki Kazahstan*, 1996, No. 17, p. 218.
17. *Finansy Kazahstana*, 1996, No. 9, 64.
18. See 'Corruption Said to be Posing Threat to National Security', *BBC Monitoring, Summary of World Broadcasts, Part I, Former USSR*, 24 April 1998.
19. *Sbornik Aktov Prezidenta Respubliki Kazahstan i Pravitel'stva Respubliki Kazakhstan*, 1996, No. 34, st 321.
20. By contrast, the previous Decree of 8 August 1994 clearly separated mandatory and negotiable terms.
21. *Vedomosti Parlamenta Respubliki Kazahstan*, 1997, No. 4, st. 36.
22. Minutes of the Session of Mazhlis (Lower Chamber of Parliament) of 26 February 1997.
23. The law contains the whole chapter on the newly established (by the Law) State Committee on Investment. Interestingly, although according to the existing legislation the capacity of the ministries and the state committees are defined by the president, in this case the authorities of the Committee were established by the law. This was done to reinforce the importance of the Committee which was chaired by A. Yesimov – a relative of the president.
24. Item 7 of Article 3 of the Civil Code includes such a clause.
25. Article 2 of the 1997 Law on State Support of Direct Investment.
26. *Vedomosti Parlamenta Respubliki Kazahstan*, 1997, No. 17, st. 218.
27. For instance, the Edict of the President having the force of law 'On Licensing', which included unjustified limitations on the activities of foreign investors, was submitted to the president in the absence of the vice-president, who opposed the draft decree, but was then on an official trip to Japan. The document was submitted intentionally in the absence of the vice-president.
28. For example, the chief argument behind the division of foreign investors into two categories was that the state annually loses 17 billion tenge (approx. US$22 million) allowing foreign companies to import alcohol and tobacco products.
29. The 1997 Law on State Support of Direct Investment was not an unexpected legislative act. For instance, the Law on Special Economic Zones of 26 January 1996, unlike a similar law passed in 1990, excluded the direct

effect of its provisions. Accordingly, the majority of articles in the 1996 law referred to other regulatory acts, and left the implementation of procedures to the discretion of the executive.

6 The Legal Regulation of FDI in the Context of Legal Reforms

1. U. Mattei (1997) 'Three Patterns of Law: Taxonomy and Change in the World's Legal Systems' 45 *American Journal of Comparative Law* 5, 19.
2. W.G. Frenkel and M.Y. Sukhman, 'New Foreign Investment Regimes of Russia and Other Republics of the Former USSR: Legislative Analysis and Historical Perspective' (1993) 16 *Boston College International and Comparative Law Review* 321, 422–3.
3. C. Gray and K. Hendley, *Developing Commercial Law in Transition Economies: Examples from Hungary and Russia*. The World Bank Policy Research Working Paper No. 1528 (1995) 1. They emphasize that 'the state must withdraw from everyday control over most aspects of economic life, and the central economic controls associated with the state's central planning apparatus must be replaced by decentralized, objective rules of the game, i.e. the "rule of law". The patron–client networks and the resulting particularism that characterized economic relations under the state socialism have to give way to relationships based on universalistic rules'.
4. Ibid., 8. They stress that market-oriented laws, institutions and market-oriented incentives are essential components for a functional commercial law in the post-Communist transitional countries. They say, for example, that banks and other creditors may not avail themselves of the rights provided under bankruptcy laws unless they are convinced that state bail-outs are not likely to be available and thus that aggressive debt collection is necessary for survival. Similarly, managers in private firms may be tempted to ignore shareholder protections and other checks and balances laid out under corporate law unless their access to inputs and their ability to sell products and raise capital depends on a law-abiding reputation. If they can raise capital by turning to the government or state banking system for subsidies, or if they have a monopoly position in the market (either as output seller or as input purchaser), why worry about reputation in private markets?
5. K. Boyle, T. Hadden and P. Hillyard, *Law and State: the Case of Northern Ireland* (1975) 1. They say that 'in settled times this fact may become obscured. The apparent independence of the legal system from current political disputes lends support to the myth that law is something above and apart from the society which it helps to regulate and control. An alternative view is that law is nothing but an instrument of domination in the hands of the property owners or the political elite. This is equally unsatisfactory. Adherence to either view serves only to obscure the kernel of truth which lies behind them both, that a legal system is the determining factor and the power structure remains very much in the background. In times of political and social disruption value systems recede into the background and the reality of political, economic and military power is likely to prevail'.

6. R.B. Siedman, *The State, Law and Development* (1978) 15–16.
7. H.V. Morais, 'Emerging Legal Strategies of Host States to Attract Foreign Investment' in *Current Developments in International Investment Law* (1996) 247–59.
8. F.A. Hoebel, *The Law of Primitive Man: a Study of Comparative Legal Dynamics* (1954) 292. G. Sawer also says: 'The material content of a legal system has always been to reflect in some sense the needs or demands of societies'. See G. Sawer, *Law in Society* (1965) 147.
9. M.D. Holmes (ed.), *The Common Law* (1963) 5.
10. L.M. Friedman, *American Law: an Introduction* (1984) 6.
11. The first and most prominent proponents of this approach were Sir Henry Maine, Durkheim, and Roscoe Pound.
12. See, for example, D.M. Trubek, *Law and Development: the Future of Law and Development Research* (1974) D.M. Trubek and M. Galanter, 'Scholars in Self-Estrangement: Some Reflections on the Crisis of Law and Development Studies in the United States' (1974) 4 *Wisconsin Law Review* 1062; D.M. Trubek, 'Toward a Social Theory of Law: an Essay on the Study of Law and Development' (1972) 82 (1) *Yale Law Journal* 1.
13. P. Nonet and P. Selznick, *Law and Society in Transition: Toward Responsive Law* (1978).
14. See P.H. Rubin (1977) 'Why is the Common Law Efficient?' 6 *Journal of Legal Studies* 51; G.L. Priest, 'The Common Law Process and the Selection of Efficient Rules' (1977) 6 (1) *Journal of Legal Studies* 65; E.D. Elliot, 'The Evolutionary Tradition in Jurisprudence' (1985) 85 *Columbia Law Review* 38; D.C. North and R.P. Thomas, 'An Economic Theory of the Growth of the Western World' (1970) 23 *Economic History Review* 1.
15. R.C. Clark, 'The Interdisciplinary Study of Legal Evolution' (1981) 90 *Yale Law Journal* 1238.
16. They considered the law as a manifestation of the will of the state and as a tool of the latter. Lenin wrote: 'Laws are political measures'. Samuel Jawitsch, a well-known Soviet professor of Theory of Law, stated: 'Laws and statutes most clearly express the will of the ruling class'. In S.L. Jawitsch, *The General Theory of Law* (1981) 43.
17. L.M. Friedman, *The Legal System: a Social Science Perspective* (1975) 270. He identifies these four types in the following terms:
    1. Change originating outside the legal system, that is, in society, but affecting only the legal system and ending there like a spent bullet.
    2. Change originating outside the legal system but moving through it with or without some internal processing) to a point of impact outside the legal system, that is, in society.
    3. Change that begins inside the legal system and which also spends whatever impact it might have inside the legal system.
    4. Change originating inside the legal system, then moving through the system and ending with its impact outside in society.
18. S. Vago, *Law and Society*, 3rd edn (1997) 216.
19. A. Podgorecki, *Law and Society* (1974) 225. More precisely, Podgorecki says: 'An abstract legal precept begins to function (and to be expressed in social behaviour) when it reaches its interpreter in the form of a complex conjunction. The constituent parts of such a conjunction are: the precept itself

and three meta-norms: the first derives from the character of the social and economic system, the second takes its content from the definite sub-culture and the third follows from the personality of the individual who makes the decision to behave lawfully'.

20. See W.M. Evan (ed.), *The Sociology of Law: a Social-Structural Perspective* (1980) 554–62; A. Allot, *The Limits of Law* (1980).
21. Podgorecki, *Law and Society*, 248.
22. T.C. Halliday and B.G. Carruthers, *The State, Professions, and Legal Change: Reform of the English Insolvency Act, 1977–1986*. American Bar Foundation Working Paper No. 9019 (1990). Some scholars concentrate on political bargaining to explain the nature and effects of legal change. See, for example, J.F. Handler, *Social Movements and the Legal System: a Theory of Law Reform and Social Change* (1978); E. Bardach, *The Implementation Game: What Happens After a Bill Becomes a Law* (1977); R.T. Nimmer, *The Nature of System Change: Reform Impact in the Criminal Courts* (1978).
23. S.A. Velkei, 'An Emerging Framework for Greater Foreign Participation in the Economies of Hungary and Poland' (1992) 15 *Hastings International and Comparative Law Review* 695, 696.
24. See R.B. Schlesinger, H. Baade, M. Damaska and P. Herzog, *Comparative Law: Cases, Text Materials* (Mineola, NY: Foundation Press, 1988) 78.
25. U. Mattei, 'Three Patterns of Law' 5, 17.
26. T.W. Waelde and J.L. Gunderson, 'Legislative Reform in Transition Economies: Western Transplants – Short-Cut to Social Market Economy Status?' (1994) 43 *The International and Comparative Law Quarterly* 347, 355.
27. Mattei identifies the common problems inherent to the countries with the political rule of law: limited control of state institutions by the society, weak courts, a high level of instability of existing democratic structures, if any; a high level of political involvement in the activity of the judiciary; high levels of police coercion; drastic governmental economic regulatory and deregulatory intervention; continuous attempts at major legal reform; a legal culture heavily influenced by foreign models and usually marginalized by the political power; a scarcity of legal literature; limited distribution of judicial opinions; scarcity of legally trained personnel; and a highly bureaucratized public decision-making process.
28. Podgorecki, *Law and Society* 80.
29. B. Rudden, 'Civil Law, Civil Society, and the Russian Constitution' (1994) 110 *The Law Quarterly Review* 56, 68.
30. See Table 6.1.
31. *Kazakhstan Survey* (1996) 4.
32. Ibid.
33. See A. Watson, *Sources of Law, Legal Change, and Ambiguity* (1985).
34. U. Mattei, 'Why the Wind Changed: Intellectual Leadership in Western Law' (1994) 42 *American Journal of Comparative Law* 195, 205.
35. Executive branch of power, too, tends to strengthen controls over the judiciary and the legal profession. For instance, the Regulation on the Ministry of Justice stipulates that the Ministry of Justice is in charge of personnel recruitment for courts as well as being a material supporter of the court system. This clause makes the whole judiciary system materially and financially dependent upon the executive branch. Similarly, the Ministry of

Justice exercises de facto controlling functions over the local bars. The 1995 Constitution has reinforced this dependence by establishing, under the chairmanship of the president, the Supreme Qualification Council, which is the screening institution before the final appointment of the judges of the Supreme Court and the regional courts.

36. A. Watson, *Society and Legal Change* (1977) 6.
37. Waelde and Gunderson, commenting on the central thesis of Watson, note: 'his strong urge to disprove the thesis that specific legal rules are intimately and inextricably linked to a society's social, political and cultural fabric by indicating numerous instances where legal rules have been transplanted to quite different societies makes him, however, focus on "technical rules" – the dogmatic core of lawyers' law, and not the part of legislation which is very much linked to a society's fabric, such as economic policies, economic regulation, competition law. Traditional contract law – Watson's main playground – needs intricate specific rules to settle cases, ... but it has little interest in social outcomes. It is for this reason that traditional contract law may survive, very much with a Roman law core, in all kind of different societies'. See T.W. Waelde and J.L. Gunderson, 'Legislative Reform in Transition Economies: Western Transplants – Short-Cut to Social Market Economy Status?' (1994) 43 *The International and Comparative Law Quarterly* 347, 369.
38. O. Kahn-Freund, 'On Uses and Misuses of Comparative Law' (1972) 37 *Modern Law Review* 1, 12–13.
39. P. Fitzpatrick, *Law and State in Papua New Guinea* (1980) chapters 1 and 2.
40. R. Pomfret, *The Economies of Central Asia* (1995) 134.
41. M.K. Kozybayev (ed.), *The Text-Book on the History of Kazakstan from Ancient Times until the Present* (1992) 144.
42. See Fitzpatrick, *Law and State.*
43. P.T. Muchlinski, '"Basic-Needs" Theory and "Development Law"' in F. Snyder and P. Slinn (eds), *International Law of Development: Comparative Perspectives* (1987) 237–70.
44. 'More Than Half Kazakh Population Live Below Poverty Line', *BBC Monitoring, Summary of World Broadcasts, Part 1, Former USSR*, 20 February 1998.
45. 'Workers Building New Capital Held Protest', *BBC Monitoring, Summary of World Broadcasts, Part I, Former USSR,* 15 January 1998; 'Kazakh Chemical Plant Workers on Strike Over Wages Arrears in Southern Town', Ibid., 19 January 1998; 'Striking Miners to Write to President Nazarbayev', ibid., 22 January 1998; 'Wage Arrears Protesters Block Rail Traffic in Southern Kazakhstan', ibid., 20 February 1998; 'Trade Unions Call for Direct Presidential Rule in the South', ibid., 24 February 1998; 'Opposition Parties Join Forces Against Leadership', ibid., 3 March 1998.
46. 'Opposition Leader Sentenced for Insulting President, ibid., 9 April 1998.
47. It is no coincidence that the president postponed the privatization of oil and gas industry and thus has maintained the state monopoly of the most attractive for FDI sector of the Kazakh economy. See 'President Nazarbayev suspends oil and gas privatization for decades', ibid., 21 April 1998.
48. U. Mattei, 'Three Patterns of Law' 5, 31.

7 The State as a Regulator of FDI

1. B.R. Cheffins, *Company Law: Theory, Structure and Operation* (1997) 213.
2. See J.J.A. Burke, 'The Economic Basis of Law as Demonstrated by the Reformation of NIS Legal Systems' (1996) 18 *Loyola of Los Angeles International and Comparative Law Journal* 207.
3. Barkey defines: 'The state can be said to be autonomous when it acts in opposition to the stated interests of the dominant classes.' See H.J. Barkey, 'State Autonomy and the Crisis of Import Substitution' (1989) 22 (3) *Comparative Political Studies* 293, 296; Hamilton, in turn, defines three distinct manifestations of this autonomy: (i) when the state pursues specific 'state ends'; (ii) when the state acts independently of dominant class interference; and (iii) when the state 'for ends opposed to the actual or perceived interests of the dominant class' See N. Hamilton, *The Limits of State Autonomy: Post-Revolutionary Mexico* (1982) 12.
4. Y. Chu, 'State Structure and Economic Adjustment of the East Asian Newly Industrializing Countries' (1989) 43 (4) *International Organization* 647, 657.
5. See P. Katzenstein, *Between Power and Plenty: Foreign Economic Policies of Advanced Industrial States* (1978); P. Katzenstein, *Small States in World Markets: Industrial Policy in Europe* (1985).
6. D. Okimoto, *Between MITI and the Market* (1989) 18.
7. K. Fields, 'Strong States and Business Organizations in Korea and Taiwan' in S. Maxfield and B. Schneider (eds), *Business and the State in Developing Countries* (1997) 131–51.
8. P.B. Evans, *Embedded Autonomy: States and Industrial Transformation* (1995).
9. See A. Amsden, 'A Theory of Government Intervention in Late Industrialization' in L. Putterman and D. Rueschhemeyer (eds), *State and the Market in Development: Synergy or Rivalry?* (1992); E. Keep and K. Mayhew, 'Towards a Learning Society – Definition and Measurement' (1996) 17 (3) *Policy Studies* 215.
10. T.W. Waelde and J.L. Gunderson, 'Legislative Reform in Transition Economies: Western Transplants – A Short-Cut to Social Market Economy Status?' (1994) 43 *The International and Comparative Law Quarterly* 347, 377.
11. L.M. Friedman, *The Legal System: a Social Science Perspective* (1975) 149.
12. Ibid., 155.
13. Sawer defines 'interests' as 'a claim actually advanced by defined individuals or groups, and considered and dealt with by defined law-makers and courts'. See G. Sawer, *Law in Society* (1965) 150.
14. Ibid., 150.
15. See J.M. Black, *Rules and Regulators* (1997).
16. A. Lijphart, *Democracies: Patterns of Majoritarian and Consensus Government in Twenty-One Countries* (1984).
17. The Law on Elections of 1995, while proclaiming the conventional freedoms of universal, equal and direct electoral right, at the same time limits the passive electoral rights of citizens in the election of MPs. In particular, because for the first time the Parliament was split into two chambers, the law establishes different requirements for the candidates to these chambers. Accordingly, the senators are elected not directly by the populace, but by

the regional representative bodies, whereas the lower chamber – the Mazhilis – is elected directly by the citizens. In addition, the Constitution stipulates that candidates to Mazhilis must be citizens of minimum age 25, to the Senate of minimum age 30, with higher education, work experience of no less than five years, and no less than three years of permanent settlement in the region from where the candidate is being elected.

The law allows mixed funding of the electoral process and, by so doing, creates equal starting conditions for the candidates; however, it also assists those candidates who are closer to the business entities. Taking into account that in Kazakhstan the absolute majority of business entities are informally linked to the state, one may assume that the sources for funding are likely to be provided to those candidates who are favoured by this state–business alliance. Therefore, this provision limits financial possibilities of the left opposition, which represents the vast majority of population and which is not associated with business structures.

In addition, the Law establishes a 'veiled' form of property qualification in the form of an irrevocable deposit which is equal to 100 times of the minimal labour wage. This also predetermines the recruitment of wealthy candidates who can afford payment of such a deposit or of those who are sponsored by the wealthy groups of society. This also prevents recruitment of the representatives of the intelligentsia, particularly from the academic field. This, in turn, decreases the intellectual capacity of Parliament.

Furthermore, the system of electoral commissions includes the Central Commission on Elections, territorial, circle and district commissions. The members of the Central Commission are recruited by the president who then proposes them to the Mazhilis for their approval. The lower-level commissions are formed accordingly by the local executives, appointees of the president, and then approved by the local representative councils. This subordinates the whole system of electoral commission to the executive. The number of electors in electoral circles may differ on 25 per cent of occasions. This also violates the principle of equal electoral right.

Neither observers nor representatives of candidates are allowed to take part as witnesses in the counting of votes. The only subject who can initiate a secondary counting of votes is the upper level commission on elections. Its representative can be present while a secondary counting is taken place. However, participation of any other non-state witnesses is again not allowed. There is the possibility of application to the court, however, because the law does not provide a procedure for preservation of ballots and conditions of access to them, this right is likely to remain ineffective.

18. See S. Mainwaring, 'Party System in the "Third Wave" ' (1998) 9 (3) *The Journal of Democracy* 67.
19. There are three main forms of elections that are adopted throughout the world: majoritarian, proportionate, and mixed. Kazakhstan employs a two-round majoritarian system of elections. A first tour is conducted in the way of the absolute majority of votes – that is, when a winning candidate receives 50 per cent + 1 of the electorates' votes. A second round is conducted on the basis of the proportionate majority, i.e. those candidate wins who receives a majority of votes.

A majoritarian system conducted in two rounds of voting allows all parties to take part in the first. The second round facilitates the establishment of alliances between the small (or/and new) parties in order to withstand stronger competitors. Nevertheless, such a system of elections allows the preservation of a multiplicity of parties (that are flexible and prone to mutual compromises and alliances) after elections.

A majoritarian system of election which is held only in one round leads to the emergence of a two-party system and hampers the process of the emergence of new parties. This happens because the votes given to the parties which lost at the elections are not represented in the Parliament. Therefore, the electorate in order to achieve their representation in the legislative body tends to vote for those parties that are likely to win. Thus, the majoritarian system with one round of elections slows the process of emergence of new parties. However, at the same time, should a new party be able to gain the necessary support of the electorate, this system accelerates the process of pushing out a party whose place is taken over by the winning party.

A proportionate system results in the emergence of a multiplicity of parties that are less flexible and independent from one another. This happens because such a system allows parties to gain access to the Parliament without winning an absolute majority of votes. Consequently, a proportionate system facilitates the process of splitting the big parties, slows the process of 'dying off' of the small parties, and does not force such small parties to merge. Additionally, this system also allows individual politicians to form new parties.

It seems that in conditions of the post-Soviet reality, which lacks a civil society, a majoritarian system slows, whereas the proportionate system would accelerate, the process of the emergence of parties. Therefore, taking this into account, one should assume that at the initial stage of democratization the proportionate system could be preferable inasmuch as it facilitates the genesis of parties. Eventually, a majoritarian system could take over. For instance, Russia accepted a mixed approach, which allows recruitment of candidates to the Parliament on the basis of both proportionate and majoritarian systems.

In Kazakhstan the existing system of elections facilitates recruitment of candidates on the basis of their personal qualities, whereas a proportionate system would facilitate the selection of candidates on the basis of their programmes or of the programmes of associations or parties which they represent.

An intention of the authors of the Law on Elections to restrain the process of formation of parties or associations of citizens can also be seen in the following clauses. The Law includes only two advantages for candidates, if they gain if they are to be suggested by the associations: (1) activists and the staff of the social movement or organization can be registered as an initiative group of citizens (Article 30 of the Code on Elections); (2) the financial deposit of the social movement, organization or association can be one of the three sources for the establishment of the election fund of a candidate. The latter is not allowed for candidates to the Senate and, accordingly, decreases the motivation on the part of social associations to propose their candidates for the Senate. In fact, according to the Law, candidates for the Senate are not allowed to form elections funds at all, and neither can they be proposed by associations, parties or social movements. Although the Law agrees to the proposals of candidates for the Mazhilis on behalf of republican and local non-governmental associations (Item 2 of Article 87), it nevertheless, allows only republican associations to contribute to the election funds of candidates (Article 92). Accordingly, this clause prevents local associations from taking an active part in an election campaign.

20. For instance, to illustrate this point one could mention a salient fact. The founding meeting of the Democratic Party of Kazakhstan in 1995 was held in the premises of the presidential administration. Financing originated from the major state-owned industrial units.
21. After the formal dissolution of the Communist Party of Kazakhstan (CPK) in September 1991, President Nazarbayev intended to lead the Socialist Party, successor to the CPK. Later, the social movement (later transformed into the Party of the People's Unity of Kazakhstan) was considered to eventually become a pro-presidential party. Finally, for the purpose of the forthcoming national elections scheduled for 1996, the Democratic Party was established, which was created to eventually become the Presidential party. However, the decision of the Constitutional Court held the 1994 elections to the Parliament to be invalid, and then followed a referendum on prolongation of the Presidential mandate until the year 2000. This prevented the Democratic Party from becoming a pro-presidential party.
22. J.S. Hellman, 'Constitutions and Economic Reform in the Post-Communist Transitions' in J.D. Sachs and K. Pistor (eds), *The Rule of Law and Economic Reform in Russia* (1997) 55–79, 73.
23. The author was involved in drafting the Law on Petroleum, which could be an example to illustrate this point. The law was drafted with the clear purpose of insulating the negotiating process associated with oil contracts from the possible corrupt influences of the civil servants involved in the negotiations with foreign companies. In order to achieve this goal a semi-licensing system was introduced, which leaves little room for discretion on the part of government officials involved in negotiations. Foreign independent experts were also involved in drafting this law. At every stage the representatives of oil companies were invited for discussions. The law was described by the *Petroleum Oilgrams News*, a major publication for the oil industry, as the best of its kind among the former Soviet republics. Kazakhstan became the first and only republic of the former USSR which introduced a system resembling the licensing system employed in western industrialized countries.
24. The post-independence Parliament was elected, as a unicameral and the only legislative and supreme representative body at the end of the Soviet period. The Parliament enacted the first, rather democratic Constitution of the republic in January 1993. According to Article 75 of the 1993 Constitution, the president was defined as the head of the state and of the executive branch. Parliament, in turn, was defined as the only legislative body and the supreme representative organ of the republic. In addition, Parliament headed the system of local representative bodies; this estab-

lished a broad social basis of its power. The right to control the executive was another substantial feature of the legislature. Led by Serikbolsyn Abdildin, who was rather independent from the president, it gradually became an advocate of a more social face of economic reforms. It included a number of strong and popular critics of the executive. In early 1993 the Parliament formed the Controlling Chamber, which revealed serious evidence of corruption among the top executives. The activities of the latter triggered a final decision of the president to curtail the too independent legislature. Thus, the first post-independence Parliament was equalled by its legitimacy and given the mechanisms provided by the 1993 Constitution independent of the influences of the executive organ. All in all, the political system that existed in 1993 could be characterized as 'parliamentary-presidential'.

25. Later, these MPs were 'rewarded' by offers of jobs in the system of executive power.
26. Initially, the president wanted to sort out the situation without dissolving Parliament. However, the assertive position adopted by the members of the Constitutional Court made this impossible. Then, the president made his decision to dissolve the legislative organ on the basis of the Court's ruling. Later, in order to avoid such unpredictable behaviour on the past of the judiciary, the president, who defined the contents of the 1995 Constitution, replaced it with the Constitutional Council. None of those members who had disagreed with the president were appointed in the newly established Council or offered jobs in the government structures. Thus, were they punished for their 'misbehaviour'.
27. From the legal point of view this decision by the president was illegal inasmuch as it violated the existing Constitution. In particular, Item 7 of Article 78 stated that the president shall after consulting with the Supreme Council (i.e. Parliament) take decisions on holding a referendum. Consequently, the president did not have the right to hold a referendum in the absence of the legislative branch of power. In order to overcome this constitutional barrier and to give a cosmetic legitimacy to his decision, the president created the Assembly of Nations of Kazakhstan, a body elected by the ethnic (cultural and similar in kind) associations. The assembly, in turn, 'requested' the president to hold premature elections. In order to justify the creation of the Assembly, the president exploited the idea of 'threat' to the 'public stability', that is, war in Chechnya. Illustrative of this was the decoration of the lobby of the House of Parliament, where the session of the Assembly took place. It was decorated with slogans like 'Everything loses its meaning when the war comes home'. Photographs of the horrors of the war in Chechnya were displayed in the foyer.
28. By contrast, the first post-independence Parliament consisted of 510 deputies. The second Parliament included 283 deputies.
29. Kazakhstan presently consists of 14 regions which, in turn, are divided into district councils. Every region, as well as every individual district, has a representative body, or council.
30. Item 4 of Article 53 of the Constitution states: '[Parliament at a joint session of the chambers shall] have the right to delegate legislative powers for a term not exceeding one year to the president by two-thirds of the votes from the total number of deputies of each chamber at the initiative of the President'.

31. By contrast, in Kyrgyztan, the referendum and amendments to the Constitution can be made by two-thirds of the members of Parliament (the issue can be initiated by one-third of the members of Parliament) or more than 300 000 citizens can claim for amendment of the Constitution.
32. According to the 1995 Constitution, the legislative initiative in Kazakhstan is given to the members of Parliament and to the Cabinet of Ministers. By contrast, in Kyrgyzstan the same right is given to the members of Parliament, the Cabinet of Ministers, the Supreme Court and 30 000 citizens.
33. By contrast, in Russia and Kyrgyzstan the committees of Parliament are entitled to call before them an individual member of the Cabinet of Ministers.
34. Hellman, 'Constitutions and Economic Reform'.
35. According to recent statistics, the current volume of FDI (approximately US$5.3 billion) is approximately equal to the external debt of Kazakhstan (approximately US$4.04 billion). See *Kazakhstan: Recent Economic Developments* (1998).
36. The practice of previous transitions shows that the target of the clientelist state is the controlling bodies of the state itself because they are able to and should, by virtue of their authority, control and inspect the activities of resource allocation. During the short period of independence this tendency is clearly witnessed in Kazakhstan, particularly a gradual process of undermining the powers of the controlling organs. For instance, the State Committee for Financial Control, established in 1993 with the purpose of supervising the financial discipline of the executive, was dissolved in 1995 and was incorporated as a unit within the Ministry of Finance. Parliament has been deprived of its controlling functions. In particular, it is deprived of the right to establish the Controlling Chamber which existed in the first post-independence Parliament and proved to be a powerful tool of control over the executive, especially, the budgetary expenditures. In the 1995 Constitution this Chamber was replaced by the estimation Committee for control of the implementation of the republican budget; however, its functions are intentionally overregulated in order to prevent it from carrying out any unexpected actions. In the interactions with the judiciary this control is exercised by way of controlling the appointment of the judges. According to the 1995 Constitution, the president is the Chairman of the Supreme Qualification Commission which approves the regional judges and members of the country's Supreme Court.
37. By contrast, for instance, the Uzbek Constitution unambiguously states that the president is the head of the state, head of the executive branch of power, and chairman of the Cabinet of Ministers, which includes the position of first minister (prime minister).
38. For example, in the neighbouring Kyrgyz Republic, Parliament has the right to demand the report of the Cabinet of Ministers and of any individual member of the Cabinet at any time. More importantly, the Cabinet is obliged by the Constitution to submit the annual report to Parliament.
39. It is important to note that the entire drafting of the 1995 Constitution was under the direct supervision of the president himself. Any changes to the draft Constitution could be included only after the approval of the president.

All meetings of the drafting committee, connected with making the amendments to the draft, was chaired personally by the president.

40. Item 2 of Article 47 states: 'The President of the Republic shall bear liability for his actions, while exercising his duties, only in the case of state treason and for this he may be discharged from office by Parliament.'
41. Item 1 of Article 46 states: 'The President of the Republic of Kazakhstan, his honour and dignity shall be inviolable'.
42. Professor K. Asanov, one of the prospective presidential candidates, was threatened with jail for the distribution of his statement during his 1999 campaign criticizing the president. The same candidate, who took part in the presidential campaign in 1991, was jailed in that year, but was released after the protests of international human rights organizations. After the assertive appeals of these organizations, the Supreme Court reconsidered the case and ruled at that time that there was no criminal content in the actions of K. Asanov. In 1992 Parliament rescinded Article 170-1 of the Criminal Code on the basis of which Professor Asanov was jailed. This was done to 'save the face' of the president who later claimed that he jailed him on the basis of the law, that is, the Criminal Code.
43. This naturally makes local executives accountable to the president, not to the populace of the region they are to serve. In addition, this rule pushes these local executives to do everything possible to make the president 'win' at the national elections. For instance, General Isengulov, who chaired the election commission for the army, recalls that the heads of the regions reported to the central Election Commission that the elections in their regions were over, although a few military units had not yet finished the counting and had not even reported to the regional election commission. In other words, the heads of the regions were forced to compete in rushing to count in order to demonstrate their loyalty to the president.
44. Barkey provides plausible arguments to prove the direct causal relationship between the state lacking autonomy and the policy of import-substituting industrialization. See H.J. Barkey, 'State Autonomy and the Crisis of Import Substitution' (1989) 22 (3) *Comparative Political Studies* 291.
45. Interestingly, for the first time the undemocratic style of governance was admitted by the president himself.
46. This was cynically commented on by the president himself at the press conference after the final results of the elections were announced. He stated: 'Do you remember the headlines when turnout was 99,99 per cent in favour? Well, you could say that we have allowed democracy to progress by 20 per cent'. Cited in 'Nazarbayev Re-elected in "Unfair" Vote' *Combined Reports by Reuters/Associated Press*, 12 January 1999 and in C. Gall, 'Smug Rulers Play for Keeps in Kazakhstan' *The Moscow Times*, 15 January 1999.
47. An international factor is skilfully used by Nazarbayev to legitimize his domestic actions. For instance, in 1995, Roland Dumas, the chairman of the French Constitutional Court, was invited to chair the advisory group on drafting the 1995 Constitution.
48. After the January 1999 elections the process of mergers of major parties was initiated. This was done with the intention of eroding the basis for the emergence of possible rivals to the president. Such a challenge is unlikely

given that the merging parties are loyal and are led by the politicians who belong to the nearest circle of people surrounding the president or even the clan of the president.

49. Barkey argues that the problems of import-substituting industrialization are directly attributable, to the lack of state autonomy. For more discussion see Barkey, 'State Autonomy'.

8 Conclusion

1. See D.C. North, 'Privatization, Incentives, and Economic Performance' in H. Giersch and H. Siebert, *Privatization: Symposium in Honor of Herbert Giersch* (1991) 3–16.
2. Senior executives of the above companies stated that their decision to refrain from investing in Kazakhstan is based mainly on the fact that the country lacks the necessary small and medium-sized companies which could act as subcontractors in future operations.
3. Professor Archie Brown, talking about the 1993 Russian constitutional reforms, has observed: 'The manner in which the 1993 Constitution was drawn up and adopted likewise provided a poor foundation on which to build either democracy or respect for the law. It was the result not of an agreement or pact between the contending institutions, or of negotiations between representatives of broad political groups and interests, or, still less, the product of deliberation by politically independent constitutional lawyers. Instead, the new fundamental law was concocted unilaterally for President Yel'tsin by his allies.' This statement is relevant to the case of Kazakhstan. See A Brown, 'The Russian Crisis: Beginning of the End or End of the Beginning?' (1999) 15 (1) *Post-Soviet Affairs* 56, 65.

Bibliography

Abramov, V.N. and Gudin, Y.M (1994) 'Vozdeistvie Politicheskogo Riska na Harakter Inostrannogo Investirovaniya v Kaliningradskii Region'. In *Regional'nye Aspekty Formirovaniya Rynochnyh Motivatsionnyh Mehanizmov*. Kaliningrad, pp. 85–91.

Adam, P.S. (1994) 'Joint Ventures in Russian Oil Production' 42 *Oil and Gas Tax Quarterly* 451.

Aganbegyan, A. (1989) *Moving the Mountain: Inside the Perestroika Revolution*. London: Bantam.

Aghion, P. and Blanchard, O. (1994) *The Economics of Enterprise Restructuring in Central and Eastern Europe*. London: Centre for Economic Policy Research.

Aghion, P. and Howitt, P. (1998) *Endogenous Growth Theory*. Cambridge, MA: MIT Press.

Aitken, B. and Harrison, A. (1999) *Do Domestic Firms Benefit from Foreign Direct Investment?: Evidence from Panel Data* 43(1) *American Economic Review* 605.

Ajani, G. (1995) 'By Chance and Prestige: Legal Transplants in Russia and Eastern Europe' 43 *American Journal of Comparative Law* 93.

Albrow, M. (1994) *Globalization: Myths and Realities*. London: Roehampton Institute.

Albrow, M. and King, E. (1990) *Globalization: Knowledge and Society. Readings from International Sociology*. London: Sage in association with the International Sociological Association.

Albucht, D.J. (1983) 'Canadian Foreign Investment Policy and the International Politico-Legal Process' 21 *The Canadian Yearbook of International Law* 149.

Alchian, A.A. (1961) *Some Economics of Property*. Santa Monica, CA: Rand Corporation.

Alchian, A.A. (1977) *Economic Forces at Work*. Indianapolis: Liberty Press.

Alchian, A.A. and Demsetz, H. (1972) 'Production, Information Costs, and Economic Organization' 62 *American Economic Review* 777.

Allen, D.W. (1991) 'What Are Transaction Costs?' 14 *Research in Law and Economics* 1.

Allen, F.R. (1971) *Socio-Cultural Dynamics: an Introduction to Social Change*. New York: Macmillan.

Allot, A. (1980) *The Limits of Law*. London: Butterworths.

Al-Shawi, K.A. (1957) *The Role of the Corporate Entity in International Law*. Ann Arbor, MI: Overbeck & Co.

Alvarez, J.E. (1992) 'The Development and Expansion of Bilateral Investment Treaties' 86 *American Society of International Law Proceedings* 532.

Aman, A.C. (1993) *The Globalization of Law, Politics, and Markets: Implications for Domestic Law Reform*. Bloomington: Indiana University School of Law.

Amantayev, Z.T. (1993) 'Kommentarii k Zakonam Respubliki Kazakhstan o Bankah, Natsional'nom Banke i Valyutnom Regulirovanii' 1 *Biznes i Pravo* 66.

Amerasinghe, C.F. (1992) 'Issues of Compensation for the Taking of Alien Property in the Light of Recent Cases and Practice' 41 *The International and Comparative Law Quarterly* 22.

Ammeen, J.J. (1994) 'Modern Russian Secured Transaction Law and Foreign Investors' Rights Thereunder' 4 *Indiana International and Comparative Law Review* 371.

Amsden, A.A. (1992) 'Theory of Government Intervention in Late Industrialization'. In L. Putterman and D. Rueschmeyer (eds), *State and the Market in Development: Synergy or Rivalry?* Boulder, CO: Lynne Reinner.

Anderson, T.L. and Hill, P.J. (1975) 'The Evolution of Property Rights: a Study of the American West' 18 *Journal of Law and Economics* 163.

Andrews-Speed, C.P. and Gao, Z. (1996) 'China's Petroleum Legal Regime for Foreign Participation in Upstream Operations: the Foreign Oil Company's View' 14 *Journal of Energy and Natural Resources Law* 161.

Aoki, M. and Kim, H. (1994) *Corporate Governance in Transitional Economies*. Washington, DC: EDI Development Studies, World Bank.

Appelbaum, R. (1971) *Theories of Social Change*. Chicago: Markham Publishing Co.

Archer, S.J. (1985) 'The Role of Administrative Agencies in Regulating Joint Ventures in China' 21 *Stanford Journal of International Law* 195.

Asante, S.K.B. (1988) 'International Law and Foreign Investment: a Reappraisal' 37 *The International and Comparative Law Quarterly* 588.

Astapovich, A.Z. and Grigoriev, L.M. (1993) *Foreign Investment in Russia: Problems and Prospects. Analytical Reports of Independent Experts*. Moscow: Informat.

Atabaki, T. and O'Kane, J. (1998) *Post-Soviet Central Asia*. London: Tauris Academic Studies in association with the International Institute for Asian Studies.

Atsegbua, L. (1993) 'Acquisition of Oil Rights Under Contractual Joint Ventures in Nigeria' 37 *Journal of African Law* 10.

Attik, J. (1994) 'Fairness and Managed Foreign Direct Investment' 32 *Columbia Journal of Transnational Law* 1.

Ayres, C.E. (1944) *The Theory of Economic Progress*. Chapel Hill: University of North Carolina Press.

Ayres, I. and Talley, E. (1995) 'Solomonic Bargaining: Dividing a Legal Entitlement to Facilitate Coasen Trade' 104 *Yale Law Journal* 1027.

Baev, A.A. (1995) 'The Transformation of the Role of the State in Monitoring Large Firms in Russia: From the State's Supervision to the State's Fiduciary Duties' 8 (2) *The Transnational Lawyer* 247.

Bailey, D. (1995) *Transnationals and Transition: the Role of Foreign Direct Investment in Hungary's Economic Transformation*. Birmingham: Research Centre for Industrial Strategy, Department of Commerce, Birmingham Business School, the University of Birmingham.

Balance, R.H., Ansari, J.A. and Singer, H.W. (1982) *The International Economy and Industrial Development: the Impact of Trade and Investment on the Third World*. Brighton: Wheatsheaf Books.

Balasubramanyam, V.N., Salish, M.A. and Sapsford, D. (1994) *Foreign Direct Investment and Growth*. Lancaster: Management School, Lancaster University.

Balbus, I.D. (1977) 'Commodity Form and Legal Form: an Essay on the "Relative Autonomy" of the Law' 11 *Law and Society* 571.

Ball, A.M. (1987) *Russia's Last Capitalists: the Nepmen, 1921–1929*. Berkeley: University of California Press.

Bardach, E. (1977) *The Implementation Game: What Happens After a Bill Becomes a Law*. Cambridge, MA: MIT Press.

Barkey, H.J. (1989) 'State Autonomy and the Crisis of Import Substitution' 22 (3) *Comparative Political Studies* 293.

Barnard, C. (1938) *The Functions of the Executive*. Cambridge, MA: Harvard University Press.

Barry, D.D. (1995) 'Toward the "Rule of Law" in Russia? Political and Legal Reform in the Transitional Period' 21 *Review of Central and Eastern European Law* 633.

Barzel, Y. (1985) 'Transaction Costs: Are They Just Costs?' 141 (1) *Journal of Institutional and Theoretical Economics* 4.

Barzel, Y. (1989) *Economic Analysis of Property Rights*. Cambridge: Cambridge University Press.

Basin, Y.G. (1993) 'Priznaniye i Ispolneniye Reshenii Suda ili Arbitrazha Drugoi Strany v Kazahstane' 1 *Biznes i Pravo* 21.

Basina, O. (1996) 'The New Law on Special Economic Zones in the Republic of Kazakhstan' 6 (21) *Russia & Commonwealth Business Law Report* 1.

Baylis, J. and Smith, S. (1997) *The Globalization of World Politics: an Introduction to International Relations*. Oxford: Oxford University Press.

Beamish, P.W. (1994) 'Joint Ventures in Less Developed Countries: Partner Selection and Performance' 34 *Management International Review* 60.

Bean, G. (1995) *Fiduciary Obligation and Joint Ventures: the Collaborative Fiduciary Relationship*. Oxford: Clarendon Press.

Beard, C.A. (1913) *An Economic Interpretation of the Constitution of the United States*. New York: Macmillan.

Becker, G.S. (1957) 'A Theory of the Allocation of Time' 75 *Economic Journal* 493.

Bell, J.F. (1967) 'Institutional Economics'. In *A History of Economic Thought*. New York: Ronald Press, pp. 539–71.

Bentham, R.W. (1993) 'A Petroleum Regime: Background and Legalities' 15 *Houston Journal of International Law* 489.

Berle, A.A. and Means, G.C. (1933) *The Modern Corporation and Private Property*. New York: Macmillan.

Berman, H.J. (1983) *Law and Revolution: the Formation of the Western Legal Tradition*. Cambridge MA and London: Harvard University Press.

Bernard, M. and Ravenhill, J. (1995) 'Beyond Product Cycles and Flying Geese: Regionalization, Hierarchy, and the Industrialization of East Asia' 47 *World Politics* 171.

Bilder, R. and Murphy, J. (1995) 'Book Review. *The International Law on Foreign Investment*. By M. Sornarajah. Cambridge: Cambridge University Press, 1994'. In 89 *American Journal of International Law* 666.

Bingman, C. (1992) 'Economic Development and Privatization in Kazakhstan' 4 *Central Asia Monitor* 27.

Birkinshaw, P.J. (1991) *Access to Justice in the Privatized and Regulated State*. Hull: Hull University Press.

Black, D.F. (1996) 'So You Want to Invest in Russia? A Legislative Analysis of the Foreign Investment Climate in Russia' 5 *Minnesota Journal of Global Trade* 123.

Black, J.M. (1997) *Rules and Regulators*. Oxford: Clarendon Press.

Blackshield, A.R. (ed.) (1983) *Legal Change: Essays in Honour of Julius Stone*. Sydney: Butterworths.

Blomstrom, M. and Kokko, A. (1997) *How Foreign Investment Affects Host-Countries*. IBRD Working Paper No. 1745. Washington, DC: World Bank, International Economic Department, International Trade Division.

Blomstrom, M., Lipsey, R.E. and Zejan, M. (1992) *What Explains Developing Country Growth?* NBER Working Paper No. 4132.

Blomstrom, M. and Persson, H. (1983) 'Foreign Investment and Spillover Efficiency in an Underdeveloped Economy: Evidence from Mexican Manufacturing Industry' 11 (6) *World Development* 493.

Boeker, P. (1993) *Latin America Turnaround: Privatization, Foreign Investment, and Growth*. San Francisco: International Centre for Economic Growth, Institute of the Americas, ICS Press.

Bogatyryov, A.G. (1992) *Investitsionnoye Pravo*. Moscow: Rossiiskoye Pravo.

Boguslavskii, M.M. (1986) *Mezhdunarodnoye Ekonomicheskoe Pravo*. Moscow: Yuridicheskaya Literatura.

Boguslavskii, M.M. (1989) *Mezhdunarodnoye Chastnoye Pravo*. Moscow: Yuridicheskaya Literatura.

Bond, E.W. and Samuelson, L. (1989) 'Bargaining with Commitment, Choice of Techniques, and Direct Foreign Investment' 26 *Journal of International Economics* 77.

Bonime-Blanc, A.R. (1987) *Spain's Transition to Democracy: the Politics of Constitution Making*. Boulder: Westview Press.

Booth, S. (1994) *Foreign Direct Investment in Eastern and Central Europe: Trends, Effects and Institutional Problems*. Reading: University of Reading, Department of Economics.

Borenzstein, E. and De Gregorio, J. (1995) *How Does Foreign Direct Investment Affect Economic Growth*? Cambridge: National Bureau of Economic Research.

Bova, R. (1991) 'The Political Dynamics of the Post-Communist Transition: a Comparative Perspective' 44 (1) *World Politics* 113.

Boycko, M. (1996) 'Privatising Russia' 22 *Review of Central and Eastern European Law* 188.

Boyer, R. and Drache, D. (ed.) (1996) *States Against Markets: the Limits of Globalization*. London and New York: Routledge.

Boyle, J. (1994) *Critical Legal Studies*. New York: New York University Press.

Boyle, K., Hadden, T. and Hillyard, P. (1975) *Law and State: the Case of Northern Ireland*. London: Martin Robertson.

Brabant, J. (1992) *Privatising Eastern Europe: the Role of Markets and Ownership in the Transition*. Dordrecht and London: Kluwer Academic.

Brada, J.C. (1993) 'The Transformation from Communism to Capitalism: How Far? How Fast?' 9 (2) *Post-Soviet Affairs* 87.

Brada, J.C. (1996) *Corporate Governance in Transition Economies: Lessons from Recent Development in OECD Member Countries*. Paris: OECD.

Braginskii, M., Butler, W. and Rubanov, A. (1993) *Foreign Investment Legislation in the Republics of the Former Soviet Union*. London: Interlist.

Bremer, L.P. (1996) 'Geopolitical Risk Assessment in Times of Turmoil' 4 *Tulsa Journal of Comparative and International Law* 117.

Breskovsky, V. (1995) 'Directors' Duty of Care in Eastern Europe' 29 (1) *The International Lawyer* 77.

Brewer, T.T. (1993) 'Government Policies, Market Imperfections, and Foreign Direct Investment' 24 *Journal of International Business Studies* 101.
Brewer, T.T. (1995) 'International Investment Dispute Settlement Procedures: the Evolving Regime for FDI' 26 *Law and Policy in International Business* 633.
Brewer, T.T. and Young, S. (1995) 'Towards a Multilateral Framework for Foreign Direct Investment: Issues and Scenarios' 4 (1) *Transnational Corporations* 69.
Breyer, S. (1979) 'Analyzing Regulatory Failure: Mismatches, Less Restrictive Alternatives and Reform' 92 *Harvard Law Review* 549.
Brink, D.J. and Li, X.L. (1995) 'A Legal and Practical Overview of Direct Investment and Joint Ventures in the "New" China' 28 *The John Marshall Law Review* 567.
Broadman, H.G. and Sun, X. *The Distribution of Foreign Direct Investment in China*. IBRD Working Paper No. 1720. Washington, DC: World Bank.
Bromley, D.W. (1989) *Economic Interests and Institutions*. New York: Basil Blackwell.
Brown, A. (1996) *The Gorbachev Factor*. Oxford: Oxford University Press.
Brown, A. (1999) 'The Russian Crisis: Beginning of the End or End of the Beginning?' 15 (1) *Post-Soviet Affairs* 56.
Bublik, V. (1995) 'Uchreditel'nyi Dogovor o Sovmestnom Predpriyatii. Novye Podhody k Ego Sostavleniyu' 8 *Hozyaistvo i Pravo* 95.
Buchanan, J.M. (1972) 'Towards an Analysis of Closed Behavioral Systems'. In J.M. Buchanan and R.D. Tollison (eds), *Theory of Public Choice*. Ann Arbor, MI: University of Michigan Press, pp. 11–23.
Buchanan, J.M. (1977) 'Why Does Government Grow?' In T. Borcherding (ed.), *Budgets and Bureaucrats: the Sources of Government Growth*. Durham, NC: Duke University Press, pp. 3–18.
Buchanan, J.M. (1980) 'Rent Seeking and Profit Seeking'. In J.M. Buchanan, R. Tollison and G. Tullock (eds), *Toward a Theory of the Rent-Seeking Society*. College Station: Texas A&M University Press, pp. 3–15.
Buchanan, J.M. (1986) *Liberty, Market and State*. Brighton, Sussex: Wheatsheaf
Buchanan, J.M. (1990) 'The Domain of Constitutional Economics' 1 *Constitutional Political Economy* 1.
Buchanan, J.M. and Tullock, G. (1962) *The Calculus of Consent*. Ann Arbor: University of Michigan Press.
Buckingham, W.S. (1958) *Theoretical Economic Systems: a Comparative Analysis*. New York: Ronald Press Company.
Buckley, P.J. (1993) 'Contemporary Theories of International Direct Investment' 44 *Revue Economique* 725.
Buckley, P.J. and Casson, M. (1991) *The Future of Multinational Enterprise*, 2nd edn. Basingstoke: Macmillan – now Palgrave Macmillan.
Burke, J.J.A. (1996) 'The Economic Basis of Law as Demonstrated by the Reformation of NIS Legal Systems' 18 *Loyola of Los Angeles International and Comparative Law Journal* 207.
Burrows, P. and Veljanovski, C.G. (1981) 'Introduction: the Economic Approach to Law'. In P. Burrows and C.G. Veljanovski (eds), *The Economic Approach to Law*. London: Butterworths, pp. 1–34.
Burton, M.G. and Higley, J. (1987) 'Elite Settlements' 52 *American Sociological Review* 295.

Butler, S.M. (1986) 'Commentary on Privatization: Forms, Limits, and Relations to a Positive Theory of Government. (Privatization: the Assumptions and the Implications)' 71 *Marquette Law Review* 551.

Butler, W.E. (1995) *Civil Code of the Russian Federation*. London: Interlist.

Butler, W.E. (1999) *Russian Law*. Oxford: Oxford University Press.

Calabresi, G. (1970) *The Cost of Accidents: a Legal and Economic Analysis*. New Haven: Yale University Press.

Calabresi, G. (1985) *Ideals, Beliefs, Attitudes, and the Law: Private Law Perspectives on a Public Law Problem*. Syracuse, NY: Syracuse University Press.

Calabresi, G. (1991) 'The Pointlessness of Pareto: Carrying Coase Further' 100 *Yale Law Journal* 1211.

Calvert, R.L. (1995) 'The Rational Choice Theory of Institutions: Implications for Design'. In D. L. Weimer (ed.), *Institutional Design*. Norwell, MA: Kluwer Academic Publishers.

Calvet, A.L. (1981) 'Synthesis of Foreign Direct Investment Theories and Theories of the Multinational Firm' 12 *Journal of International Business Studies* 43.

Cameron, P. (1994) 'Creating a Legal Framework for Investment in the Commonwealth of Independent States Energy Sector: Lessons from the Energy Charter Experiment' 1 *Tulsa Journal of Comparative and International Law* 233.

Carter, A. (1989) *The Philosophical Foundations of Property Rights*. New York and London: Harvester Wheatsheaf.

Cerny, P.G. (1995) 'Globalization and the Changing Logic of Collective Action' 49 (4) *International Organization* 595.

Charap, J. and Zemplinerova, A. (1994) 'Foreign Direct Investment in the Privatization and Restructuring of the Czech Economy' 10 *Development and International Cooperation* 27.

Cheffins, B.R. (1997) *Company Law: Theory, Structure and Operation*. Oxford: Clarendon Press.

Chu, Y. (1989) 'State Structure and Economic Adjustment of the East Asian Newly Industrializing Countries' 43 (4) *International Organization* 647.

Chuhan, P., Perez-Quiroz, O. and Popper, H. (1997) *International Capital Flows: Do Short-Term Investment and Direct Investment Differ?* IBRD Policy Research Working Paper No. 1669. Washington, DC: World Bank.

Chung, E. (1996) 'Petroleum Investment in the Russian Federation: Russian Federation Federal Law No. 225-FZ on Production Sharing Agreements (December 30, 1995)' 37 *Harvard International Law Journal* 551.

Chung, K.S. (1988) 'The Internationalization of the Korean Securities Market: Legal and Economic Perspectives' 27 *Columbia Journal of Transnational Law* 27.

Churakov, Y. (1993) 'Vozmozhnosti Privlecheniya Inostrannogo Kapitala' 2 *Ekonomist* 88.

Clark, I. (1997) *Globalization and Fragmentation: International Relations in the Twentieth Century*. Oxford: Oxford University Press.

Clark, R.C. (1981) 'The Interdisciplinary Study of Legal Evolution' 90 *Yale Law Journal* 1238.

Cleeve, E. (1993) *Transnational Corporations and the Theory of Internationalization*. Manchester: Department of Economics and Economic History, Manchester Metropolitan University.

Coase, R.H. (1992) 'On the New Institutional Economics: Comments'. In L. Werin and H. Wijkander (eds), *Contract Economics*. Cambridge, MA: Basil Blackwell, pp. 48–65.

Coase, R.H. (1993) 'Law and Economics at Chicago' 36 *Journal of Law and Economics* 239.

Coleman, J. (1980) 'Efficiency, Utility, and Wealth Maximization' 8 *Hofstra Law Review* 509.

Collet-White, M. (1999) 'Nazarbayev Reasserts Control in Kazakhstan' *The Moscow Times*, 12 January.

Comeaux, P.E. and Kinsella, N.S. (1997) *Protecting Foreign Investment Under International Law: Legal Aspects of Political Risk*. Dobbs Ferry, NY: Oceana Publications.

Commander, S., Fan, Q. and Shaffer, M.E. (1996) *Enterprise Restructuring and Economic Policy in Russia*. Washington, DC: World Bank.

Commons, R. (1934) *Institutional Economics*. New York: Macmillan.

Conforti, B. (1993) *International Law and the Role of Domestic Legal Systems*. Dordrecht and London: Martinus Nijhoff.

Cook, P. and Kirkpatrick, C.H. (1995) *Globalization, Regionalization and Third World Development*. Manchester: Institute for Development Policy and Management, University of Manchester.

Cooter, R. and Ulen, T. (1988) *Law and Economics*. Reading, MA and London: Addison Wesley.

'Corruption Said to be Posing Threat to National Security', *BBC Monitoring, Summary of World Broadcasts, Part I, Former USSR*, 24 April 1998.

Cox, R. (1987) *Production, Power, and World Order: Social Forces in the Making of History*. New York: Columbia Press.

Dahlman, C.J. (1989) *Impact of Technological Change on Industrial Prospects for the LDCs*. Washington, DC: World Bank.

Dallago, B., Ajani, G. and Grancelli, B. (1992) *Privatization and Entrepreneurship in Post-Socialist Countries*. London: St Martin's Press.

Dalrymple, C.K. (1996) 'Politics and Foreign Direct Investment: the Multilateral Investment Guarantee Agency' 29 *Cornell International Law Journal* 161.

Dannreuther, R. (1994) *Creating New States in Central Asia: the Strategic Implications of the Collapse of Soviet Power in Central Asia*. London: Brassey's for the International Institute for Strategic Studies.

Dasgupta, S., Mody, A. and Sinha, S. (1996) *Japanese Multinationals in Asia: Capabilities and Motivations*. IBRD Policy Research Working Paper No. 1634. Washington, DC: World Bank.

Daviddi, R. (1994) *Privatization in the Transition to a Market Economy*. Florence: European University Institute.

Davis, D.R., Weinstein, D.E., Bradford S.C. and Shimpo, K. (1996) *The Heckscher–Ohlin–Vanek Model of Trade: Why Does it Fail? When Does it Work?* Cambridge, MA: National Bureau of Economic Research.

De Alessi, L. (1980) 'The Economics of Property Rights: a Review of the Evidence' 2 *Research in Law and Economics* 1.

Dean, R.N. (1996) 'The Russian Legal System: Ten Years Later' 39 *Private Investments Abroad* 12.1.

De Mello, L.R. (1997) 'Foreign Direct Investment in Developing Countries and Growth: a Selective Survey' 34 (1) *The Journal of Development Studies* 1.

Denisova, L.I. (1995) 'Fondovyi Rynok i Inostrannye Investitsii. Tendentsii Razvitiya Fondovogo Rynka' 4 *EKO* 65.

Dimolitsa, A. (1988) 'Arbitration Agreements and Foreign Investments: the Greek State Between Contractual Commitment and Sovereign Intervention' 5 *Journal of International Arbitration* 17.

Diver, C.S. (1989) 'Regulatory Precision'. In K. Hawkins and J. Thomas (eds), *Making Regulatory Policy*. Pittsburg, PA: University of Pittsburgh Press.

Dolzer, R. and Stevens, M. (1995) *Bilateral Investment Treaties*. The Hague: Kluwer Law International.

Doner, R.F. and Hawes, G. (1995) 'Southeast and Northeast Asia'. In M. Dorraj (ed.), *The Changing Political Economy of the Third World*. Boulder, CO: Lynne Reinner.

Dongarov, I.N. (1990) *Inostrannyi Kapital v Rossii v SSSR*. Moscow: Mezhdunarodnye otnosheniya.

Doronina, N.G. and Semilyutina, N.G. (1993) *Pravovoye Regulirovaniye Inostrannyh Investitsii v Rossii i za Rubezhom*. Moscow: Finstatinform.

Draeger, P. (1994) 'The Legal Framework for Doing Business in Russia: a Summary' 32 *Alberta Law Review* 310.

Dunning, J. (1990) *Structural Change in the World Economy*. London: Routledge.

Dunning, J. (1991) *Prospects for Foreign Direct Investment in Eastern Europe*. Discussion Papers in International Investment and Business Studies No. 155. Reading: University of Reading, Department of Economics, 1–16.

Dunning, J. (1993a) *Globalization: the Challenge for National Economic Regimes*. Dublin: Economic and Social Research Institute.

Dunning, J. (1993b) *Multinational Enterprise and the Global Economy*. Wokingham: Addison-Wesley.

Dunning, J. (1993c) *The Globalization of Business: the Challenge of the 1990s*. London: Routledge.

Dunning, J. (1996) *Foreign Direct Investment and Governments: Catalysts for Economic Restructuring*? London: Routledge.

Dunning, J., Kogut, B., and Blomstrom, M. (1990) *Globalization of Firms and the Competitiveness of Nations*. Lund and Bromley: Lund University Press, Chartwell-Bratt.

Elliot, E.D. (1985) 'The Evolutionary Tradition in Jurisprudence' 85 *Columbia Law Review* 38.

Ellman, M. and Kantorovich, V. (1998) *The Destruction of the Soviet Economic System: an Insider's History*. Armonk, NY and London: M.E. Sharpe.

El Sheikh, F.R.A. (1984) *The Legal Regime of Foreign Private Investment in Sudan and Saudi Arabia: a Case Study of Developing Countries*. Cambridge and New York: Cambridge University Press

Evan, W.M. (ed.) (1980) *The Sociology of Law: a Social-Structural Perspective*. New York: Free Press.

Evans, P.B. (1986) 'State, Capital, and the Transformation of Dependence: the Brazilian Computer Case' 14 (7) *World Development* 791.

Evans, P.B. (1995) *Embedded Autonomy: States and Industrial Transformation*. Princeton: Princeton University Press.

Evans, P., Rueschmeyer, D. and Stephens, E.H. (1995) *States Versus Markets in the World System*. Beverly Hills and London: Sage.

Evstratov, S.Y., Kozlov, N.B. and Kuznetsov, A.I. (1991) *Inostrannye Investitsii v SSSR: Voprosy Pravovogo Regulirovaniya*. Moscow: Finansy.

Fatehi-Sedeh, K. and Safizadeh, M.H. (1989) 'Association Between Political Instability and Flow of Foreign Direct Investment' 29 (4) *Management International Review* 4.

Fatouros, A.A. (1962) *Government Guarantees to Foreign Investors*. New York and London: Columbia University Press.

Fatouros, A.A. (1996) 'Towards an International Agreement on Foreign Direct Investment'. In *Towards Multilateral Investment Rules*. Paris: OECD.

Feathers, L.A. (1992) 'Western Opportunities for Investment in the Oil Industry of the Former Soviet Union' 7 *The American University Journal of International Law and Policy* 703.

Feldbrugge, F.J.M. (1993) *Russian Law: the End of the Soviet System and the Role of Law*. Dordrecht and London: Martinus Nijhoff.

Fenwick A. (1985) 'Equity Joint Ventures in the PRC: an Assessment of the First Five Years' 40 *The Business Lawyer* 839.

Fields, K. (1997) 'Strong States and Business Organizations in Korea and Taiwan'. In S. Maxfield and B. Schneider (eds), *Business and the State in Developing Countries*. Ithaca, NY: Cornell University Press.

Fischell, W.A. (1995) *Regulatory Takings: Law, Economics and Politics*. Cambridge, MA and London: Harvard University Press.

Fitzpatrick, P. (1980) *Law and State in Papua New Guinea*. London: Academic Press.

Foster, N.G. (1993) *German Law and Legal System*. London: Blackstone.

Frenkel, W.G. and Sukhman, M.Y. (1993) 'New Foreign Investment Regimes of Russia and Other Republics of the Former USSR: a Legislative Analysis and Historical Perspective' 16 *Boston College International and Comparative Law Review* 321.

Freund, O. (1928) 'Economic Organization, Commercial Regulations and Concessions in the Soviet Union' 22 *Illinois Law Review* 852.

Fridman, T.L. (1960) *Inostrannyi Kapital v Dorevolyutsionnom Kazahstane*. Alma-Ata: Kazgosizdat.

Friedberg, J.J. (1982) 'Monitoring Foreign Investment in Energy Resources: Problems and Proposals' 84 *West Virginia Law Review* 1093.

Friedman, L.M. (1975) *The Legal System: a Social Science Perspective*. New York: Russel Sage Foundation.

Friedman, L.M. (1984) *American Law: an Introduction*. New York: W.W. Norton.

Friedman, M. (1962) *Capitalism and Freedom*. Chicago, IL: University of Chicago Press.

Froot, K.A. (ed.) (1993) *Foreign Direct Investment*. Chicago and London: University of Chicago Press.

Gabriel-Castel, J. (1986) 'Privatization: Is International Law Relevant?' 24 *The Canadian Yearbook of International Law Annual* 368.

Gall, C. (1999) 'Smug Rulers Play for Keeps in Kazakhstan' *The Moscow Times*, January 15.

Gann, P. (1985) 'The US Bilateral Investment Treaty Program' 21 *Stanford Journal of International Law* 373.

Geddes, B. (1990) 'Building "State" Autonomy in Brazil, 1930–1964' 22 (2) *Comparative Politics* 217.

Geist, M.A. (1995) 'Toward a General Agreement on the Regulation of Foreign Direct Investment' 26 *Law and Policy in International Business* 673.

Genov, N. (1991) 'The Transition to Democracy in Eastern Europe: Trends and Paradoxes of Social Rationalization' 128 *International Social Science Journal* 331.

Gereffi, G. (1995) 'Global Production Systems and Third World Development'. In B. Stallings (ed.), *Global Change, Regional Response*. Cambridge: Cambridge University Press, pp. 100–42.

Giddens, A. (1990) *The Consequences of Modernity*. Cambridge: Polity Press.

Gill, S. (1997) *Globalization, Democratization and Multilateralism*. Basingstoke: Macmillan – now Palgrave Macmillan.

Gillespie, J. (1994) 'Private Commercial Rights in Vietnam: a Comparative Analysis' 30 *Stanford Journal of International Law* 325.

Globerman, S. (1988) 'Government Policies Toward Foreign Direct Investment: Has a New Era Dawned?' 23 *Columbia Journal of World Business* 41.

Gochenour, D.T. (1992) 'Current Difficulties in Forming Policy and Atracting the Foreign Oil Industry to the Former Soviet Union: International Energy Law Symposium' 27 *Tulsa Law Journal* 705.

Goldsmith, A. (1995) 'Democracy, Property Rights and Economic Growth' 32 (2) *The Journal of Development Studies* 157.

Goldstein, W. (1992) 'The Future Role of Multinational Enterprises and Foreign Direct Investment' 27 *Foreign Trade Review* 257.

Gordley, J. (1995) 'Comparative Legal Research: its Function in the Development of Harmonized Law' 43 *American Journal of Comparative Law* 555.

Gordon, D. (1990) 'The Polish Foreign Investment Law of 1990' 24 *International Lawyer* 335.

Graham, E.M. (1996a) 'The (not Wholly Satisfactory) State of the Theory of Foreign Direct Investment and the Multinational Enterprise' 20 *Journal of International and Comparative Economics* 183.

Graham, E.M. (1996b) *Global Corporations and National Governments*. Washington, DC: Institute for International Economics.

Graham, H.J. (1996) 'Foreign Investment Laws of China and the United States: a Comparative Study' 5 *Journal of Transnational Law & Policy* 253.

Grant, W. (1992) *Economic Globalization, Stateless Firms and International Governance*. Coventry: Department of Politics and International Studies, University of Warwick.

Gray, C. (1995a) *Hungary's Bankruptcy Experience, 1992–1993*. Washington, DC: World Bank, Policy Research Department, Transition Economics Division.

Gray, C. (1995b) 'Law and the Regulation of Foreign Direct Investment: the Experience from Central and Eastern Europe' 33 *Columbia Journal of Transnational Law* 1.

Gray, C. (1996) *In Search of Owners: Lessons of the Experience with Privatization and Corporate Governance in Transition Economies*. Washington, DC: World Bank, Office of the Chief Economist and Senior Vice President, Development Economics.

Gray, C. and Hendley, K. (1995) *Developing Commercial Law in Transition Economies: Examples from Hungary and Russia*. The IBRD Policy Research Working Paper No. 1528. Washington, DC: World Bank, Policy Research Department, Transition Economics Division.

Green, F. (1974) 'The Management of Political Risk' *Bests Review* (July).

Griffin, K. and Khan, A.R. (1992) *Globalization and the Developing World: an Essay on the International Dimensions of Development in the Post-Cold War Era*. New York: UNDP.

Grigoriev, L. (1992) 'First Step for Former Soviet Republics: Rapid Privatization' 105 *The Los-Angeles Daily Journal*, 3 January, 6.

Gross, D. and Steinherr, A. (1995) *Winds of Change: Economic Transition in Central and Eastern Europe*. London: Longman.

Grzesiak, C. (1993) 'The Denationalization of Kazakhstan' 21 *Denver Journal of International Law and Policy* 441.

Gudgeon, K.S. (1986) 'United States Bilateral Investment Treaties: Comments on Their Origin, Purposes, and General Treatment Standards' 4 *International Tax & Business Lawyer* 105.

Gwiazda, A. (1992) 'New Conditions and Environment for Direct Foreign Investment in Poland' 28 *Russian and East European Finance and Trade: a Journal of Translations* 69.

Haggard, S. (1986) 'The Newly Industrializing Countries in the International System' 38 (2) *World Politics* 343.

Haile-Mariam, Y. (1993) 'Privatization of State-Owned Enterprises and the Law: Issue and Problems' 7 *Emory International Law Review* 35.

Hall, P.A. and Taylor, R.C.R. (1996) 'Political Science and the Three Institutionalisms' XLIV *Political Studies* 936.

Halliday, T.C. and Carruthers, B.G. (1990) *The State Professions and Legal Change: Reform of the English Insolvency Act, 1977–1986*. American Bar Foundation Working Paper No. 9019. Chicago: American Bar Foundation.

Hamilton, N. (1982) *The Limits of State Autonomy: Post-Revolutionary Mexico*. Princeton, NJ: Princeton University Press.

Handler, J.F. (1978) *Social Movements and the Legal System: a Theory of Law Reform and Social Change*. New York: Academic Press.

Hayek, F. (1944) *The Road to Serfdom*. Chicago, IL: University of Chicago Press.

Hayward, S. and Lay, J. (1997) 'The New Foreign Investment Law of Vietnam: Catalyst for Change?' 8 *International Company and Commercial Law Review* 233.

Heckscher, E.E., Flam, H., Flanders, M. and Ohlin, B. (1991) *Heckscher–Ohlin Trade Theory*. Cambridge, MA: MIT Press.

Heleniak, D.W. and Farrel, T.C. (1988) 'Developments in the Law of Mergers and Acquisitions: Cross Border Transactions' 20 (2) *Institute on Securities Regulation* 143.

Hellman, J.S. (1997) 'Constitutions and Economic Reform in the Post-Communist Transitions'. In J D. Sachs and K. Pistor (eds), *The Rule of Law and Economic Reform in Russia*. Boulder, CO: Westview Press, pp. 55–79.

Henderson, J. (1989) *The Globalization of High Technology Production: Society, Space and Semi-Conductors in the Restructuring of the Modern World*. London: Routledge.

Henderson, J. (1998) *Uneven Crisis: Institutional Foundations of East Asian Economic Turmoil*. Oxford: University of Oxford, Transnational Communities Programme.

Henderson, S.K. (1995) 'Legal Eye on Hedging's Newest Club' *Euromoney*, May, 95–6.

Hendley, K. (1995) 'The Spillover Effects of Privatization on Russian Legal Culture' 5 *Transnational Law & Contemporary Problems* 39.

Herbiet, M. (1993) 'The Constitutional Basis of the Economic Order During a Period of Transition from a Planned to a Market Economy'. In *Rule of Law and Transition to a Market Economy*. Sofia: UNIDEM Seminar Papers, European Commission for Democracy Through Law, October.

Hettne, B. (1990) *Globalization of Development Theory*. Budapest: Institute for World Economics of the Hungarian Academy of Sciences.

Highest, K. (1989) 'The Enigma of the Lex Mercatoria' 63 *Tulane Law Review* 613.

Hirst, P.H. (1995) *Globalization in Question*. Sheffield: Political Economy Research Centre, University of Sheffield.

Hirst, P.H. and Thompson, G. (1996) *Globalization in Question: the International Economy and the Possibilities of Governance*. Cambridge: Polity Press.

Hoebel, E.A. (1954) *The Law of Primitive Man: a Study of Comparative Legal Dynamics*. Cambridge, MA: Harvard University Press.

Hoenig, C. (1992) 'Investing in Eastern Europe Through the Austrian Holding Company' 26 *The International Lawyer* 303.

Holmes, O.W. (1963) *The Common Law*, ed. by M.D. Howe. Cambridge, MA: Harvard University Press.

Hoogvelt, A.M.M. (1997) *Globalization and the Post-Colonial World: the New Political Economy of Development*. Basingstoke: Macmillan – now Palgrave Macmillan.

Hooton, M.E. (1994) 'Structuring and Negotiating International Joint Ventures' 27 *Creighton Law Review* 1013.

Houde, M.-F. (1997) *International Direct Investment: Policies and Trends in the 1980s*. Paris: OECD.

Howell, M.J. (1994) *Investing in Emerging Markets*. London: Euromoney in association with the World Bank.

Hrasky, M. and Hraska, A. (1995) 'International Joint Ventures in the Czech Republic' 23 *International Business Lawyer* 63.

Hughes, J. (1994) 'The Americanization of Russian Politics: Russia's First Television Election 1993' 10 (2) *Journal of Communist Studies and Transition Politics* 125.

Huntington, S. (1991) *The Third Wave: Democratization in the Late Twentieth Century*. Norman and London: University of Oklahoma Press.

Huntington, S. and Nelson, J. (1976) *No Easy Choice*. Cambridge, MA: Harvard University Press.

Hunya, G. (1992) 'Foreign Direct Investment and Privatization in Central and Eastern Europe' 4 (4) *Communist Economics and Economic Transformation* 501.

Hymer, S. (1976) *The International Operations of National Firms*. Cambridge, MA: MIT Press.

Ioffe, O.S. (1989) *Development of Civil Law Thinking in the USSR*. Milano: Giuffre.

Ionescu, G. (1993) *Globalization: the Interweaving of Foreign and Domestic Policy-Making*. London: Government and Opposition Ltd.

Isabayeva, A. (1992) 'Zony Svobodnye, Tseli Konkretnye' 8 *Kazahstan: Ekonomika I Zhizn'* 22.

Jackson, G.D. (1994) 'Doing Business in Russia: a Practical Guide for American Investors' 3 *Journal of International Law and Practice* 111.

Jadach, C.L. (1985) 'Ownership and Investment in Poland' 18 *Cornell International Law Journal* 63.

Jawitch, S.L. (1981) *The General Theory of Law*. Moscow: Progress Publishers.
Johnston, J.S. (1990) 'Law, Economics, and Post-Realist Explanation' 24 (5) *Law and Society Review* 1217.
Jungnickel, R. (1993) *Foreign Direct Investment: Recent Trends in a Changing World*. Hamburg: HWWA.
Kahn-Freund, O. (1972) 'On Uses and Misuses of Comparative Law' 37 *Modern Law Review* 1.
Kaloupek, M.T. (1992) 'Drafting Dispute Resolution Clauses for Western Investment and Joint Ventures in Eastern Europe' 13 *Michigan Journal of International Law* 981.
Karass, A.V. (1927) 'Kontsessii v Sovetskom Prave' 2 *Sovetskoye Pravo* 30.
Karl, T.L. and Schmitter, P.C. (1991) 'Modes of Transition in Latin America, Southern and Eastern Europe' 128 *International Social Science Journal* 269.
Kartheiser, R. and Mashlenko, I. (1994) 'Exploiting Natural Resources in Russia' 13 (2) *International Financial Law Review* 24.
Kaser, M. (1992) *The Central Asian Economies After Independence*. London: Royal Institute of International Affairs.
Kaser, M. (1995) *Privatization in the CIS*. London: Royal Institute of International Affairs.
Kaser, M. (1997) *The Economies of Kazakhstan and Uzbekistan*. London: Royal Institute of International Affairs.
Katzenstein, P. (1978) *Between Power and Plenty: Foreign Economic Policies of Advanced Industrial States*. Madison: University of Wisconsin Press.
Katzenstein, P. (1985) *Small States in World Markets: Industrial Policy in Europe*. Ithaca, NY: Cornell University Press.
Kazakhstan Survey. London: International Tax and Investment Centre. June 1996.
'Kazakh Chemical Plant Workers on Strike Over Wages Arrears in Southern Town', *BBC Monitoring, Summary of World Broadcasts, Part I. Former USSR*, 19 January 1998.
'A Kazakh Sham' *Financial Times*, 12 January 1999.
'Kazakhstan: Seven Years of Bad Luck?' *The Economist Intelligence Unit*, February 1999.
'Kazakhstan: Foreign Investment' *Oxford Analytica Daily Brief*, 12 February 1999.
Kennedy, K.H. (1986) *Mining Tsar: the Life and Times of Leslie Urquhart*. Sydney and London: Allen & Unwin.
Kennedy, P. (1989) *The Rise and Fall of the Great Powers: Economic Change and Military Conflict from 1500–2000*. London: Fontana.
Kennedy, P. (1994) *Preparing for the Twenty-First Century*. London: Fontana.
King, A. (1991) *Culture, Globalization and the World System*. Basingstoke: Macmillan in association with the Department of Art and Art History, State University of New York at Binghampton.
Klimkin, S.I. (1997) *Pravovye Formy Predprinimatel'stva v Respublike Kazahstan*. Almaty: Baspa.
Kline, J.M. (1993) 'International Regulation of Transnational Business: Providing the Missing Leg of Global Investment Standards' 2 *Transnational Corporations* 153.
Kobrin, S.J. (1977) *Foreign Direct Investment, Industrialization and Social Change*. Greenwich, CT: JAI Press.

Kobrin, S.J. (1982) *Managing Political Risk Assessment: Strategic Responses to Environmental Change*. Berkeley: University of California Press.
Kofele-Kale, N. (1990) 'Host-Nation Regulation and Incentives for Private Foreign Investment: a Comparative Analysis and Commentary' 15 *The North Carolina Journal of International Law and Commercial Regulation* 361.
Kofele-Kale, N. (1992) 'The Political Economy of Foreign Direct Investment: a Framework for Analysing Investment Laws and Regulations in Developing Countries' 23 *Law and Policy in International Business* 619.
Kojima, K. (1977) 'Direct Foreign Investment Between Advanced Specialized Countries' 28 *Hirotsubashi Journal of Economics* 1.
Kokko, A. (1994) 'Technology, Market Characteristics and Spillovers' 43 (2) *Journal of Development Economics* 279.
Kokko, A. and Blomstrom, M. (1995) 'Politics to Encourage Inflows of Technology Through Foreign Multinationals' 23 (3) *World Development* 1.
Kolo, A. (1994) *Managing Political Risk in Transnational Investment Contracts*. Dundee: University of Dundee, Centre for Petroleum and Mineral Law and Policy.
Kolodkin, A. (1994) 'Russia and International Law: New Approaches' 26 *Revue Belge de Droit International* 552.
Komarov, A.S. (1996) 'International Commercial Arbitration in Russia as a Means of Resolving International Economic Disputes' 22 *Review of Central and Eastern European Law* 19.
Konoplyanik, A. (1993) 'Russian Oil Industry and Foreign Investments: Legal Aspects and the Problem of Business Risk' 11 *Journal of Energy and Natural Resources Law* 248.
Koslow, L.E. (1992) 'Mexican Foreign Investment Laws: an Overview' 18 *Law and Policy in International Business* 441.
Kozybayev, M.K. (ed.) (1992) *The Text-Book on the History of Kazakhstan from Ancient Times until the Present*. Alma-Ata: Ministry for Education, Institute of History and Ethnology of the Academy of Sciences of the Republic of Kazakhstan.
Kreuzer, K. (1990) *Legal Aspects of International Joint Ventures in Agriculture*. Rome: Food and Agriculture Organization of the United Nations.
Krieger, J. (ed.) (1993) *The Oxford Companion to Politics of the World*. New York and Oxford: Oxford University Press.
Kronfol, Z.A. (1972) *Protection of Foreign Investment: a Study in International Law*. Leiden: A.W. Sijthoff.
Krugman, P. (1990) *Integration and the Competitiveness of Peripheral Industry*. London: Centre for Economic Policy Research.
Krugman, P. (1995) *Development, Geography, and Economic Theory*. Cambridge, MA and London: MIT Press.
Kuusi, J. (1979) *The Host-State and the Transnational Corporation: an Analysis of Legal Relationships*. Farnborough: Saxon House.
Kuznetsov, Y. (1992) 'Gosudarstvennoye Regulirovaniye Investitsii: Aktsent Smeshayetsya na Mikrouroven' 9 *Rossiiskii Ekonomicheskii Zhurnal* 50.
Landau, B.A. and Bernstein, I.N. (1930) *Pravovye Usloviya Kontsessionnoi Deyatel'nosti v SSSR*. Moscow.
Lapidus, G. (1995) *The New Russia: Troubled Transformation*. Boulder, CO and Oxford: Westview Press.

Latynina, Y. (1999) 'Inside Russia: Looking with Pride at the Mess in Kazakhstan' *The Moscow Times*, 12 January.
Lauterpacht, E. (1997) 'International Law and Private Foreign Investment' 4 *Indiana Journal of Global Legal Studies* 259.
Lawson, C.M. (1982) 'The Family Affinities of Common Law and Civil Law Systems' 6 (1) *Hastings International & Comparative Law Review* 85.
Leamer, E.E. (1995) *The Heckscher–Ohlin Model in Theory and Practice*. Princeton, NJ: International Finance Section, Department of Economics, Princeton University.
Lee, K. (1991) *Chinese Firms and the State in Transition: Property Rights and Agency Problems in the Reform Era*. Armonk, NY: M.E. Sharpe.
Leff, A. (1975) 'Economic Analysis of Law: Some Realism about Nominalism' 60 *Virginia Law Review* 451.
'Legal Principles and Practices Relating to Private Foreign Investment: a Panel' (1993) 77 *American Society of International Law Proceedings* 292.
Lev, D.S. (1997) 'Book Review. *Russian Law. Trying to Make Law Matter: Legal Reform and Labour Law in the Soviet Union*. By Kathryn Hendley. University of Michigan Press, 1996' In 44 *American Journal of Comparative Law* 531.
LeVine, S. (1998) 'Is 90 per cent of Vote Suspicious? Kazakh Leader is Puzzled' *Dallas Morning News*, 6 December.
Levy, B. and Spiller, P. (1994) 'The Institutional Foundations of Regulatory Commitment: a Comparative Analysis of Telecommunications Regulation' 10 (2) *Journal of Law, Economics and Organization* 201.
Lewis, N. (1996) *Choice and the Legal Order: Rising Above Politics*. London: Butterworths.
Lii, S.-Y. (1994) 'Japanese Direct Foreign Investment and Trade Flows in the Asia-Pacific Region' 8 *Asian Economic Journal* 181.
Lijphart, A. (1984) *Democracies: Patterns of Majoritarian and Consensus Government in Twenty-One Countries*. New Haven and London: Yale University Press.
Lillich, R.B. (1965) *The Protection of Foreign Investment: Six Procedural Studies*. Syracuse, NY: Syracuse University Press.
Lillich, R.B. (1989) 'Joint Ventures and the Law of International Claims' 10 *Michigan Journal of International Law* 430.
Lin, L. and Allison, J.R. (1994) 'An Analysis of Expropriation and Nationalization Risk in China' 19 *The Yale Journal of International Law* 135.
Lind, H. (1996) 'East–West Joint Ventures: Contractual Aspects' 24 *International Business Lawyer* 116.
Lindblom, C. (1959) 'The Science of Muddling Through' 19 *Public Administration Review* 79.
Lindblom, C. (1977) *Politics and Markets: the World's Political-Economic Systems*. New York: Basic Books.
Linz, J. (1993) 'Authoritarianism'. In J. Krieger (ed.), *The Oxford Companion to Politics of the World*. New York Oxford University Press.
Linz, J. and Stepan, A. (1996) *Problems of Democratic Transition and Consolidation: Southern Europe, South America, and Post-Communist Europe*. Baltimore and London: John Hopkins University Press.
Lipsey, R.G. (1993) *Globalization, Technological Change and Economic Growth*. Belfast: Northern Ireland Economic Development Office.

Louvard, F. (1995) 'Privatization in Russia' 23 *International Business Lawyer* 260.

Luard, E. (1990) *The Globalization of Politics: the Changed Focus of Political Action in the Modern World*. London: Macmillan.

Lussenburg, S.M. (1985) 'Joint Venture Investment in the People's Republic of China: a Continuing Challenge' 63 *The Canadian Bar Review* 545.

Lyandau, L.G. (1930) *Inostrannvi Kapital v Dorevolyutsionnoi Rossii i SSSR*. Moscow and Leningrad.

Lyusov, A.N. (1993) 'Investitsii i Investitsionnaya Deyatel'nost' 10–11 *Den'gi i Kredit* 43.

MacPherson, C.B. (1962) *The Political Theory of Possessive Individualism*. Oxford: Oxford University Press.

Madura, J. and Whyte, A.M. (1990) 'Diversification Benefits of Direct Foreign Investment' 30 (1) *Management International Review* 73.

Mainardi, S. (1992) 'Foreign Direct Investment in Latin America and South East Asia: Relevance of Macroeconomic and Policy-Related Factors' 51 *Giornale Degli Economisti e Annali di Economia* 259.

Mainwaring, S. (1998) 'Party System in the "Third Wave" ' 9 (3) *The Journal of Democracy* 67.

Mainwaring, S., O'Donnell, G. and Valenzuela, J.S. (eds) (1992) *Issues in Democratic Consolidation: the New South American Democracies in Comparative Perspective*. Notre Dame: University of Notre Dame Press.

Mairal, H.A. (1989) 'Foreign Investments and Municipal Laws: the Argentine Experience' 4 *Connecticut Journal of International Law* 635.

Malfriet, K. (1987) 'The Hungarian Quest for a Valid Theory of "Socialist" Property: Still a Long Way to Go' 13 *Review of Socialist Law* 241.

March, J.G. and Olsen, J.P. (1984) 'The New Institutionalism: Organizational Factors in Political Life' 78 (3) *American Political Science Review* 734.

March, J.G. and Olsen, J.P. (1989) *Rediscovering Institutions: the Organizational Basis of Politics*. New York: The Free Press.

Masuyama, S., Vandenbrink, D., Chia, S. and Nomura, S. (1997) *Industrial Policies in East Asia*. Tokyo and Singapore: Nomura Research Institute, Institute of South East Asian Studies.

Matecki, M. (1989) 'Legal Aspects of East–West Investment (Joint Ventures)' 34 *Osteuropa Wirtschaft* 224.

Mattei, U. (1994) 'Why the Wind Changed: Intellectual Leadership in Western Law' 42 *American Journal of Comparative Law* 195.

Mattei, U. (1997) 'Three Patterns of Law: Taxonomy and Change in the World's Legal System' 45 *American Journal of Comparative Law* 5.

Maulenov, K.S. (1993) 'Konstitutsiya Respubliki Kazahstan o Zash'ite Predprinimatel'skoi Deyatel'nosti Inostrannyh Investorov'. In *Konstitutsiva Respubliki Kazahstan I Aktual'nye Problemy Gosudarstva i Prava*. Almaty: AGU, pp. 45–51.

Maulenov, K.S. (1993) 'Zakonodatel'stvo ob Inostrannyh Investitsiyah v Respublike Kazahstan' 1 *Biznes i Pravo* 18.

Maulenov, K.S. (1994a) 'Sovmestnye Predpriyatiya v Kazahstane' 12 *Hozyaistvo Pravo* 79.

Maulenov, K.S. (1994b) 'Sovmestnye Predpriyatiya s Inostrannymi Investitsiyami' 12 *Kazahstan: Ekonomika i Zhizn'* 69.

Maulenov, K.S. (1995a) 'Osvoenie Prirodnyh Resursov Kazahstana: Pravovye Aspekty' 7 *Hozyaistvo i Pravo* 90.

Maulenov, K.S. (1995b) 'Zakon ob Inostrannyh Investitsiyah v Respublike Kazahstan' 7 *Vneshnyaya Torgovlya* 25.

McGrory, D.P. (1988) 'Privatization in the United Kingdom and Economic Regulation in the United States: Lessons in Administrative Law' 11 *Liverpool Law Review* 117.

McMillan, C.H. (1992) 'Foreign Direct Investment Flows to the Soviet Union and Eastern Europe: Nature, Magnitude and International Implications' 23 *Journal of Development Planning* 305.

McMillan, C.H. (1993) 'The Role of Foreign Direct Investment in the Transition From Planned to Market Economies' 2 *Transnational Corporations* 97.

Mellot, T.R. (1996) 'Changes in the Russian Tax System to Encourage Foreign Investment' 45 *Oil and Gas Tax Quarterly* 303.

Messing, J.W. (1997) 'Towards a Multilateral Agreement on Investment' 6 (1) *Transnational Corporations* 123.

Mikesell, R.F. (1971) *Foreign Investment in the Petroleum and Mineral Industries: Case Studies of Investor–Host Country Relations*. Baltimore and London: John Hopkins University Press.

Molkner, K (1993/1994) 'A Comparison of the Legal Regimes for Foreign Investment in Russia, Kazakhstan and Kyrgyzstan' 11 *International Tax and Business Lawyer* 71.

Morais, H.V. (1996) 'Emerging Legal Strategies of Host States to Attract Foreign Investment'. In *Current Developments in International Investment Law*. London: Butterworths.

'More Than Half Kazakhs Population Live Below Poverty Line', *BBC Monitoring, Summary of World Broadcasts, Part I, Former USSR*, 20 February 1998.

Mosk, R.M. (1993) 'Expropriation: What to Do About It?' 5 *California International Practitioner* 11.

Muchlinski, P. (1987) ' "Basic Needs" Theory and "Development Law" '. In F. Snyder and P. Slinn (eds), *International Law and Development: Comparative Perspectives*. Abingdon: Professional Books, pp. 237–70.

Muchlinski, P. (1995) *Multinational Enterprise and Law*. Oxford: Blackwell.

Muller, W.J. and Stern, T.G. (1989) 'The Evolution of Petroleum Contracts in Argentina. Issues of the Foreign Investors' Legal Protection' 7 *Journal of Energy and Natural Resources Law* 189.

Munck, G.L. (1994) 'Democratic Transitions in Comparative Perspective' 26 (3) *Comparative Politics* 355.

Musin, V.A. (1991) 'Pravovye Voprosy Inostrannyh Investitsii v SSSR' 4 *Pravovedenie* 14.

Nazarbayev, N. (1996) *Kazakhstan-2030. Message of the President of the Country to the People of Kazakhstan*. Almaty.

'Nazarbayev Re-Elected in "Unfair" Vote' *Combined Reports by Reuters/Associated Press*, 12 January 1999.

'Nazarbayev's 20 Per Cent of Democracy' *The Moscow Times*, 12 January 1999.

Nelson, L.D. (1994) 'Property to the People: the Struggle for Radical Economic Reform in Russia' 439 *Economic Journal* 1846.

Nelson, L.D. (1995) *Radical Reform in Yel'tsin's Russia: Political, Economic and Social Dimensions*. Armonk, NY: M.E. Sharpe.

Nimmer, R.T. (1978) *The Nature of System Change: Reform Impact in the Criminal Courts*. Chicago: American Bar Foundation.

Nomura, S.K. (1995) *The New Wave of Foreign Direct Investment in Asia*. Singapore: Institute of Southeast Asian Studies.

Nonet, P. and Selznick, P. (1978) *Law and Society in Transition: Toward Responsive Law*. New York: Harper and Row.

North, D.C. (1981) *Structure and Change in Economic History*. New York: Norton.

North, D.C. (1984) 'Transaction Costs, Institutions, and Economic History' 140 (1) *Journal of Institutional and Theoretical Economics* 7.

North, D.C. (1990) *Institutions, Institutional Change and Economic Performance*. Cambridge: Cambridge University Press.

North, D.C. (1992) 'Privatization, Incentives, and Economic Performance'. In H Giersch and H Siebert (eds), *Privatization: Symposium in Honor of Herbert Giersch*. Kiel: Institute fur Weltwirtschaft an der Universitat Kiel.

North, D.C. (1993) 'Institutions and Economic Performance'. In U. Maki and C. Knudsen (eds), *Rationality, Institutions and Economic Methodology*. London: Routledge, pp. 242–61.

North, D.C. (1997a) *The Contribution of the New Institutional Economics to an Understanding of the Transition Problem*. WIDER Annual Lectures. Helsinki: UNU World Institute for Development Economics Research.

North, D.C. (1997b) *The Process of Economic Change*. WIDER Working Papers No. 128. Helsinki: UNU World Institute for Development Economics Research.

North, D.C. and Thomas, R.P. (1970) 'An Economic Theory of the Growth of the Western World' 23 *Economic History Review* 1.

Nystrom, N.N. (1996) 'Entity Characterization Issues in the PRC' 21 *William Mitchell Law Review* 839.

Ocran, T.M. (1987) 'Bilateral Investment Protection Treaties: a Comparative Study' 8 *New York Law School Journal of International and Comparative Law* 401.

Ocran, T.M. (1988) 'International Investment Guarantee Agreements and Related Administrative Schemes' 10 *University of Pennsylvania Journal of International Business Law* 341.

Odle, M. (1993) 'Foreign Direct Investment as Part of the Privatization Process' 2 (2) *Transnational Corporations* 7.

O'Donnell, G. and Schmitter, P. (1986) *Transitions from Authoritarian Rule: Tentative Conclusions about Uncertain Democracies*. Baltimore: John Hopkins University Press.

O'Driscoll G.P. and Rizzo, M.J. (1985) *The Economics of Time and Ignorance*. Oxford: Blackwell.

OECD (1996) *Globalization of Industry Overview and Sector Reports*. Paris: OECD.

Ohmae, K. (1995) *The End of the Nation State: the Rise of Regional Economies*. New York: The Free Press.

Okimoto, D. (1989) *Between MITI and the Market*. Stanford, CA: Stanford University Press.

Olcott, M.B. (1999) 'US Gives up on Democracy' *Boston Globe*, 13 January.

Olson, M. (1993) 'Dictatorship, Democracy, and Development' 87 *American Political Science Review* 567.

'Opposition Parties Join Forces Against Leadership', *BBC Monitoring, Summary of World Broadcasts, Part I, Former USSR*, 24 February 1998.

Osakwe, C. (1989) 'The Death of Ideology in Soviet Foreign Investment Policy: a Clinical Examination of the Soviet Joint Venture Law of 1987' 22 *Vanderbilt Journal of Transnational Law* 1.

Osakwe, C. (1993) 'Navigating the Minefields of Russian Joint Venture Law and Tax Regulations: a Procedural Compass' 25 *Vanderbuilt Journal of Transnational Law* 799.

O'Sullivan, P.J. (1993) 'An Assessment of Ireland's Export-Led Growth Strategy via Foreign Direct Investment, 1960–1980' 129 *Weltwirschaftliches Archiv* 139.

Pardinas, C.M. (1991) 'The Enigma of the Legal Liability of Transnational Corporations' 14 *Suffolk Transnational Law Journal* 405.

Parra, A.R. (1995) 'The Scope of New Investment Laws and International Instruments' 4 (3) *Transnational Corporations* 27.

Parsons, K.H. (1942) 'John R. Commons Point of View' 18 *Journal of Land and Public Utility Economics* 245.

Pastor, M. and Hilt, E. (1993) 'Private Investment and Democracy in Latin America' 21 (4) *World Development* 489.

Perkins, R.B. (1995) 'Corporate governance in the New Russia' 14 (6) *International Financial Law Review* 12.

Peter, C.M. (1988) 'Settlement of Investment Disputes' 5 *Journal of International Arbitration* 67.

Pfeffer, I. (1956) *Insurance and Economic Theory*. Homewood, IL: R.D. Irwin.

Pfeffermann, G. and Weigel, D.R. (1988) 'Private Sector and the Policy Environment' 25 *Finance and Development* 51.

Pirrwitz, B. (1988) 'Annulment of Arbitral Awards Under Article 52 of the Washington Convention on the Settlement of Investment Disputes Between States and Nationals of Other States' 23 *Texas International Law Journal* 73.

Podgorecki, A. (1974) *Law and Society*. London: Routledge & Kegan Paul.

Pomfret, R. (1994) 'Foreign Direct Investment in a Centrally Planned Economy: Lessons From China. Comment on Camath' 42 *Economic Development and Cultural Change* 413.

Pomfret, R. (1995) *The Economies of Central Asia*. Princeton, NJ: Princeton University Press.

Popondopulo, V.F. (1994) 'The Legal Regulation of Foreign Direct Investment in Russia' 42 *Cleveland State Law Review* 599.

Popova, T. (1992) 'Privatizatsiya: Tempy, Masshtaby, Prioritety' 2 *Ekonomist* 65.

Posner, R.A. (1989) *Economic Analysis of Law*, 1st edn. Boston: Little, Brown.

Posner, R.A. (1975) 'The Economic Approach to Law' 53 *Texas Law Review* 757.

Posner, R.A. (1987) 'The Law and Economics Movement' 77 *American Economic Review* 1.

Posner, R.A. (1993) 'What Do Judges Maximize? (The Same Thing Everybody Does)' 3 *Supreme Court Economic Review* 1.

Posner, R.A. (1996) *Law and Legal Theory in England and America*. Oxford: Clarendon Press.

Posner, R.A. (1997) 'The Future of the Law and Economics Movement in Europe' 17 *International Review of Law and Economics* 3.

Powell, W.W. and DiMaggio, P.J. (eds) (1991) *The New Institutionalism and Organizational Analysis*. Chicago: University of Chicago Press.

Pratten, C. (1996) *The Valuation of Inward and Outward Direct Investment: a Report for CSO*. Cambridge: University of Cambridge, Department of Applied Economics.

Pridham, G. (1994) 'Democratic Transitions in Theory and Practice: Southern European Lessons for Eastern Europe'. In G. Pridham and T. Vanhanen (eds), *Democratization in Eastern Europe: Domestic and International Perspectives*. London: Routledge.

Priest, G.L. (1977) 'The Common Law Process and the Selection of Efficient Rules' 6 (1) *Journal of Legal Studies* 65.

Pritchard, R. (1996) *Economic Development, Foreign Investment and the Law: Issues of Private Sector Involvement, Foreign Investment and the Rule of Law in a New Era*. London: Kluwer Law International and International Bar Association.

Pritchard, R. (1997) 'The Transformation in Foreign Investment Law – More Than a Pendulum Swing?' 8 *International Company and Commercial Law Review* 233.

Przeworski, A. (1986) 'Problems in the Study of Transition to Democracy'. In G. O'Donnel, P. Schmitter and L. Whitehead (eds), *Transitions from Authoritarian Rule: Comparative Perspectives*. Baltimore and London: John Hopkins University Press.

Przeworski, A. (1991) *Democracy and the Market: Political and Economic Reforms in Eastern Europe and Latin America*. Cambridge: Cambridge University Press.

Putnam, R. (1988) 'Diplomacy and Domestic Politics: the Logic of Two-Level Games' 42 *Organization* 427.

Pyatkin, A. (1992) 'Inostrannye Investitsii – Rezerv Economicheskogo Razvitiya' 4 *Rossiskii Economicheskii Zhurnal* 10.

Radygin, A. (1995) *Privatization in Russia: Hard Choice, First Results, New Targets*. London: Centre for Research into Communist Economies.

Rapakko, T. (1997) *Unlimited Shareholder Liability in Multinationals*. Stanford, CA: Kluwer Law International.

Reading, M.R. (1992) 'The Bilateral Investment Treaties in ASEAN: a Comparative Analysis' 42 *Duke Law Journal* 679.

Reihel, M. (1927) 'Kontsessii v Sovetskom Zakonodatel'stve i Praktike' 4 *Sovetskoye Pravo* 3.

Reiter, T.M. (1993/1994) 'The Feasibility of Debt–Equity Swaps in Russia' 15 *Michigan Yearbook of International Legal Studies* 909.

Rinehart, T.M. (1995) 'Forming a High Technology Joint Venture in Hungary' 11 *Santa Clara Computer and High Technology Law Journal* 287.

Rizzo, M.J. (1979) 'Uncertainty, Subjectivity, and the Economic Analysis of Law'. In M.J. Rizzo (ed.), *Time, Uncertainty and Disequilibrium: Exploration of Austrian Themes*. Lexington, MA: Lexington Books.

Robertson, D. (1995) *Investment Liberalization and Market Forces: the New OECD Initiative*. Canberra: Research School of Pacific and Asian Studies, Australian National University.

Robertson, R. (1992) *Globalization: Social Theory and Global Culture*. London: Sage Publications Company.

Robock, S.H. 'Political Risk: Identification and Assessment' 6 (4) *Columbia Journal of World Business* (1971) 6.

Rojec, M. (1994) 'Foreign Direct Investment in the Transformation Process: Some Operational Characteristics of Foreign Subsidiaries and Joint Ventures in Slovenia' 10 *Development and International Cooperation* 5.

Root, F. (1968) 'US Business Abroad and the Political Risks'. *MSU Business Topics* 73. Winter.

Rubin, S. (1956) *Private Foreign Investment: Legal and Economic Realities*. Baltimore: John Hopkins University Press.
Rudden, B. (1994) 'Civil Law, Civil Society, and the Russian Constitution' 110 *The Law Quarterly Review* 56.
Rustow, D. (1973) 'Transitions to Democracy: Towards a Dynamic Model' 2 (3) *Comparative Politics* 337.
Ruttan, V.W. and Hayami, Y. (1984) 'Toward a Theory of Induced Institutional Innovation' 20 *Journal of Development Studies* 203.
Sachs, W. (1984) 'The "New" US Bilateral Investment Treaties' 2 *International Tax and Business Lawyer* 192.
Sagandykova, S. 'Inostrannye Investitsii i Rabochie Mesta' 10 *Kazakhstan: Ekonomika I Zhizn'* 16.
Salacuse, J.W. (1990) 'BIT by BIT: the Growth of Bilateral Investment Treaties and their Impact on Foreign Investment in Developing Countries' 24 *International Lawyer* 655.
Salani, S. and Sloan, J. (1995) 'An Overview of Legal and Financing Aspects for Doing Business in Hungary, Poland, and the Czech Republic' 9 *Temple International and Comparative Law Journal* 27.
Saler, T.D. (1996) *All About Global Investing*. New York and Chichester: Wiley.
Sally, R. (1995) *States and Firms: Multinational Enterprises in Institutional Competition*. London: Routledge.
Saltz, I.S. (1992) 'Negative Correlation Between Foreign Direct Investment and Economic Growth in the Third World: Theory and Evidence' 39 *Rivista Internazionale di Scienze Economiche e Commerciali* 617.
Samuels, W.J. (1971) 'Interrelations Between Legal and Economic Processes' 14 *Journal of Law and Economics* 435.
Samuels, W.J. (1981) 'Maximization of Wealth as Justice: an Essay on Posnerian Law and Economics as Policy Analysis' 60 *Texas Law Review* 147.
Samuels, W.J. (1992) *Essays on the Economic Role of Government*. New York: New York University Press.
Samuels, W.J. and Schmid, A.A. (1981) *Law and Economics: an Institutional Perspective*. Boston: Kluwer-Nijhoff.
Sanchez-Mejorada-Velasco, R. (1992) 'Foreign Investment in Mining in Mexico' 23 *St Mary's Law Journal* 821.
Sarsembayev, M.A. (1995) *Pravovoye Regulirovanie Vneshneekonomicheskoi Deyatel'nosti*. Almaty: Gylym.
Sattarova, G.S. (1996) 'Mezhdunarodno-Pravovoye Regulirovanie Investitsii (Na Primere Dvustoronnih Soglashenii Respubliki Kazahstan o Pooshrenii i Zashite Investitsii'. In *Aktual'nye Voprosy Kommercheskogo Zakonodatel'stva Respubliki Kazahstan i Praktika Ego Primeneniya*. Almaty: Adilet Press, 135–50.
Sawer, G. (1965) *Law in Society*. Oxford: Clarendon Press.
Schmidt, A.A. (1992) 'Legal Foundations of the Market: Implications for the Formerly Socialist Countries of Eastern Europe and Africa' 26 *Journal of Economic Issues* 707.
Schmidt, A.A. (1994) 'Institutional Law and Economics' 1 *European Journal of Law and Economics* 33.
Schmidt, K.-D. (1994) 'Foreign Direct Investment in Central and Eastern European Countries: State of Affairs, Prospects and Policy Implications' 633 *Kiel Working Papers* 1. Kiel: Institut fur Wirtschaft an der Universitat Kiel.

Schneider, R.C. (1994) 'Privatization in One Country: Foreign Investment and the Russian Privatization Dynamic' 17 *Hastings International and Comparative Law Review* 697.

Scott, N.C. (1995) 'Foreign Investment Laws and Foreign Direct Investment in Developing Countries: Albania's Experiment' 29 (3) *The International Lawyer* 577.

Scott, R.E. (1990) 'A Relational Theory of Default Rules for Commercial Contracts' 29 *Journal of Legal Studies* 598.

Seebach, S.L. (1995) 'Bankruptcy Behind the Great Wall: Should US Business Seeking to Invest in the Emerging Chinese Market be Wary?' 8 *Transnational Lawyer* 351.

Sekushin, O.I. (1990) *Ottorzhenie NEP i Kommandno-Administrativnaya Sistema*. Leningrad: Lenizdat.

Shah, A. and Slemrod, J. (1991) 'Do Taxes Matter for Foreign Direct Investment?' 5 *World Bank Economic Review* 473.

Shil'manov, K.A. (1994) 'Mezhdunarodno-Pravovoye Obespecheniye Vneshneekonomcheskoi Deyatel'nosti' 1 *Biznes i Pravo* 12.

Shishido, Z. (1992) 'Problems of International Joint Ventures in Japan' 26 *The International Lawyer* 303.

Shum, C. (1991) 'Recent Development in Equity Joint Ventures Law in the PRC' 1991 *Lloyd's Maritime and Commercial Law Quarterly* 403.

Shwartz, B. (1971) *The Bill of Rights: a Documentary History*, vol. II. New York: McGraw Hill Book Company.

Siedman, R.B. (1978) *The State, Law and Development*. London: Croom Helm.

Silliman, E. and Kayukov, E. (1996) 'New Company Formation in Russia: Legal Regulation' 3 *Parker School Journal of East European Law* 175.

Simidjiski, Y. (1994) 'A Comparative Study of the Bulgarian Law on Foreign Investment and the Foreign Investment Laws of Hungary, Poland, and the Czech Republic Through the Prism of the World Bank Guidelines for treatment of Foreign Investment' 9 *Florida Journal of International Law* 277.

Siqueiros, J.L. (1993/1994) 'Bilateral Treaties on the Reciprocal Protection of Foreign Investment' 24 *California Western International Law Journal* 255.

Skelton, J.W. (1993) 'Investing in Russia's Oil and Gas Industry: the Legal and Bureaucratic Obstacles' 8 *Natural Resources and Environment* 26.

Sklyarov, S. (1998) 'Beskonechnaya Skazka: Kazakhstan. Diktatura s Chelovecheskim Litsom' 34 *Expert*, 14 September, 56–7.

Slay, B. (1994) 'Rapid Versus Gradual Economic Transition' 3 (31) *RFE/RL Research Report*, 12 August.

Smith, A. (1991) *National Identity*. London: Penguin.

Smith, G. (1996) *Reforming the Russian Legal System*. Cambridge: Cambridge University Press.

Smith, M. (1992) 'Commercial Legal Systems Crystalize in Hungary, Poland, and Czechoslovakia: Now There is a Room for any Size Investor' 19 *Ohio Northern University Law Review* 99.

Sornarajah, M. (1986) 'State Responsibility and Bilateral Investment Treaties' 20 *Journal of World Trade Law* 79.

Sornarajah, M. (1988) 'Supremacy of the Renegotiation Clause in International Contracts' 5 *Journal of International Arbitration* 97.

Sornarajah, M. (1995) *International Law on Foreign Investment*. Cambridge: Cambridge University Press.

Spybey, T. (1996) *Globalization and World Society*. Cambridge: Polity.

Stansbury, P.R. (1995) 'Managing Legal and Business Risks in Newly Emerging Areas: Structuring Investments to Reduce Risks' 1995 *Private Investments Abroad* 11.1.

Starr, R. (1994) 'Foreign Participation in Oil and Gas Projects in the Former Soviet Union: a Legal Perspective' 12 *Journal of Energy and Natural Resources Law* 442.

Stockmayer, A. (1986) 'Bilateral Investment Promotion Protection and Treaties: a Model for Community Promotion of Mining Investment?' 4 *Journal of Energy and Natural Resources Law* 247.

Stoleson, M.A. (1997) 'Investment in an Impasse: Russia's Production Sharing Agreement Law and the Continuing Barriers to Petroleum Investment in Russia' 7 *Duke Journal of Comparative & International Law* 671.

'Striking Miners to Write to President Nazarbayev', *BBC Monitoring, Summary of World Broadcasts, Part I, Former USSR*, 22 January 1998.

Strong, F. (1997) *Judicial Function in Constitutional Limitation of Government Power*. Durham, NC: Carolina Academic Press.

Stulz, R.M. (1995) *Foreign Equity Investment Restrictions, Capital Flight and Shareholder Wealth Maximization*. London: Centre for Economic Policy Research.

Suchman, M.C. and Edelman, L.B. (1996) 'Legal Rational Myths: the New Institutionalism and the Law and Society Tradition' 21 (4) *Law and Social Inquiry* 903.

Suleimenov, M.K. (1994) 'Pravovoye Obespecheniye Ekonomicheskoi Reformy (V Tom Chisle Ryada Voprosov Vneshneekonomicheskoi Deyatel'nosti' 4 *Izvestiya Natsional'noi Akademii Nauk Respubliki Kazakhstan. Seriya Obshestvennyh Nauk* 52.

Sutton, A.C. (1968) *Western Technology and Soviet Economic Development 1917 to 1930*. Stanford, CA: Stanford University Press.

Swamy, D.S. (1994) *The Political Economy of Industrialization: From Self-Reliance to Globalization*. New Delhi and London: Sage.

Tang, S.S. (1993) 'Legislative Framework for Direct Foreign Investment in ASEAN' 10 *ASEAN Economic Review* 155.

Tarakov, A. (1993) ' "Tengizchevroil": Aspekty Sdelki Veka' 6 *Kazahstan: Ekonomika i Zhizn'* 35.

Terry, S. (1993) 'Thinking About Post-Communist Transitions: How Different Are They?' 52 (2) *Slavic Review* 333.

Thelen, K. and Steinmo, S. (1992) 'Historical Institutionalism in Comparative Politics'. In S. Steinmo, K. Thelen and F. Longstreth (eds), *Structuring Politics: Historical Institutionalism in Comparative Analysis*. New York: Cambridge University Press, pp. 1–32.

Thomas, P. (1993) 'Talking Kazakhstan' 146 *Energy Economist* 20.

Thomas, P. (1995) *Kazakhstan: Investment Opportunities in the Energy Sector*. London: Financial Times Energy Publishing.

Thompson, T.L. (1993) 'If it's Tuesday, This Must Be Kazakhstan' 13 *California Lawyer* 22.

Tolentini, P.E.E. (1990) 'Overall Trends of Foreign Direct Investment' 29 *CTC Reporter* 28.

'Trade Unions Call for Direct Presidential Rule in the South', *BBC Monitoring, Summary of World Broadcasts, Part I, Former USSR*, 24 February 1998.

Tribe, L. (1988) *American Constitutional Law*, 2nd edn. Mineola, NY: The Foundation Press.

Trubek, D.M. (1972) 'Toward a Social Theory of Law: an Essay on the Study of Law and Development' 82 (1) *Yale Law Journal* 1.

Trubek, D.M. (1974) *Law and Development: the Future of Law and Development Research*. Report of the Research Advisory Committee on Law and Development of the International Legal Centre. New York: International Legal Centre.

Trubek, D.M. and Galanter, M. (1974) 'Scholars in Self-Estrangement: Some Reflections on the Crisis of Law and Development Studies in the United States' 4 *Wisconsin Law Review* 1062.

Tsebelis, G. (1990) *Nested Games: Rational Choice in Comparative Politics*. Berkeley and Los Angeles: University of California Press.

Tuganbayev, A.S. (1963) 'Iz Istorii Vneshnih Ekonomicheskih Otnoshenii Kazahstana' 2 *Vestnik Akademii Nauk Kazahskoi SSR* 21.

Turro, J. (1993) 'Kazakhstan Negotiating to Develop Oil – and Taxes are on the Table' *Tax Notes International*, 31 May, 1304–06.

Umbeck, J. (1981) 'Might Makes Right – A Theory of the Formation and Initial Distribution of Property Rights' 19 (1) *Economic Inquiry* 38.

Urzhumov, S. (1992) 'SEZ: Za i Protiv' 6 *Kazahstan: Ekonomika I Zhizn'* 22.

Vago, S. (1997) *Law and Society*, 5th edn. Upper Sadle River, NJ: Prentice-Hall.

Vandevelde, K. (1993a) 'Of Politics and Markets: the Shifting Ideology of the BITs' 11 *International Tax and Business Lawyer* 159.

Vandevelde, K. (1993b) 'US Bilateral Investment Treaties: the Second Wave' 14 *Michigan Yearbook of International Legal Studies* 621.

Varanese, J.B. (1996) 'The Regulation and Pledge of Immovables in Kazakhstan' 19 (4) *Middle East Executive Reports* 11.

Vaughan, K.I. (1979) 'Does It Matter That Costs Are Subjective?' 46 *Southern Economic Journal* 702.

Vaughan, K.J. (1994) 'Russia's Petroleum Industry: an Overview of its Current Status, the Need for Foreign Investment, and Recent Legislation' 25 *Law and Policy in International Business* 813.

Veeder, V.V. (1998) 'The Lena Goldfields Arbitration: the Historical Roots of Three Ideas' 47 *International and Comparative Law Quarterly* 747.

Veljanovski, C.G. (1982) *The New Law-and-Economics*. Oxford: Centre for Socio-Legal Studies.

Velkei, S.A. (1992) 'An Emerging Framework for Greater Foreign Participation in the Economies of Hungary and Poland' 15 *Hastings International and Comparative Law Review* 695.

Vernon, R. (1966) 'International Trade and International Investment in the Product Cycle' 83 (1) *Quarterly Journal of Economics* 190.

Vernon, R. (1971) *Sovereignty at Bay: the Multinational Spread of US Enterprises*. New York: Basic Books.

Vitriyanskii, V.V. (1995) 'The Concept and Varieties of Legal Persons According to the Civil Code of Russia' 21 *Review of Central and East European Law* 501.

Voznesenskaya, N.N. (1975) *Inostrannye Investitsii i Smeshannye Predpriyatiya v Stranah Afriki*. Moscow: Nauka.

Voznesenskaya, N.N. (1989) *Sovmestnye Predpriyatiya kak Forma Mezhdunarodnogo Sotrudnichestva*. Moscow: Nauka.

Waelde, T.W. (1995a) 'Book Review. *Kazakhstan: Investment Opportunities in the Energy Sector*. By Paul Thomas. London: Financial Times Energy Publishing, 1995'. In 4 *Journal of Energy and Natural Resources Law* 352.

Waelde, T.W. (1995b) 'The 1994 Energy Charter Treaty' 5 *Journal of World Trade* 5.

Waelde, T.W. (1996) 'International Energy Investment' 17 *Energy Law Journal* 191.

Waelde, T.W. and Gunderson, J.L. (1994) 'Legislative Reform in Transition Economies: Western Transplants – a Short-Cut to Social Market Economy Status?' 43 *The International and Comparative Law Quarterly* 347.

'Wage Arrears Protesters Block Rail Traffic in Southern Kazakhstan', *BBC Monitoring, Summary of World Broadcasts, Part I, Former USSR*, 20 February 1998.

Wallace, C.D. (1982) *Legal Control of the Multinational Enerprise*. The Hague and London: Martinus Nijhoff.

Wallerstein, I. (1974–1989) *The Modern World-System*. New York and San Diego: Academic Press.

Watson, A. (1977) *Society and Legal Change*. Edinburgh: Scottish Academic Press.

Watson, A. (1981) *The Making of the Civil Law*. Cambridge, MA and London: Harvard University Press.

Watson, A. (1985) *Sources of Law, Legal Change, and Ambiguity*. Edinburgh: T. & T. Clark.

Welsh, H. (1994) 'Political Transition Processes in Central and Eastern Europe' 26 (4) *Comparative Politics* 379.

Wes, M.A. (1996) *Globalization: Winners and Losers*. London: Institute for Public Policy Research.

Whitehead, L. (1996) *The International Dimensions of Democratization: Europe and the Americas*. Oxford: Oxford University Press.

Wigand, W. (1991) 'The Reception of American Law in Europe' 39 *American Journal of Comparative Law* 229.

Willet, A. (1951) *The Economic Theory of Risk and Insurance*. Philadelphia: University of Pennsylvania Press.

William, C. and Heins, R. (1964) *Risk Management and Insurance*. New York: McGraw-Hill.

Williams, P.R. and Wade, P.E. (1995) 'Bankruptcy in Russia: the Evolution of a Comprehensive Russian Bankruptcy Code' 21 *Review of Central and East European Law* 511.

Williamson, O.E. (1985) *The Economic Institutions of Capitalism: Firms, Markets, Relational Contracting*. New York: Free Press.

Williamson, O.E. (1988) 'The Logic of Economic Organization' 4 *Journal of Law, Economics and Organizations* 65.

Williamson, O.E. (1993a) 'The Evolving Science of Organization' 149 *Journal of Institutional and Theoretical Economics* 35.

Williamson, O.E. (1993b) 'Transaction Cost Economics Meets Posnerian Law and Economics' 149 *Journal of Institutional and Theoretical Economics* 99.

Winiecki, J. (1993) *Post-Soviet-Type Economies in Transition*. Aldershot: Avebury.

Wolf, C. and Sufrin, S. (1955) *Capital Formation and Foreign Investment in Underdeveloped Areas: an Analysis of Research, Needs and Program Possibilities*. Syracuse, NY: Syracuse University Press.

Wolf, K.M. (1995) 'The Legal Framework for Joint Development of China's Onshore Oil Resources: Negotiation Strategies and Future Prospects' 9 *Journal of Chinese Law* 141.

'Workers Building New Capital Held Protest', *BBC Monitoring, Summary of World Broadcasts, Part I, Former USSR*, 15 January 1998.

Yin, R. (1989) *Case Study Research: Design and Methods*. Beverly Hills, CA: Sage Publications Company.

Zakariya, H.S. (1986) 'Insurance Against the Political Risks of Petroleum Investment' 4 *Journal of Energy and Natural Resources Law* 217.

Zhang, X.J. (1993) 'Role of Foreign Direct Investment in Market-Oriented Reforms and Economic Development: the Case of China' 2 *Transnational Corporations* 121.

Zimbler, B.L. (1993) 'Russian Foreign Investment Laws and Natural Resources' 14 *Whittier Law Review* 477.

Index